BILL AND PATIENCE

BILL AND PATIENCE

*An Eccentric Marriage
at Stowe and Beyond*

Harriet Hall

The Book Guild Ltd
Sussex, England

The Book Guild Ltd
25 High Street,
Lewes, Sussex

First published 2000
© Harriet Hall, 2000

Set in Times
Typesetting by Keyboard Services, Luton

Printed in Great Britain by
Bookcraft (Bath) Ltd, Avon

A catalogue record for this book is
available from the British Library

ISBN 1 85776 408 0

CONTENTS

FOREWORD

I feel very honoured to be asked to write an introduction to Harriet Hall's *Bill and Patience: An Eccentric Marriage at Stowe and Beyond* a masterly biography of her parents. Her father, Bill McElwee, was History Tutor at Stowe and taught me there before the war. He and Patience lived at Vancouver Lodge, Dadford, an old house belonging to the school. It was there that Historians gathered for Sunday tea, an invitation to this being in itself an accolade. It was not renewed; it did not need to be, it meant that you belonged. What was remarkable was not the tea (though the marmalade sandwiches were delicious), but the talk. Never have I heard such talk. It was real freedom of speech. All were expected to join in from the great head of the school himself, Noel Annan, to the merest new boy, and Bill and Patience often had guests. I can remember meeting the historian A. J. P. Taylor and his wife, Simon Ramsey (later Lord Dalhousie), Isaiah Berlin, old Historians and their friends as well as an occasional parent. Discussion ranged over any subject that occurred to us, much of it trivial school gossip. Only the great J. F. Roxburgh was exempt. It was often very funny and the characters of boys and masters were freely dissected. Bill, though at heart an establishment figure (Patience was not), could not resist making a point out loud if he saw it coming.

Such were Vancouver tea parties as I remember them as a boy before the war, and, at intervals, throughout the late forties and fifties. All the time Patience went on writing her 'sunny romances' (her phrase) and, later, pony books. Among other history books. Bill wrote a definitive life of Charles V and poetry hidden in novels. He revealed that his gift for spotting a winner extended beyond boys to art, architecture and food in Western Europe where he guided us on remarkable 'culture tours'. He started an annual Historians' Shakespeare play, put on out of doors at the Queen's Temple.

For a time, the war brought an end to all this, but afterwards Bill emerged in a more serious uniform to command the Stowe 'Combined Cadet Force', a body in which he had already served when it was an 'Officer's Training Corps'. He had fought with distinction in Normandy. Patience produced Harriet.

After the war, I was lucky to be able, in the intervals of foreign service, to see more of Bill and Patience at Vancouver. My affection for them both deepened and I owe them a very great deal. This introduction can only be a token tribute to them, and to Harriet for her splendid book.

Stephen Whitwell

ACKNOWLEDGEMENTS

I have received an enormous amount of help with this book for which I am deeply grateful. Many old Historians made time either to see me or to write down their memories of my parents and I have tried to reflect their views and impressions faithfully. Obviously, there are many more people that I might have contacted and possibly I was biased in favour of people I already knew or whom I remembered my parents talking about. Having an up-to-date address was also a factor. I can only apologise to those who would have wished to describe different aspects of my parents' lives or have other stories to tell.

I first went to see Robert Kee with the idea of writing about my parents almost ten years before I began and am grateful to him for telling me that I must find my own voice in which to describe their lives. I regret the length of time it took me to do this since it has meant that I have missed being able to tap the memories of several early Historians. There have, nonetheless, been many people who were at Stowe in the thirties, who have given me wonderful material. Noel Annan, to whom Bill always referred proudly as his first scholar, both talked to me and wrote at length. I am also grateful for having been able to make extensive use of his life of J. F. Roxburgh and of his book *Our Age*. Mouse Vickers gave me time and lent me the minutes of the Viveur Club. Wayland and Liz Kennet gave me lunch and valuable material, while Charles Alexander, Peter Orde, Carroll Macnamara, Michael Scholfield and John Stoye all wrote, and Roland Oliver very kindly sent me part of his autobiography. Edmund Rolfe has regularly talked to me about my parents. Of the prewar Historians though, it is to Stephen Whitwell that I owe the greatest debt. He not only wrote a vivid description of his own experiences of the History Side and life at Vancouver, but has supported me throughout the whole process, including reading several drafts.

Above all however, he has made the publication of this book possible, something for which I am unable to express my gratitude strongly enough.

The postwar contributors are inevitably more numerous, not least because I know them. Simon Digby also gave me part of his autobiography and, most generously, has given financial help towards the production of the book. Sam Adshead, Simon Brown, Anthony Chamier, Angus Fairrie, Hector MacLean, Antony Phillipi and Toby Robertson all wrote. In addition I have gratefully used a letter William Hayter wrote to a one-time master at Stowe when my father died. Colin Anson, Brian Brindley, Alan Caiger-Smith, Charles Cox, Adrian Evans, Christopher Gauvain, Jeremy Jessel, Peter Leslie, Tim Manville-Hales, Piers Plowright, Brooks Richards, Giles Rooke, Richard Temple, David Sabberton, Robert Skepper, Tom Waine and Paul Whitfield gave me time, their impressions, and, in many cases, lunch. Christopher Kenyon not only allowed me to see the reports Bill wrote on him, but is, with great generosity, giving the book its launch and again I am enormously grateful.

Because of the McElwee travelling scholarship at Stowe, I have collected the views and memories of David Part who, together with Colin Anson, initiated the prize, of John Wates who is a trustee of the fund, and of Andrew Rudolf who, when he was History Tutor at Stowe, organised the presentations made by the winners of the prize.

Of Bill's former colleagues, Cyril Atkins, Joe Bain, John Hunt, and Colin James all either wrote to me or gave me time and hospitality. I am also indebted to Cyril for the photographs of us all taken in the Rec Room. Brian Stephan, who, sadly, has since died, but who was not a fan of Vancouver, provided me with balanced and perceptive impressions.

I am grateful to the Headmaster of Stowe, Jeremy Nichols, for allowing some of the administrative staff to give their time in helping me. A vast chunk of the book would be missing were it not for Sandra Amdor who worked hard to dig out details of Bill's Stowe career including his file which proved vital to the story. Her support and enthusiasm have been most encouraging. I have also had help from Alison Ewens and Frances Orger.

It was Philip Cottam, who is now history tutor at Stowe, who was kind enough to put me in touch with Eileen Griffiths, the librarian at Sedbergh to whom I am enormously grateful for giving her time and interest in helping me trawl the school archives. Through her, I was able to track down Gabriel Carritt and Philip Mason both of whom were contemporaries of Bill's at Sedbergh and who provided me with vivid descriptions of him and life at the school in the twenties. Sadly, I am unable to show them the fruits of their contributions as they have both since died.

Mary and Theodore Connor together with Bob and Doreen Wheeler, and my own contemporary, June Hall, all gave me views and stories from outside the immediate Stowe circle.

For the period when Bill was at the Royal Military Academy Sandhurst, I am greatly indebted to Bill Jenkins, Kenneth Ingham, Kathleen Rumbold, Richard Snailham and Philip Warner to whom I am particularly grateful for his checking of the relevant chapters.

I have also received particular help from Jeffrey Gill who knew nothing of Stowe, my parents or any of the background. He nobly read the book with great thoroughness, producing highly constructive comments which went a long way towards shaping the book to its present form.

I am also grateful for being given permission by Harper Collins to quote from *W. H. Auden, A Biography* by Humphrey Carpenter, to David Higham Associates and Hamish Hamilton for the use of material from *A Personal History* by A. J. P. Taylor and to The Orion Publishing Group for quotations from *Tricks of Memory* by Peregrine Worsthorne. The copyright of the letter to Patience from Wystan Auden belongs to his estate and Professor Edward Mendelson, Literary Executor of the Auden Estate, kindly gave me permission to use it. Dr Ronald Roxburgh has allowed me to quote extensively from the letters of his uncle, J. F. Roxburgh, for which I am most grateful.

The number of quotations from the *Buckingham Advertiser* that I have used throughout the book are reprinted with the kind permission of the *Buckingham and Winslow Advertiser* and I am grateful for being allowed by the *New Statesman,* to whom the copyright belongs, to reprint the review by Alan Taylor on pages 198 to 199. *The Northampton Mercury* has kindly let me use the article quoted on pages 244 to 245.

I have, in addition, made grateful use of: *Gavin Maxwell, A Life* by Douglas Botting, *A Sparrow's Flight* by Lord Hailsham of St Marylebone, *Christabel, The Russell Case and After* by Eileen Hunter, *T. H. White: A Biography* by Sylvia Townsend Warner, and *Temples of Delight, Stowe Landscape Gardens* by John Martin Robinson. I am unable to identify the source of the article on Christabel Ampthill by Catherine Stott, but I much appreciated being able to use the information it contained.

The staff at The Book Guild have all given me great support and encouragement for which I am deeply grateful.

Finally, I could never have achieved this volume at all without the help I have received from my husband, David. He has supported my working part time, carefully and constructively read each chapter and encouraged me when I felt daunted. I could not have done it without him.

1

Gambling and Underdogs

My arrival in the world on 11 September 1942 was, according to my mother, accompanied by a ferocious Luftwaffe attack on the hospital. Since even the smallest event in her life was grist to her storytelling mill, this could well be exaggerated – particularly the bit about the matron trying to calm her supposed fears by attributing the noise to nurses banging bedpans about on the floor above. However, there were regular raids on the South Coast and Worthing Gasworks, which were next to the hospital, might well have been viewed as a suitable just-over-the-coast target. 'Anyway,' she would state heroically, 'I was much too far gone in labour to care about a few German bombs.'

By the time I was born my parents, Patience Kennington and Bill McElwee, were already in their thirties and established in their eccentricities as well as their mutual dedication to the education of public schoolboys. This is the story of their backgrounds, how they met, what they achieved and the powerful influences they exerted on one another, as well as those with whom they came in contact. It is also about a large part of the lifetime of Stowe, a school founded in 1923 and to which Bill went to teach in 1934. He was away for five years during the war, and finally left in 1962. Bill and Patience were a team, she being the one who nurtured the boys he taught, picking up the pieces when the brutalities of public school life got them down. They also wrote 13 books apiece, had a variety of interests and some remarkable friends. Their friendships are also part of their history.

Having a child after 12 years of marriage was a triumph for Patience, and she made the most of it. In the short term, coming when I did meant that apart from a brief stint working in the Educational Book Department of the Red Cross in Oxford, she was able to avoid doing any war work, a considerable achievement as she had always loathed the thought of formal employment. She had so far managed to avoid it by becoming engaged to Bill at the age of 17 and marrying at 20, both these states then being regarded as full-time occupations for women. She had a narrow escape since shortly before she conceived, she was interviewed for a job in the War Office. She always alleged that her interviewer had asked her if she were the sort of woman who started pieces of knitting and then left them unfinished. This was highly perceptive, there being several potential garments languishing in drawers being eaten by what my grandmother called 'the morth'. She never revealed the nature of the job for which she was being interviewed or how her future employment would have been affected by her inability to complete her knitting.

Patience, a misnomer if ever there was one, was born in July 1910, though her father, when once asked to confirm the year of her birth, said that she was born the year Craigenure was disqualified from winning the Derby, which happened in 1912. This would have made her 15 when she became engaged to my father and 13 when she wrote her first novel, which was rejected by a publisher for being 'decadent and morbid', so it was generally assumed that my one-track-minded grandfather had made a mistake. When she was born, her parents, Syd and Maudie Kennington, together with her older brother Alan, were living in Ilkley, where Syd owned a prep school. I never knew Syd, who died when I was still a baby, but Bill liked him enormously, describing a slightly raffish charm enhanced by his nose having been broken in his youth during a boxing bout. He was a successful sportsman when up at Cambridge, and presumably achieved some sort of degree. He went down to run his prep school, which he then proceeded to gamble away. Patience always alleged that Syd came from a long line of gamblers, saying proudly that one of his ancestors gambled away the monopoly of playing cards to a gentleman called De La Rue in the course of one night's card play, conjuring up a picture of aristocratic regency bucks entertaining themselves at Whites. Family research has tracked down a Kennington who worked as a card-maker in Holborn in the latter part of the last century and married the boss's daughter, so there could be some truth in the story – even if the facts are less glamorous than Patience would have liked. Syd's only other ancestor of note was a Miss Jenner of the Edinburgh department store family, which has enabled some members of the family to obtain satisfactory discounts on their goods. He was one of seven children and Eric Kennington the distinguished sculptor was a relation, as was the actress Anne Kennington. It was probably someone in Maudie's family who was reputed to be descended from Shakespeare's mother. Patience was sufficiently enamoured of this legend to have me christened Harriet Mary Arden.

In the highly nuanced social structure of their day, it is likely that Patience's mother, Frances Maud Hay Grant, was seen as coming from a rather grander family. (Why she was always called Maudie, rather than the much nicer Frances, is baffling.) They came from Tonbridge, and Maudie presumably met Syd when he was at school there. The Tonbridge *Free Press* of 21 July 1905 described their wedding in Tonbridge Parish Church as 'a fashionable and exceedingly pretty marriage ceremony'. The honeymoon was spent in Barton-on-Sea 'for golf'. Maudie's father, John Hay Grant, belonged to the Indian Civil Service and was sufficiently senior to be asked to turn the first sod when the construction of the Bombaugh sewage works was begun 1878. The heavily chased silver spade commemorating this event is a family heirloom. I know little about Maudie's mother, apart from the fact that she died of breast cancer and that she was a tall, handsome woman with a formidable jawline which she bequeathed to her five daughters. Possibly her one son was similarly blessed, but I do not remember ever seeing Maudie's brother Johnny who, like Syd, owned a prep school, but remained a shadowy figure. Of Maudie's sisters, Toto was the smallest and least formidable, being rather silly and invariably dressed in mauve with touches of black, which suggests that she was a widow by the time I knew her. Theo was the youngest and a lesbian, something always openly accepted, but dealt with by defensive jokes and excused by the fact that all the young men she might have married had been killed in the First World War. Her partner, always referred to as 'my friend', wore soft, feminine clothes, while Theo had short hair and invariably wore trousers, a style that entirely suited her strong features. They were a devoted couple, only parted by Theo's death.

Annie and Isobel were the successful sisters, in that they made 'good' marriages which enabled them to bail out poor Syd and Maudie when things got really bad. Maudie, entirely understandably, loathed going cap-in-hand to them, and inevitably they became enemies of the family, being depicted as both unpleasant and frightening, though their actual crimes were rarely specified, apart from the fact that they gave bridge parties and put on hats for lunch. Aunt Isobel was apparently

3

the most disapproving, though Patience was delighted by a rumour that when she was in her eighties and bedridden, Isobel took to sending the District Nurse out with regular bets. Patience had to stay regularly with Isobel and her family when she was adolescent, her cousin Jean being about her age and always held up as an example she should follow. This added to the sense of inadequacy engendered by these visits. Jean had made herself forever odious to Patience when, as a child, she allegedly threw a kitten onto the fire.

It seems, however, that the two sisters enabled the Kennington family to survive. With the prep school gone they moved south and Syd became Bursar at Lancing College, but clearly his salary was insufficient to finance his betting and maintain the family. There was apparently an occasion when things got so bad that they considered putting themselves and the two children into a boat and rowing out to sea – perhaps on an occasion when the sisters had refused to help. Something turned up though, and they lurched on to the next crisis, still managing to live to some extent in the manner that befitted their class. There were nurses for the children when they were small, one of them being revealed to be quite mad when she threw the infant Patience into the sea, from whence she was only just rescued in time. Having been taught by Maudie until she was eleven, Patience subsequently went to school in Worthing, to which she had to bicycle. She hated both the daily journey and the school, being thankful to leave at 16. Alan went to his Uncle Johnny's prep school in Seaford, to Lancing and up to Merton College, Oxford, where he took Garbo punting, generally led a fairly expensive and enjoyable life, coming down with a third-class degree.

They were not, I think, a particularly happy family. Though Syd apparently enjoyed his work and was extremely popular at Lancing, such compulsive gambling does not suggest contentment and clearly meant that life for Maudie was a continuous strain. I suspect her attitude to sex was of the 'lie back and think of England' sort. My father remembers an evening when they were celebrating their wedding anniversary, and Syd implied that he was unlikely to receive any physical benefit from the occasion. Whether because of the finances, or from something in her past, Maudie was consumed with an anxiety that pervaded all our lives. A satisfactory day would have to be paid for with a bad one, superstitions abounded, and her children's lives were profoundly affected. Alan, who was delightful, but as bad a gambler as his father, refused to have a child of his own in case it should be a

4

failure, while my mother remembered such things as being asked as she left for a party, 'Darling, are you sure you want to go? Suppose you get a headache or nobody is nice to you?' Maudie encouraged her to smoke on the grounds that it would prevent her breath smelling, and, when following her marriage, Patience discovered herself to have an apparently thickened hymen, her mother dissuaded her from having an operation to correct this, because she 'might die under the knife'. This kind of worry is a difficult and pervasive inheritance to shake off. It lessened somewhat in Patience, but a share inevitably descended to me.

Another characteristic of Maudie's was her passionate espousal of the underdog. She invariably voted Liberal simply because they attracted so few votes, and she became deeply sorry for the Germans the moment they were beaten. On VE day, I, then aged two and a half, was given a Union Jack and told to shout 'Hurrah for South Africa, Mafeking has been relieved' rather than any anti-German slogan. My only memory of the day is ending it in tears. The strain of living with such anxiety was leavened, however, by her enormous charm and her humour. She remained a handsome woman, but dressed eccentrically in layers of clothing, some of which would be of Victorian elegance, while others would clearly have originated from a jumble sale. Thick stockings were held up with black elastic garters, and she had a collection of stylish pointed shoes with buttoned straps. She was tall enough to carry off heavy Victorian jewellery, and the smell of amber beads brings her back to me instantly. Her voice was a distinctive upper-class drawl, and she had a delightful ability to alter words, such as 'eginmatic' for enigmatic.

The allusive humour was a family trait, and Bill recalls the difficulty of keeping up with the literary backchat when he first knew them. Patience may have loathed school, but read at great speed, giving herself a wide education, and Alan shared her literary enthusiasms. Quotations fell thickly, not only from Shakespeare, a wide variety of poets and well-known novelists, but also from a delightful series called the Nelson Classics, which included such titles as *The Making of a Marchioness*, *The Fortune of Christina McNab*, and *The Lame Dog's Diary*. It was from this last that one of the most durable of family quotations came, 'Just the husband for Emily' being used in the book to describe a string of dubiously eligible young men, and in the family for any object or idea that seemed to solve a current problem. Bill clearly became a Nelson Classics fan, since I noted recently when

5

rereading *The Expensive Miss Du Cane*, that he had written on the flyleaf 'Worthing, 12th September 1942', so he must have found it in a secondhand bookshop the day after I was born. Another family allusion, baffling to outsiders, was their habit of describing grubby underclothing as being 'Isabella-coloured'. This referred to a Crusader's lady who had refused to change her vest until her husband returned from foreign parts.

Patience's adolescence was probably happier than her childhood. She enjoyed the contact with Lancing occasioned by Syd's job, getting to know J. F. Roxburgh, who was then a housemaster there, and being remembered by Andrew Croft, the distinguished explorer, who was to accompany Roxburgh when he went to Stowe. She was close to Alan and shared his love of Brighton, seeing romance in the criminality of the race course gangs. *Brighton Rock* was one of her favourite books. She also adored the antique shops which in those days were a wonderful source of beautiful, if damaged, objects, that could be bought for very little. There were local parties, games of tennis which she apparently enjoyed, which is surprising in the light of her later determination never to take part in any form of sporting activity, and acrimonious family games of bridge, a game at which she became adept. She also enjoyed the gambling. While never becoming as addicted as her father and brother, she nonetheless shared much of their excitement and to the end of her life, never failed to bet on the major races of the year.

She loved Shadwells, the pretty red-brick house that was owned by Lancing College and let to the Kenningtons at a peppercorn rent, and seemed inured to its discomforts. I remember being told that it was Queen Anne, but given that it was also reputed to have a secret room, it may well have been earlier. It had two large rooms, a bathroom and an incredibly dark and primitive kitchen area downstairs, with a complete Victorian period piece of a drawing-room and four bedrooms upstairs. The garden was large, with lovely red-brick walls thickly coated with ivy which, when I was small, Bill would part to show me birds' nests. There were a greenhouse, cold frames and a magnificent mulberry tree.

The house also appears to have been haunted. One night Patience heard footsteps come up to her door and then retreat. Having ascertained that no member of the family had been stirring, she and Alan tied string across the top of the stairs, being unsurprised to find it intact after the footsteps again approached. Shortly after this, Patience saw

6

a man in what she said was eighteenth-century dress on the path behind the house. She mentioned this to a neighbour, who said: 'Oh you've seen the old gentlemen, how nice.' The story is inconclusive, since no one seems to have known who he was or why he should have been walking about inside Shadwells. Both Patience and Alan relished this episode, since they believed in and were without fear of ghosts. Indeed, they loved the house, seeming impervious to the dark corners that scared me as a child, and inured to the erratic gas lighting which remained in place until Maudie's death. There never seems to have been a suggestion that Patience should, like Maudie and Bill's mother, spend time abroad. No doubt in the twenties, Germany would have been seen as unsuitable, and anyway she would probably have resisted any such idea. However, home-loving though she was, at the age of 17, Patience was packed off to Oxford to acquire secretarial skills – and there she met Bill.

2

Family History

Compared with Patience's, Bill's upbringing was considerably more ordered and austere. His family is also much better documented, with copious and muddled family trees compiled by his younger brother Patrick, tracing both McElwees and his Lloyd mother's connections with half the minor landed gentry of Wales and Ireland. There is also a large collection of sepia-ish photographs. In social terms, Bill's mother, Katherine Lloyd, like Maudie Hay-Grant, married slightly beneath her. The Protestant McElwees were reasonably prosperous farmers in Donegal, having settled there after emigrating from Scotland in the seventeenth century, when they spelt their name Mc Ell Wee. However, it is likely that in getting a scholarship to Queen's College, Galway, followed by a BA with Honours in biological science after studying medicine at the Royal University of Ireland in Dublin, John McElwee, Bill's father, was bettering himself. He was born in 1861 and joined the British Navy in 1887 as a surgeon, glowing 'testimonials' having been written about him by Dublin doctors whose appointments and qualifications took up more space on the paper than their commendations.

John's position in the family of five is not clear, one tree making him the third child and another the youngest. The first may stem from the contemporary practice of automatically putting boys first on family trees. My great-grandfather's will, made in 1884, leaves the farm to his eldest son James on condition that 'he shall support his mother respectably during her life or until she may marry again', but James died the same year as John joined the Navy, and as Andrew, the second son, had emigrated to America, John took on the responsibility for his mother. This resulted in a lengthy non-courtship of Katherine since he felt he could not keep both wife and mother 'respectably'.

Of his two sisters, Martha's fate is unknown to me, but Sarah married a John Duncan whom Bill remembered with affection sewing up *The Times* every morning saying, 'I have to do this before your aunt gets at it.' I have a photograph of John McElwee looking solemn, with a sad-looking sister – possibly Martha and a deeply disapproving mother. His father's will adds to the sense of austerity conjured up by this picture, leaving five pounds to the 'Donegal Protestant Orphans' Society', and five pounds to the 'Sustentation Fund of the Church of Glenties, Donegal'.

One of the earliest of my collection of photographs shows a young woman with corkscrew ringlets holding a baby in a flowing christening robe. On the back is written: 'Katherine P. Lloyd, Dec 15th 1871, aged three months, one week'. The elegant young woman, Bill's grandmother, was Phoebe, the daughter of William Vincent, an Indian Army General whose portrait hangs in the Indian Army Museum at the Royal Military Academy Sandhurst – not because he was a particularly distinguished soldier, but because it is an example of a particular uniform. There is also a document, dated 1804 and signed by The Most Noble Marquis Wellesley, commissioning William Vincent, Gentleman, as an Ensign in the service of the Honourable East India Company on the Bengal Establishment. Family legend has it that through him we descend from an Afghan princess, but sadly it seems likely that it was his first wife who had this interesting background and that Phoebe was a child of his subsequent marriage. The family dark-brown eyes are the only thing that give any credence to the legend. The Vincents are reputed to stem from a Huguenot refugee who, with the surname Vincent de Lisle, arrived in Dublin in the eighteenth century and supported himself by teaching fencing and dancing.

Bill's maternal grandfather was William Lloyd, one of a numerous clan, descended from Denbighshire princelings who, in the tenth and eleventh centuries, spent much time fighting first the Saxons and then the Normans. Some Lloyds moved to Ireland in the seventeenth century, where they did some dirty work on behalf of the English before settling down, mostly eschewing politics and making a series of prudent marriages to heiresses who were often their own first cousins. This inbreeding and regular emigration have largely removed Protestant Lloyds from Ireland. Bill's grandfather was one of ten children, but only three of them survived to reproduce. Bill would tell stories of his great-uncles who roamed the world, coming home at intervals to drink up their profits, his favourite being Tom, who survived the drink only to be killed by a charging rhinoceros on the banks of the Zambezi. Many of the Lloyds' small but elegant Georgian houses remain standing, suggesting that, in spite of their initial support for the English powers, they were tolerable landlords.

Vivid glimpses of the lives of nineteenth-century Lloyds are provided by the diary of Deborah Lloyd, born in 1786 and a cousin of Bill's great-grandfather, who was also called William. She married her first cousin and they settled in Lloydsborough, a pretty house which she had inherited from her father and which, eerily, still contains some of her furniture. She was consistently rude about William, who regularly stayed at Lloydsborough, generally finding him 'not at all improved'. However, she relented when he married Kate Harris, writing: 'I like Kate very much, she is quiet and domestic.' He went on to become a respected Waterford lawyer.

Bill's grandfather, born in 1836, chose, like his future son-in-law, to qualify as a surgeon and join the navy. One of his earliest commissions was in HMS *Calcutta*, in whom he sailed to China in 1858. When anchored in the mouth of the Pekin River, he wrote to his mother with a pleasing description of the situation in which the expedition found itself:

> 'We found here 14 ships. French, Yankie, Russians and our own. Lord Elgin and the French and Yankie plenipotentiaries have been trying to open negotiations with Pekin and have failed they sent up an ultimation the day before we came in allowing them six days to come to terms and if they fail to do so, it is said that we are to take the posts at the two entrances of the river and afterwards be guided by circumstances however I don't think they know themselves what to do and they say Lord Elgin is sorry he ever came up here however I shall I hope be able to tell you more before I close this, as owing to the loss of one of the P & O steamers, everything in the mail line has gone astray and there may be no opportunity of sending this for a fortnight.'

William goes on to note the unattractive nature of their anchorage as 'it is composed of mud flats and not a sign of a hill to be found', and to deplore the cold, wet weather, before ending by saying 'the Chinamen don't seem inclined to come to terms and the attack is to commence on Monday'. He signs himself formally: 'I remain, my dear mother, ever your affectionate son, William H. Lloyd.' The erratic punctuation is quoted verbatim.

William Lloyd was eminently respectable, possibly in contrast to some of his brothers. He had a highly successful career in the Navy, ending up as an Inspector General of Naval Hospitals and Fleets, in which capacity he attended a conference for Military Surgeons in Washington in 1887. A delightful contemporary newspaper cutting describes him as: 'The typical middle-aged Englishman in appearance, handsome and neat, with clear-cut features and a well-made figure. He is inclined to be slender. He wears the conventional side-whisker, and the touch of grey in it sets off, with good effect, the ruddy, healthy English glow of his face.' Other cuttings recording the same occasion also mention 'his typically British face, a little florid with iron-grey side-whiskers' and as 'speaking with a decidedly English accent'. He was required to acknowledge the welcome of one Secretary Bayard, and did so in a 'brief and neatly-worded speech'. His obituary in *The Times* notes that he joined the Navy at the age of 20, was on the active list for 40 years, and that his first ship was the *Calcutta*. In her, he took part in the China War of 1857–8 'winning the medal with clasps for Canton and Taku'. Having served in North America, he was then taken out of ships and into hospitals in Portsmouth, Plymouth, Lisbon and Hong Kong. He retired in 1896, but having been an Honourary Surgeon to Queen Victoria, continued in that capacity to both Edward VII and George V until his death in April 1923. When he died, my grandmother received the following letter from Windsor Castle:

Dear Madam,

The King has learnt with regret of the death of his old friend, Inspector General Lloyd who was in the *Bacchante* with his Majesty as far back as 1879, and was honorary surgeon to three successive Sovereigns.

I am commanded to convey to you the expression of his Majesty's heartfelt sympathy in your loss.

Yours very truly,

Clive Wigram.

William Lloyd married Phoebe Vincent in 1870 and had two daughters, Katherine, generally known as Kitty or Katie, and Eileen. It is impossible to know whether it was a happy marriage, but it cannot

11

have been easy for Phoebe. A number of letters written to the 17-year-old Kitty when she was in Germany, studying music and German, suggest a lonely, almost stifling life, dogged by ill health. William was away at the time, as he must have been for much of their married life, Eileen was at school, and Phoebe's chief preoccupations seem to have been the Church, music and her health. At one stage she describes hearing voices, which would suggest some form of psychosis, but generally the impression she gives is of chronic exhaustion. Her most frequent visitors were various uncles, while aunts seemed to die regularly, with her often remarking gloomily that she was again in mourning. It would not be surprising if she were seriously depressed. She died in 1890 aged 40, and with 1990s hindsight it is tempting to think that she cannot have had much of a life, but probably it was what her birth and upbringing would have led her to expect.

Eileen Lloyd also seems to have had a limited life. Born ten years after her sister in 1881, she suffered severely from a thyroid imbalance which could then be operated on, but with only a 50 per cent chance of her surviving the surgery. Possibly this was inherited from Phoebe. One photograph shows her with slightly protruding eyes, and thyroid problems would account for the symptoms she described. Her father refused his consent to her having the operation, and she died in 1917, when she would have been 36. Bill always felt that it was wrong of his grandfather to have withheld his permission, since she was likely to die young anyway and there was at least a chance that she might have survived and had a much happier life. A lengthy obituary in *The Church League for Women's Suffrage* details her considerable work for that organisation. She began as librarian and before she died became responsible for 'acknowledging and forwarding gifts to the Serbians'. The write-up goes on to say that:

'in spite of her weak health the interests, which she entered into with such zest, were most varied. Her artistic bent found outlet in beautiful silken embroidery and lacemaking and in landscape and portrait photography. For the country she had an intense love, and we will not forget how boxes of primroses came to remind us in London of the Spring when she was away.'

She apparently sang in the Lambeth choir, learnt shorthand and typing for the League and undertook social work for Christ Church in Westminster Bridge Road, where she had a class of women 'who regarded her with great affection'. She belonged to the Girls Diocesan Association and, as well as helping to sustain Serbians, had also packed parcels for Belgians. Some of Eileen's embroidery survives, as does a photograph entitled 'Billy' taken of my father sitting in a high chair looking pensive, which won a medal from the Reigate Photographic Society. Bill remembers her as being frequently irritable, which probably went with the illness. Her discomfort and distress must have had to go somewhere when she was clearly sweetness and light for the Church League.

The Inspector General appears to have abandoned his travels after Phoebe died, his final appointment being in Plymouth. He would therefore have been able to provide a home for his daughters, at which Kitty probably acted as hostess and where she is likely to have met John McElwee. The romantic idea that they met at a Naval Ball is fostered by my discovery in a little rosewood writing desk that belonged to Kitty, of a collection of dance programmes in which his name occurs frequently. Clearly 'nothing was said' on account of his family obligations, but they corresponded while he travelled across the world. Sadly, none of Kitty's letters survive, but there is a large bundle from John written from various ships and stations redolent of power and Empire. They come from HMS *Hannibal*, *Pioneer*, *The Empress of India*, *Centurion*, *Medusa* and others. From the Channel Squadron, the Mediterranean Fleet, Singapore and the Naval sick quarters in Yokohama. The letters are formal and deprecating, invariably beginning 'Dear Miss Lloyd' and ending 'Yours sincerely, J. McElwee.' He is apologetic about his lack of ability, and admires her skills. He describes things seen on his travels and books he has read, but there is little about people and he never writes about his work. The impression he gives is of a somewhat stoical loneliness, unsure of himself in many ways, but prepared to explore a limited philosophical range of ideas. In one letter, written in May, 1901, he enclosed photographs of Mycenae, appearing in one, heavily suited and hatted, with a Greek in national dress standing slightly behind him, mirroring his pose.

Kitty, with her period in Germany, must have been widely educated. She seems to have been a serious woman with even greater skill with a needle than her sister. Two delightful embroidered pictures exist as testament to her skills, one of the house in Devon to which the family moved in the twenties, and one of an enchanting garden with a dovecote, which she made for me when I was a baby. John's letters to her frequently note her knowledge and breadth of reading matter. She finally married him in July 1906, their having corresponded for ten years. They were, respectively, 44 and 34. Bill, always known as Billy as a child, was born in September 1907, and his brother Patrick in July 1911. Bill could just remember the distressing occasion on which Kitty miscarried a daughter, who was to have been called Nancy. The McElwees were living somewhere in Hampstead when Bill was born and at some point moved to Sheerness, ever afterwards referred to by him as 'Sheernasty'.

However, it was the posting to Malta that made the biggest impression on Bill, both because of the place itself and the apparent consequences of his father's going there. Throughout the letters to Kitty, there is mention of illnesses suffered by John and, according to Bill, one of these was Malta fever, following a bout of which, John was told that he must never return to Malta or it might recur fatally. Possibly the outbreak of war left John feeling unable to refuse the posting, so off they went, accompanied by that formidable mentor of Bill and Patrick's youth, their governess Miss Spraggs, and vast quantities of their belongings, including a grand piano. The date of their departure is not recorded, but by 1915 Patrick is noted in a faded cutting as coming second in a swimming race for the over-fours and under-sevens, at a gymkhana run at the Ladies Bathing Club, Tigne. The description of this event is splendid, the scene depicted as being of 'more than usual animation', with the prowess of the children, the numbers taking part and the 'graceful diving' by the participators in the 'standing and running dive' event, all being detailed eulogistically. It goes on to mention that 'the fine band of a Warship now in Harbour enlivened the proceedings' and that 'At the conclusion of the Gymkhana the prizes – a carefully selected and appropriate collection – were distributed to the fortunate winners by Lady Limpus, the President of the Club.' Three 'hearty Cheers' for Lady L and the organisers of the event 'terminated a pleasant and healthy afternoon's recreation'.

Bill's and Patrick's youth was thoroughly and engagingly documented photographically, starting with them in voluminous dresses held in the arms of their nurse, Flowerday, and proceeding via sailor suits to shorts with snake belts and, finally, proper suits. Their time in Malta spawned a vast collection of faint, sepia-tinted prints, showing a huge variety of outdoor activities, but in none of these does John McElwee appear. No doubt, because of the war there was little time for the men to take part in family outings, but it does fit with Bill's sense of him as a distant and disapproving parent, whose irascibility was exacerbated by ill health. His most abiding memories were of his father throwing his boots at a beloved kitten and his insistence that Bill learn to knit. This was to encourage dexterity when tying knots, it being assumed that Bill would go into the Navy. His red/green colour blindness, about which he minded a great deal, thwarted that ambition and possibly added to his sense that he would have been unable to live up to his father's expectations. He always felt that Patrick, probably more relaxed and ebullient, like many second children, was John's favourite. In spite of all this, Bill seemed to have some happy experiences on Malta.

More difficult to discern is whether John and Kitty had a happy marriage. Before the posting to Malta, they took a number of bicycling holidays in France, a practice presumably instigated by Kitty who had done the same with her father. They kept meticulous, if rather dull, diaries of their travels, with Kitty recording architectural detail minutely while John commented on the countryside and on what he probably felt were the 'natives'. In the record of what was likely to have been their first holiday together, Kitty writes sadly: 'John does not take very kindly to sight-seeing', while in a later diary, John wrote: 'passed a Church in (illegible) succeeded in not entering it'. The following sentence is characteristic of him: 'An uninteresting looking town. Folk alert-looking and minding their own business; civil when asked the way.' Diaries written by John also contain detailed and exact accounts, with all expenditure worked out down to the last centime, including a reminder to himself to recover from Kitty the amount he had lent her to buy some postcards.

Tragically, the doctors who had warned John not to return to Malta turned out to have been all too right. He became ill again and was sent home in the autumn of 1916, managing, in spite of his health, to guide his party back to England, travelling overland as much as possible, and again keeping meticulous accounts. When they got back, Kitty and the children went to her father's house in South Kensington, while John went into the Naval Hospital at Haslar in Portsmouth. There is a slim packet of letters to Kitty that record the progress of his disease. The first is dated 17 October 1916, and says:

Sweetheart,
 The post brought nothing from you – rather unkind of it. I had another from Sarah [his sister] written after she got my telegram

15

from Southampton. From what she tells me of Johnny McCormick I'm afraid he is failing rapidly. She had no other news worth sending you.

I have just written a scribble of congratulations on his promotion to Stenhouse. For the rest all I have done today is to read *The Times*, read a little Theosophy (my book is interesting), eat and sleep. The rest in bed here and the complete peace have done me good but my fever continues just the same. For the past couple of nights the sweating has not been as profuse as it had been.

Forgive such a short scrawl, but I've absolutely nothing to write about. I trust the kiddies are behaving well in Miss Spraggs absence. Love to you all.

Yours,

J. McElwee.

In another brief note, written in pencil, he apologises for not having written for two days, describing himself as: 'almost glued to the bed on my back – such pain across my loins! – and other, not very minor discomforts, not much improvement yet. Temperature still up. Nights sweats continue, but not so profusely. Report on my blood examination not yet to hand, but I've not any doubt myself I've got Malta fever.' He looks forward to seeing her the following Thursday. An expert on tropical diseases can throw no light on what Malta fever might have been, and John's obituaries state that he died of 'Malignant Endocarditis'.

Subsequent letters written during the last days of October detail slight ups but many more downs in the progress of his illness. They touch on the problems of retrieving their belongings from Malta and occasionally mention a book he has enjoyed. In one, he writes: 'I gather from a casual remark of yours that you intend coming here next Friday. I shall be VERY GLAD to see you; but isn't it both troublesome and expensive for you?' In the penultimate letter in the collection, he thanks her formally for the gift of a dressing gown, and in the last one, which is simply dated Thursday, he says: 'I'm not sure if this is Thursday – the days go by anyhow for me now, and my *Times* is not within reach to consult. I hope you got home all right last night and that nothing had gone amiss in your absence; if I hear that Patrick gave aunty Eileen and grandpa trouble I shall be very cross.' He records that he had 'sweated through 2 flannel pyjama suits – pain in back

16

perhaps a little better.' There is a postscript expressing concern about which school Bill might attend in the future.

I find these austere, stoical letters infinitely sad and wonder why my grandmother was with him so little. However, she should not be judged at this distance, and possibly she was with him more as the end approached. This came on 16 December 1916, when he was 55 and they had been married only ten years. His obituaries detailed the prizes he had won as a student and his prowess as a rugger player. Echoes of the Empire are evoked by their also noting that, in 1891, he took part in an expedition up the Gambia which resulted in the capture of Tambi and Tomataba, for which he received the Ashanti medal and clasp. He was buried with Naval honours, but, because of the war, was deprived of a band and a firing party. Bill, aged nine, attended the funeral and for ever afterwards was undone by the sound of the Last Post. Even more traumatic for him was the outburst from his mother, who flung her arms round him crying, 'Oh Billy, Billy, you must be the man of the family now.' He later felt that this outburst left him with a permanent legacy of uncertainty about his ability to live up to adult responsibilities.

3

Sedbergh

Following John McElwee's death, Kitty and the boys continued to live with her father in Alfred Place, South Kensington. There must have been further sadness for her when Eileen died, but at least, given his long life, the Inspector General would have offered support through a difficult period. He remained, from Bill's description, wholly in charge of his faculties. It was, for the two boys, a somewhat severe, Victorian upbringing.

Bill remembered being hit over the head with a tablespoon by his grandfather for some minor misdemeanour at table, and any attempt to preserve a favourite mouthful till last would be frustrated by the application of salt if it were something sweet, and sugar on a savoury treat. 'You love your mother, but not your food', was a constant precept, and helpings had to be finished or they would reappear at subsequent meals. The battle to get Patrick to eat rice pudding was apparently epic. Bill described his mother as 'gruff', and my vague memories of her do not include any physical demonstration of affection. However, the message on the back of the picture she embroidered for me was loving and, as her only grandchild, I must have mattered enormously to her. A solitary remaining letter of hers, written to Patience during the early days of the marriage, is affectionate and helpful. To the end of her life, she signed her letters to Bill, 'Ever your loving mother, Katherine P. McElwee', which, by the forties, does seem a touch distant. Bill always seemed clear, though, that it was inability to express feeling that dogged her, rather than a lack of love for her family.

It is likely that Miss Spraggs was also pretty brisk, though Bill yielded to no one in his admiration for her teaching abilities. All his subsequent academic success he reckoned he owed to her, citing his success in the College of Preceptors exam, which he took at the age of nine after being sick in an Underground train on the way, as laying the foundations of his skill in passing examinations. He seems to have been a widely read child, being enthusiastic about such traditional boys' authors as G. A. Henty and Seton Merriman, but the literature he was given when he was very young he found frightening. *Grimms' Fairy Tales* he found uncomfortable, particularly the splitting in half of *Rumplestiltskin*, which gave him nightmares and he also deeply disliked *Struwwelpeter*, finding, as a thumb-sucker, the *Long-Legged Scissor Man* quite terrifying. His reaction did not stop him encouraging me to read both authors, but I coped with Grimm and as for *Struwwelpeter*, was merely irritated that my name constantly invoked comparison with *Harriet and the Matches*.

Bill must have gone to his prep school at Great Brickhill near Bletchley soon after his father's death. He was bullied there, but seems to have mitigated this by teaming up with two other boys, their little gang being referred to as 'The Three Musketeers'. He clearly felt sufficient enthusiasm for the place to keep a small collection of shadowy photographs which depict a pleasant house surrounded by gloomy shrubs. It was here that Bill and Patrick encountered a pernicious method of teaching languages. The children would be required to recite French irregular verbs while the teacher paraded behind them with a small switch. Each mistake would be rewarded by a cut on the back of a bare leg. For Bill this concentrated the mind wonderfully and he rarely faltered, but Patrick became transfixed by the thought of the switch and the process gave him a serious stammer. This was eased by subsequent therapy, but he retained a slight hesitancy in his speech all his life. Perversely, he went on to study and teach Modern Languages. Bill though, must already have made History his principal subject, since he entered a History competition in his last term at prep school and clearly did well. A letter from a Mr Henry written to the Headmaster says: 'I enclose the results of the History Competition and beg to congratulate you on the performance of McElwee. He did exceedingly well in the second paper and with a little more luck in the first, would certainly have been among the Prize Winners.'

Bill must have told me why his mother chose to send her sons north to Sedbergh, to which he went in September 1921, but I only remember his saying that it had been a mistake to send Patrick to the same schools, allowing him to be overshadowed by Bill's achievements. It

19

is probable that Kitty felt a tough school was appropriate for father-less boys, but in fact, though he can have had little in common with the rugger-playing sons of northern businessmen and the austere regime may have contributed to his subsequent ill-health, Bill was, overall, happy and successful there.

Two Sedberghian contemporaries of Bill's, Philip Mason and Gabriel Carritt, remember Bill as being different as they were them-selves, from the majority of other boys at the school. Gabriel Carritt remembered how little music and pictures featured in their lives, though Bill recalled a piano recital at the school by Moiseiwitsch, after which the rugger coach was heard to wish that he could have those wrists on a scrum-half. All of them were influenced by the beauty of the surrounding countryside, which remains unchanged, with the small town and rather austere school buildings appearing to be much as they were in the 1920s. Computers and the elegantly restored library sug-gest some progress and alteration, but there are still desks that clearly date from the last century, and the absence of girls seemed to com-pound what felt like a lack of colour and variety when comparing Sedbergh with other contemporary schools.

Lupton House, in which they were all placed, is at some distance from the main school and seems to have engendered an intimate fam-ily atmosphere which, in spite of the sparse furnishing and decoration, persists to this day. Bill remembered arriving to a series of initiation ceremonies, including being made to sing a song while being show-ered with boots and shoes, but his contemporaries have no such rec-ollections. He did resent the fact that his mother had failed to get all his clothes and equipment right, but judging from his later career, he cannot have been seriously hampered by this. There exists a photo-graphic and handwritten termly record of the boys in Lupton, provid-ing a brief but rather cosy record of their progress from being one of the herd in a general house room to the more exclusive studies and prefectorial status. Gabriel Carritt described the 'five' study, to which at different times he and Bill were assigned, as a 'terrible little slum', but would probably agree that it was an improvement on the house room, where he recalls the boys exciting themselves into getting erec-tions which they would then measure using instruments taken from their geometry sets. He feels this activity was rooted in their boredom and that no link was made between erections and relationships. Bill made the 'five study' in 1923 when he was 16 and, from one of the photographs in the house record, still childish in appearance. His dark good looks are already apparent, but his black hair is thick and unruly while his expression is rather anxious. At this stage the boys are still wearing shorts. Two years later, when a member of the 'prefects' study', his stance is infinitely more confident, though in both photographs he has his arms tightly folded. In the later photograph there are again five of them, their smooth hair and formal suits making them look older than modern 18-year-olds.

Gabriel Carritt also described the discomfort of returning from a run or game of rugger, cold, wet and caked in mud, and then having to queue to use one small basin in order to clean up. He has written about the 'crowded space, the squalid passages, the bare windswept dormitories' together with 'only four lavatories outside without doors'. Both he and Bill condemned the food, Gabriel describing breakfasts of porridge, underdone bacon with bread and margarine, lunches that almost invariably consisted of local lamb and a solid suet pudding, with a rudimentary tea to follow the ferocious exercise expected by the school. The school provided bread and butter, but in spite of being given limited storage space, boys were expected to bring well-stocked tuck boxes to supplement this, in particular needing cocoa and condensed milk to create what was known as a 'brew', the hot water being provided by the matron.

Bill simply said the food was sparse and unappetising, his other major complaint about the physical conditions being that since they had to have their bedroom windows open in all weathers, in winter he would frequently wake up to find snow on his pillow. This cannot have helped an already delicate chest and must have contributed to his life-long contention that fresh air was bad for you. However, his health seems to have allowed him to take part in the 'Ten', an annual race so-called because of the number of tors traversed by the runners, failure to take part in which, even if they were at death's door, damned boys for the rest of their careers. Success on the rugger field was of course the key to real fame at Sedbergh, and Bill just about scraped through by being in the Second Fifteen. Though just under six feet in height, he was quite slight, but nonetheless managed to make himself a moderately successful hooker. Philip Mason recalls him making a hundred in a house cricket match, which must have been pleasing. Gabriel Carritt was in the First Fifteen and therefore assured of high status in the school.

Philip Mason's memories are more of outside and academic activities. He does not recall the squalor and discomfort described by

21

Gabriel Carritt – perhaps because of a rather different focus, he was able to ignore the physical limitations. He remembers a strong liking for Bill who, in spite of being younger, filled space created by early-leaving contemporaries. They were both interested in the fledgling League of Nations and in Toc H, an organisation run by a man called Tubby Clayton which provided a forum for doing good works in a constructive and un-pious way. In a jointly written article in the *Sedberghian*, Bill and Philip Mason describe the Toc H ideals of community and fellowship, depicting it as being a movement aimed at cutting through the class, caste and hierarchical systems within the Church. They also spent a weekend in a Bradford boy's club during which they were 'chaperoned' by T. H. White, later to be a colleague of Bill's at Stowe, and tried unsuccessfully to learn Italian together.

Philip Mason also produced two house plays, *Arms and The Man*, in which he played Raina while Bill was Luka, and a play by H. A. Vachell called *Quinnies*, in which Bill was the daughter of an old man who kept a furniture shop played by Mason.

On the teaching side, Mason described the Headmaster, Weech, as having appointed a team of eccentrics with varying teaching abilities. Having been told by Weech, whom Gabriel Carritt described as 'fat and lazy', that English Literature was a subject 'only for women', Philip Mason joined 'Clio', the History Sixth, which was run by the brilliant and splendidly erratic Neville Gorton, who was later to become Bishop of Coventry. In his autobiography, Philip recalls an occasion when, having become a bishop and processing towards his Cathedral, Neville stopped to talk to an elderly woman standing by her garden gate, went into her house and vanished for the rest of the afternoon.

The boy whom Bill most often recalled was Freddy Spencer Chapman, later to behave heroically in the Burma Campaign and to take part in a number of expeditions. At Sedbergh, for most of his career he seems to have been wild to a fault, spending time poaching and generally breaking bounds.

Gabriel Carritt, who liked him very much, nonetheless suffered from complex behaviour on Chapman's part in that he would regularly steal money from Gabriel, but would then use it to buy him presents of cocoa and other goodies. I suspect that the then rather conformist Bill was attracted by his lawlessness, regularly recounting with relish the fact that Freddy Chapman had been beaten 13 times in 14 days. They seem to have had a mutual masturbatory relationship, but not one that was seriously involved. Both Bill and Gabriel Carritt were attractive to homosexuals, and were each later to become the object of Wystan Auden's affections. While at Sedbergh Carritt received a series of passionate love letters from another boy, which were subsequently pinched by Auden, who intended to use then in a play which never materialised. Carritt himself says that all the boys in Lupton House were in love with Edie, their matron, whom he describes as tending 'our sores and bruises, devouring us with doglike devoted eyes.'

Bill's school career must have been highly active. Besides playing rugger and the activities he undertook with Philip Mason, he fenced, was a member of the Debating Society, and in 1925 is recorded as having won prizes for History, Divinity, French and 'The Rankin Shakespeare Prize'. Also a member of 'Clio', Neville Gorton's teaching was meat and drink to him, engendering a lifelong passion for seventeenth-century English history. There does seem to have been a point, though, when his academic success was not entirely assured. In August 1925, Weech wrote to him as follows:

My Dear McElwee,

I have been going through the examination reports recently, and I have come to the conclusion that it would not be wise for you to delay your scholarship effort till the Balliol Group comes round. I don't want to discourage you in any way, and I have every confidence that you are going to get a scholarship, but the examiners seem to think you will not be of the requisite standard for New College or Balliol. Unless I misunderstand the situation, the size of the scholarship will be of importance to you, and I shall want you to obtain an £80 scholarship. This, I am afraid, probably bars the two colleges I have mentioned.

In this same connection, I am going to cut you off from extraneous activities, such as Secretaryships to Toc. H. or League of Nations; I think you will have to concentrate all next term on purely Scholarship work, and doubtless you will do a little historical reading in September.

But don't let this disturb your holidays.

Yours sincerely,

W. N. Weech.

A splendid headmasterly letter that no doubt concentrated Bill's mind. He was always able to work effectively under pressure.

His housemaster, a man called Meister who was much loved by his charges, wrote to Bill at the end of December that same year:

My Dear McElwee,

I know you have been wondering during the last few days whether you or Chapman would be Head of House.

I talked it over with Rea [who must have been the departing Head of House] and was a good deal exercised over the problem. You see I have for a long time kept Chapman back from his natural place by virtue of seniority, but he has lately done so well that it would be unfair to let the past weigh any more. Eventually we decided that he should be Head, my only sorrow being that you might be disappointed. And for this term therefore I decided that you should go on as second Prefect. If you hadn't lived so far away I should have liked a talk which was impossible in the crowded hours of yesterday. Please understand that it is not that I do not think you would make an excellent Head of House. I am perfectly confident that you would. It is only after weighing things very carefully that I have decided that Chapman, who is now entering his 6th year of schooltime, has the slightly greater claim.

You are big enough, I know, to realise that these problems are not always easy for a Housemaster: and I believe you will do all in your power to back Chapman up in what is always a difficult task.

Also I want you to be Captain of House Football: this term we have had cruel luck from the weather, and I am not sure what the plan is for next term: but I want you to be ready for whatever may happen. It's a job that needs tact and thought: you've got fairly good material to work on; but you will have some gaps to fill.

I want to take this opportunity of telling you that I am very conscious of your loyal support and keen work for the House; and I am very grateful for it. And for many reasons I am very sorry that you are not going to be head. But so long as you realise that it is not due to any shortcomings of your own but merely what seems justice to another I don't think you need have any cause for envy or disappointment.

May you have a glorious holiday: you deserve it after your triumphant success.

Yours very sincerely,

G. C. Meister.

24

The 'triumphant success' was the achievement, in spite of Weech's reservations, of a History Scholarship to Christ Church. Possibly New College and Balliol were then more highly regarded academically. However, Bill averred to the end of his life that Christ Church was superior to *any* other College and was only to be compared with Kings, Cambridge, but it is unclear whether this conviction predated his being there. He was certainly warmly welcomed:

Christ Church,
Oxford.
Dec 18th

Dear McElwee,
It was a great pleasure to be able to elect you to a modern history scholarship and to think you will become a member of the House. I believe that you said you were going to leave Sedbergh before the end of the School Year and go to Germany. I hope that you will carry this out and get to Marburg or some good place like that, when you can read widely and settle down for a time in an atmosphere that is academic, but not scholastic. But see something of life and opinion too. We look forward to having you here.

Yours sincerely,

E. F. Jacob.

Ernest Jacob, a distinguished Renaissance scholar, was to become a close friend of Bill's, the promise of nurture implicit in that letter being amply fulfilled. In the meantime, Bill had a final term at Sedbergh, presumably free to enjoy running the football and playing second fiddle to Freddy Chapman, before he did indeed go to Marburg University.

Travel, Oxford and Getting Engaged

Bill's sojourn in Marburg after he left Sedbergh in 1926 was in fact a continuation of his European and linguistic education, which had begun with his spending a summer holiday in 1924 or 1925 with Georges and Ludmilla Pitoeff in Paris and Biarritz. I should have taken copious notes about this riveting episode while Bill was still alive. As it is, I can remember very little. It was at about the time that 'Les Pitoeff' as they were known in French theatrical circles, opened their own theatre in Paris. They were highly thought of, scoring successes with plays by Ibsen, Shaw and Pirandello among others. They had a number of children, there being a particular play they would put on that informed *les tout Paris* that Ludmilla was again pregnant.

Bill seems to have been taken on as a kind of summer tutor, and one brief vignette remains in my mind. The youngest child, called, I think, Sacha, was difficult to feed, and a lengthy process had to be undertaken by which everyone else shared spoonfuls of his food. Thus, it was: 'Un pour Maman, un pour Papa, un pour Monsieur Bill et un pour Sacha'. The family had a holiday villa in Biarritz, then a fashionable resort, at which some of the time was spent. The only record of this period available is a photograph which could well have been taken in a Biarritz garden, of Georges in a virulently striped jacket reading a letter while Bill, looking over his shoulder, has an arm round a small boy – possibly Sacha. Ludmilla poses self-consciously under a parasol, an unidentified man peers theatrically over Georges' other shoulder, and two young girls grin cheerfully at the camera. Apart from the stimulus of spending time with such a family, Bill acquired fluent French, it being a matter of great pride that in France he would be mistaken for a Belgian, but never an Englishman.

Exciting though his stay with Les Pitoeff must have been, Marburg was the more defining experience for Bill. In 1950 he wrote what was known in the family as his 'war novel'. While much of *Final Objective* is taken up with a description of fighting across Germany in the winter of 1945, it is interwoven with his hero's earlier experience of spending a happy post-school period there. It is the story of a love affair and of a country community, but with little about any academic milieu. This does not fit with Bill's tales of young men proudly decorated with duelling scars among whom he mixed at Marburg, but it does depict the complex, clear-eyed affection he developed for the Germans, mixed with the insight and excitement that were, for him, engendered by early experiences of travel. Because of his familiarity with the country, Bill's hero McCann has 'a fundamental difference of outlook which cut him off, to some extent, from everybody else in the Battalion'. He goes on to write: 'Had he been challenged to do so, McCann would in fact have found it difficult to describe, even to a sympathetic person who shared his feelings, exactly what it was that had first touched Germany with romance for him. Yet he believed that his experience had been a normal one and one which was common to all young men of normal sensibility who, like him, received the usual, perhaps slightly insular British education, and were then suddenly plunged in late adolescence into the comparative freedom and total novelty of a foreign background.'

His thesis was that the first time 'foreignness' is encountered, ordinary things, in the book a country railway station, his German hosts and the village in which they live, are seen with 'the observant, excited eye with which every child greets a new aspect.' Everything, he felt, including the people, were 'romanticised and so remained in the memory, touched, like the memories of childhood with a magic which was no more deserved by those particular circumstances than by others on occasions less sensitively appreciated'. This rather ponderous paragraph is followed by one which vividly illustrates what was likely to have been his state of mind when he went to Marburg: 'There was another element which such an experience shared with the experiences of childhood, which also served to endow it with a golden quality in retrospect – the element of irresponsibility. For the first time in years and probably the last time in life there was no examination round the corner, no job waiting to be done, no neglected duty elsewhere to tug at the conscience or oppress the mind with thoughts of the future. No holiday again would ever offer such completeness of escape; and it was inevitable that the disillusioned and harassed mind of later life

27

should cherish the unique experience as an unreal, almost unbeliev-able, memory.'

Though it is rather too obvious a device, landing McCann back on the same station platform ten years later gives Bill further opportunity to illustrate another aspect of adolescence, that was also, I suspect, self-revelatory. 'It had been a very awkward, unsure youth who had stepped out on to that platform ten years ago – one who seemed to bear little relation to the tired, disillusioned soldier who stood now leaning against the signal box of that same station.' He goes on to detail the social gaffes committed during that earlier journey: under-tipping the waiter in the dining-car, finding himself in the ladies' lavatory by mistake, and failing to send a telegram to his hosts when the train was delayed. All of which had made him 'miserable with shame' and which 'still had the power, when remembered, to sting him with embarrassment'. What powerful bells are rung by that description.

In reality, able after his six months stay to speak fluent German, Bill travelled home from Germany through France, where he discovered that learning another language had temporarily bereft him of his French. Conscious that German was still wildly unpopular, he found himself struggling to communicate in Latin. The home to which he went was, by now, in the small village of Culmstock on the borders of Devon and Somerset, where Kitty had found a delightful house called Tapscott, to which Philip Mason remembers a happy visit. The Lloyds had long had links with Devon, which probably accounts for her choice of county. They seem to have acquired friends, and Bill was able to learn to ride on the horses of local farmers.

One of the people he met was Mary McClelland, a woman then in her late twenties, living with her mother and being the 'daughter at home'. She too had Irish connections, linking somewhere with the Lloyds in the labyrinthine family trees cobbled together by Patrick, and was one of that sad generation of young women deprived of possible partners by the wartime destruction of young men. She fell in love with Bill and, indeed, he with her. He would later describe this episode rather defensively, emphasising her prettiness and his immaturity. She kept extensive diaries of their innocent boy-and-girl relationship, which many years later, in what I think was an act of unforgivable self-humiliation, she sent to Bill. Having read them from cover to cover, I rather priggishly threw them away, feeling, I think, that she should not be further exposed, but now of course, I wish I

28

had them. Bill in later years, would ask exasperatedly if she had really felt there could be any future in their relationship given the age gap, but she had clearly convinced herself that somehow this could be overcome and that she could be more to him than a calf-love.

This affair had started before Bill went up to Oxford in the autumn of 1926, but was always of infinitely greater importance to poor Mary than to Bill, who rapidly became absorbed into the delights of University life and contact with some remarkable contemporaries. He must have worked reasonably hard, though he always said it was not hard enough and that it had been fatal to admit to playing bridge. However, apart from his enjoyment of being taught by Ernest Jacob, I have little picture of his academic life, though it almost certainly confirmed the love of British and European history of the sixteenth and seventeenth centuries that he had acquired under Gorton at Sedbergh. It would not just have been the games of bridge that hampered his work, since his looks and charm clearly ensured his social success. He was not a member of the Bullingdon Club and was not, I think, prone to the sort of excesses described by Evelyn Waugh in *Decline and Fall*, but he did recall with pleasure going round the exquisite Peckwater Quad in Christ Church one night, breaking ALL the ground-floor windows with a polo mallet. He excused such vandalism by saying that he had paid for the damage the following day.

Where particular friends were concerned, he is one of four people listed by Lord Hailsham, then Quintin Hogg, in his autobiography as being his closest friends, and in a recent letter Lord Hailsham reiterated this, describing a common circle of friends and saying that he was 'a dear person'. When they were all still at Oxford, Hailsham, his friend Richard Best, who was the son of an Orangeman, and Bill, also an Irish Protestant, were all invited to a meal with the Jesuits at Campion Hall. According to an article on Lord Hailsham written by Geoffrey Lewis, he later discovered that this invitation, which came out of the blue, had been issued because two young Jesuit students needed to be cured of their fear of 'Protestants and public schoolboys'. While Bill never wavered from his Church, he much admired the compassion of the Catholics and knew Father Martin D'Arcy, of whom he would speak with warmth.

Dick Crossman must also have been at Oxford then and was certainly a friend of Bill's after the war. Rex Warner was close enough to be asked to Bill's twenty-first birthday party. A favourite story of Bill's was of the occasion when Rex Warner, who had been drinking

29

heavily, asserted that 'absolute beauty' had floated in through his window one night. Among the remarkable dons of that era, Bill clearly knew 'Sligger' Urquhart well, and he would talk familiarly of A. J. Ayer and Maurice Bowra. When, in 1961, I met him on a Swan's Hellenic cruise, Bowra recalled Bill affectionately. Bill's most notable and well-documented friendship, however, was that with Wystan Auden.

Auden, who had been up at the House for a year, seems to have spotted Bill almost immediately. In his biography of Auden, Humphrey Carpenter describes their contact extensively. After documenting Auden's early contact with Louis MacNeice, Carpenter writes: 'More important to Auden was a friendship of a different kind, in effect a love-affair. During this Autumn he became very attached to a freshman at Christ Church, a history scholar named W. L. (Bill) McElwee, who had just come up from Sedbergh School. Auden made his feeling clear to McElwee; an unpublished poem entitled "Quique amavit" and bearing the dedication "To the only begetter Mr W. L." is in part a declaration of love though it goes on to consider in obscure terms the complexities of the process of loving.' Carpenter goes on to say, 'It is impossible to be certain what sort of relationship Auden had with McElwee. Most of Auden's friends had the impression that McElwee was not prepared to respond to Auden's love and would not go to bed with him, though he was flattered by the attention. According to one undergraduate contemporary, however, Auden reported that he and McElwee had made an arrangement to go to bed regularly once a week. If this was true, Auden mentioned it to no one else and most people had the impression that his feelings for McElwee left him unhappy and unsatisfied.' Auden and Bill apparently went to Austria together during the Christmas vacation of 1926, after which Auden reported to a friend: 'I had a very good three weeks in Austria with McElwee and no complications thank God!' Carpenter takes this to mean that there was no sex between them.

I think that Bill did experience some uncertainty about his sexuality, but I do not think he was physically in love with Auden. While he may well have been flattered by the attention of one who was not only senior to him, but was already gaining a considerable reputation, he also regarded him with enormous affection, remaining close friends long after Auden's affections had been transferred elsewhere. Bill would describe Auden walking down the High wearing carpet slippers, clutching a china tobacco jar and loudly humming Bach cantatas.

He was also impressed by the fact that Auden managed to break my grandmother's habit of reading everyone's postcards by writing a card of such outstanding obscenity that she never dared to read one again. Auden visited Tapscott in April 1927 and was apparently in some awe of Kitty, but was immediately taken with Patrick, which according to Carpenter upset Bill and caused him to refer to himself as 'the discarded mistress'.

Carpenter notes that shortly after this Bill became engaged to be married, there being the faint implication that this happened on the rebound from Auden, but this seems highly unlikely to me. The exact date of this occurrence is not recorded, but must have been in Bill's first year. Patience, having escaped from her hated school, had got a place in a secretarial college in Oxford, a move which was probably designed to allow her to meet young men rather than to gain a useful qualification. Judging by passages in a subsequent novel of hers, she found learning typing and shorthand difficult. I doubt if she ever used the latter, and though she typed fast and reasonably accurately, it was always with two fingers on each hand.

Pretty and entertaining, she was much more successful in meeting young men. She would recount with relish the occasion on which she was taken out in a punt by a wealthy undergraduate from Christ Church. He, or rather the College Kitchens, had provided a lavish picnic lunch, most of which she threw to a group of swans by whom she was frightened, though she did manage to eat enough to throw up later when the motion of the punt got to her. 'And he still proposed,' she would say triumphantly. This episode illustrates two constants in Patience's life, her motion sickness and her fear of swans. It was a matter of pride to her that she had been sick in one of the very earliest Rolls-Royces, and merely watching films of ships at sea would cause her to go green. She spent much of the film *Battle of the River Plate*, which she adored, with her eyes shut. As for swans, Bill recalled fondly the time they were fishing from one of the islands in the Stowe lakes. Patience was out of sight round a corner, but in earshot, and he suddenly heard her say with anguish, 'Oh do go away, you horrid creature. Oh, how Leda *could*.'

They met at the bridge table. Patience was a skilled player, and Bill was instantly enchanted when she sat down to play and announced that she had to win or would be unable to get home, as she did not have her bus fare. They never recounted how she did get home, but the next day they went racing with friends and became engaged in the

31

back of the car on the drive back to Oxford. She was 17 and he was 20. Mary wrote despairingly in her diary, 'Billy is engaged' and went on to speculate miserably about someone else bearing him 'dark-eyed babies'. Patience felt sorry for her and insisted on making her Godmother to their solitary dark-eyed baby when eventually it arrived.

She also seems to have felt sorry for Auden and wrote soon after they became engaged: 'Wystan worries me. I expect he will go on feeling hurt you know'. This does not suggest that the attachment to Patrick was long-lasting, and indeed it was soon superseded, as Humphrey Carpenter notes, when Bill introduced Auden to Gabriel Carritt, who went up to Christ Church in the autumn of 1927. They were both at Bill's twenty-first birthday party, which took place in September 1928 and for which Auden had written a charade. According to Carpenter and to my uncertain memories, this was not in fact performed. I suspect that the Devon neighbours would have disapproved. Given that company, some kind of charades would have been part of the entertainment, and possibly that was the occasion on which Ernest Jacob appeared with an inadequate sheet doing duty for a toga.

By the time I knew my parents, Patience was apt to remark cynically that they had to get married since they had taken on a vast number of bets that their engagement would not last until Bill had a degree and some gainful occupation. Neither had the wherewithal to honour their commitments. The hundreds of letters Patience wrote to Bill during the three years belie this, suggesting that in fact she adored him and was entirely looking forward to getting married. From comments in her letters, Bill clearly wrote to her as well, but sadly none of his letters survive. This is a particular deprivation as he was not given to writing letters, being convinced throughout his life that all letters answered themselves if left long enough. He wrote when he felt it was really necessary, which made the results valuable. One letter from Auden who had by then left Oxford, started: 'It is high time one of us wrote to the other, and as you certainly never will it has to be me.' Patience never dated her letters, so it is impossible to know at what stage many of them were written, but it would seem likely that the following dates from comparatively early in their relationship:

Darling Bill,
Mummy has just said 'Don't pester the poor boy with letters' but in spite of that – I never thought this longing for you would get

worse instead of better. It's ever present. I had an odd tea-party yesterday. The girl admitted she was in love with me. Of course I got rattled and said some rather childish things. We have agreed to have a purely mental friendship. She is an interesting person, rather pedantic, an absolute intellectual snob. She told me I'd improved since I've been engaged – that's one for you.

You're much nicer to me in your letters than I am to you. But I think you know I love you equally. I feel it will make me incredibly happy just to see you again. I can't do much for you. I hope the time will come soon when I will be able to.

It's no use just at the moment writing down things like that, because I want to see you. I keep everything to tell you.

Goodnight darling,

Patience.

Similarly to Bill, Patience was apparently attractive to lesbians and later made a good story out of the occasion when, during the war, a female member of the Scottish aristocracy made a pass at her in the still room of a castle while making cream cheese. She never seemed to be repelled by these advances, but confusingly, always stated that she disliked women in general. In one of her letters to Bill she says 'Men worry me and I hate women', and I remember her frequently saying how much she disliked being touched by women. This would probably now label her as a closet lesbian, but that does not feel accurate to me. She was dubbed 'the only female homosexual I know' by someone up at Oxford, the most likely candidate for this statement being Auden, who clearly liked and appreciated her greatly. This statement feels right and though difficult to define, is probably best illustrated by the fact that Auden could write to her in the following terms:

My Dear Patience,
I was very touched to get a card from you. Its whiff of clean English boyhood nearly gave me a stroke and for nights I shan't be able to sleep without three orgasms. Berlin is a buggers daydream. There are 170 male brothels under police control. I could say a lot about my boy, a cross between a rugger hearty and Josephine Baker. We should make D.H. Lawrence look rather blue. I am a mass of bruises. Perhaps you can give me some news of Bill? He is not likely to write but I should like to know how

his health is. I am perfectly convinced the disease is psychological, and taking him to throat specialists a waste of time and
money. Perhaps a sanatorium life will be psychologically right
but I doubt it. You are much more likely to cure him than anyone else. Having written something about his work, the letter ends:
'please write sometime. Love Wystan.'

Undoubtedly Patience liked adolescent boys, felt comfortable with
them and found them less daunting than adults, but it is remarkable
that she could be written to in those terms in 1928, when she was only
18. She was apparently concerned, though, when she got a letter from
Auden, while staying with her formidable Aunt Isobel in their large
house in Yately, and wrote to Bill: 'I had another letter from Wystan
today. He put some rash remark about male brothels on the flap of
the envelope which I can only pray wasn't seen'. She might, in fact,
have enjoyed shocking what seems to have been a pretty stuffy
family.

More generally, Patience's letters describe what was probably a
fairly conventional, slightly flapperish, way of life for a young woman
of her class in what was then a small seaside town, with Lancing
College providing considerable social cachet. By the time I knew her,
watching sporting events was something she enjoyed, but taking part
in them was anathema to her. Then she set out to learn to ride, probably to please Bill, and was concerned with the correct clothing. 'This
morning I was quite snowed under with patterns and whipcord from
the Bedford Riding Co. Shan't I look a little pet in jodhpurs?' She
also played a great deal of tennis, mostly with someone called Geoffrey
whom she found boring. Describing him to Bill, she wrote, 'I don't
like him. I think he has no blood in his veins, only the whitening stuff
they use for tennis courts'. Other letters depict Kennington family life
vividly.

Soon after Bill left England to spend time in a sanatorium, her
brother Alan, always known in the family as Dumpy, went off to spend
some time in Germany. Since he was slightly older than Bill, he must
already have come down from Oxford and decided to put in his travel
the other way round. He wrote his best novel following the year he
spent there. Patience described his departure graphically:

Dumpy went on Friday. I couldn't mind so very much. I was
drained of tears already – I shall never get used to your not being

34

with me. Dumpy's going off was extraordinarily confused. Mummy with tears streaming down her face imploring him to remember he was Herren and not Damen – I looking on the bright side of things saying what about this three-year-old handicap – Pop saying My God, this bicycle is over oiled – and Dumpy utterly unmoved playing the *Rhapsody in Blue*.

The reference to the 'three-year-old handicap' confirms how much Patience condoned and joined in with the gambling habits of her father and brother. Other letters illustrate this: 'I've discovered I've got a new vice, Greyhound racing. It's right in my blood. I cleaned up big money at Hove last night, and all Dumpy's dogs sat down and had a think in the middle of the course. You are lucky to be marrying anything so competent as myself.' In another written just before Bill returned: 'If you come back on the 25th, say, you'd be back in time to hold my hand during the Lincoln.' The betting continued all her life, but was mostly on major races and was never the all-encompassing activity it was for her father and brother.

In spite of her devotion, Patience was not above describing other encounters to Bill. On another visit to Aunt Isobel, she writes of 'an old flame' whose mother said she had 'an evil face'. She goes on to say: 'Robert and I were in love in the way one is for two years, when his mother forbade me to see him again.' She can only have been 15 when this affair started. She is clearly worried about Bill's reaction to her confessions and urges him to write, but also says: 'Oh by the way, don't think I am trying to badger you into marrying me. Take your time about making me an honest woman.' After all this rather muddled emotion, she ends her letter characteristically, 'I've discovered a P. G. Wodehouse in this arid waste, so no more time must be lost, Goodnight darling, Patience.' He seems to have responded satisfactorily to all this, prompting the reply, 'I knew of course you would be helpful, and I told Robert you would be nice about it. Let's get married as soon as we can – not to unload superfluous' [I think – the word is almost illegible] 'sex, but because you are such an angel.' It sounds rather as if, in spite of the fact that they had no means of subsistence, she was pressuring him to marry her quickly.

The illness to which Auden refers and the reason for his departure to a sanatorium was not in Bill's throat, but in his lungs. The details are slightly hazy, but it seems to have started with the removal of his appendix. After the operation, he developed a cough which somehow aggravated the unhealed scar, resulting in an abscess in one lung. It was desperately painful and Bill would later describe being given what he said was heroin, but was presumably morphine, with euphoric results. He remained understanding about addiction ever afterwards. Whatever the exact reason, he now had a damaged lung which no one seemed able to treat. The major fear was that it was, or would develop into, tuberculosis, hence the idea of his going to a sanatorium. This meant that he delayed taking his degree by a year, going out to Leysin in the French Alps in November 1929, and returning the following April. Here, judging by Patience's letters, his health and state of mind fluctuated a good deal. Tests for TB were at that time done by injecting wretched guinea pigs with, presumably, blood samples, and then waiting to see what happened. 'How is your guinea pig,' wrote Patience, 'you had better not tell me if it is dead.' Later she wrote again: 'I'm rather glad that guinea pig is still flourishing. It will probably die of natural causes. I had a guinea pig called Edward and he died very soon.'

The experience of these six months had a profound effect on Bill. He wrote a play about it called *Local Colour* which, though the dialogue is a touch stilted and the plot over-contrived, does give a vivid picture of the violent mood swings, intense relationships and constant worry induced by the daily monitoring of everyone's physical state. The plot concerns a young journalist who manages to infiltrate the sanatorium in order to get background for a book and ends up finding that he actually does have the disease. It is a device that enables Bill to depict the intrigues, tensions and fears befalling a small group of people and the literally feverish gaiety with which they deal with their predicament. Patience's letters, however, reveal Bill as becoming deeply disheartened at times and as well as urging him not to work too hard, 'something will turn up even if you get a Fourth'. She begs him not to become hopeless, 'otherwise I shall feel you ought to be marrying someone brisk and pushing.' At one point there is clearly a fear that if he returns, it will be only to go out there again, but eventually he apparently gets better, though it is never clear how or from what. He was left with a bronchiectasis and only one functioning lung, the other being collapsed. The doctors told him that he would be lucky if he survived for five years, and at this point he seems to have resolved to stop listening to them and get on with his life. In order to survive, he had to cough up a quantity of phlegm every morning of his life; it was the one thing about which he remained wholly disciplined. He was prone to bronchitis and, at times, bouts of pneumonia that would come close to killing him, but was triumphant on the day he drew his old age pension.

5

Marriage and Employment

During Bill's absence in Leysin and immediately following his return, Patience alternated between expressing anxiety about his health, when she would urge him not to risk further damage by overwork, and fear of the future, when she would ask tentatively whether he was doing enough work. As the months passed, her varied speculations about his future employment increased. Going into the Diplomatic Service is mentioned, though he did not apparently get to the point of applying, and there seems to have been serious consideration given to taking on a Sussex farm, though its size and viability is not discussed. In one letter Patience wonders if they could survive entirely on the minute allowances they each received from their parents, she having early expressed her antipathy to 'toiling and moiling in an office'. The erratic nature of both families' finances would swiftly have rendered this idea ineligible. In one letter Patience writes: 'It's a pity about your not having any money. A great blow has fallen on the K (Kennington) family, something to do with income tax.' This must have been a particular problem, coming on top of the constant drain occasioned by Syd's gambling.

However, finances were better in the other family: 'It's good news the McElwee finances prospering like this'. No details are given, but it is possible that, for once, Kitty's investments had been successful. On the whole her financial speculations were legendary for their disastrous nature. Endowed, like most members of her class at that time, with a certain amount of capital, she had an unerring ability, Bill always alleged, to spot a country with an approaching disaster and her enthusiastic investments would invariably precede the failure of a vital crop or a major revolution. The allegation that she invested in Warsaw Gas, Coal and Coke in 1939 was almost certainly a characteristic invention by Patience, but there was, when she died, little money left for her sons.

It is likely that while Bill may have joined in with Patience in fantasising about the future, his sights and those of his tutors were set on an academic career. This meant that a First-class degree was vital, and accounts for the anxieties aroused by the amount of time he had to take out because of his health. When he had completed his papers, Bill telephoned Maudie and told her that he thought he had got a Second. Patience subsequently wrote full of further speculation about what they might do if he had got a Third, though this may have been occasioned by her determination never to tempt fate. Her mood of determined pessimism continued right up to the moment when he telephoned to say that he had got his First, since her letter of congratulation is clearly the second of the day. It is headed:

Lancing, 3.30.

My Darling Bill,

My letter of this morning was sufficiently gloomy and resigned. I feel completely overcome. I think the telephone man thought I was quite mad. I am so terribly proud and pleased. Mum seems to be getting on tremendously fast with her letter even though she has just burst into tears. Stout little Mrs Hargreaves has just been told the news. She said she was glad because she always thought you were a nice boy.

Darling, I do feel so absolutely happy.

Are you terribly tired? I hope you will have been able to write, but I'll let you off if you've been getting drunk.

Don't think I shall love you any more just because you have got a First. I'll tell you a secret, I couldn't love you any more.

God bless you, darling.

Patience.

It was a characteristic of both Maudie and Patience that good news always made them cry.

Keith Feiling, who must also have taught Bill, and who had written cheeringly to him in Leysin, wrote a letter that began 'My Dear McElwee' rather than 'My Dear Man', which was his usual opening. He went on: 'My warmest congratulations on your 1st which is a splendid performance. Apart from its material advantage to you I am sure

39

you will find it a help to yourself that you have overcome many obstacles and won. On the future we must write or speak much more.'

Two postcards remain, one simply saying 'Heartiest Congratulations' and signed Denys Page with an artistic slant, and the other from a Donald Allan, saying 'Naturally! but many congrats'. The letter Bill would probably have treasured most though, was one from his Scout, the man who looked after him at Christ Church:

Dear Sir,
Well done, Ho-blooming-ray, I am so glad. That's how I feel. I know I ought to write, Dear Sir, please accept my humble congratulations on your First.

I expect you feel like my outburst too. You must have a good rest now Sir.

You will be pleased to know that my boy will see again with his bad eye. Yesterday the matron told us that they were quite pleased with him, and that in time he would see again. Perhaps not so strong, but he would see. This world is not such a bad place after all.

I wish you always the best of luck, and your lady.
I am Sir Always yours respectfully
T. Hicks

There is no clear picture of how Bill filled the months following the news of his degree. Presumably he based himself at Tapscott, visited Oxford to discuss possibilities with Keith Feiling and others, then waited for news of his various applications. One letter from Patience says: 'Why do you apologise for discussing ways and means in a letter? You must know that it comforts me to have our marriage mentioned. If you get any sort of a job we must marry, because otherwise I should never see you at all. I think we could manage all right on five hundred.' In another letter she asks if he is thinking of applying to become a Fellow of All Souls, but I can find no mention of his having applied for a Senior Scholarship from Christ Church, only that he was waiting to hear if he had got one. Perhaps he applied for both, since she says at one point: 'I hear that Bowen got his fellowship. How soon shall we know about you? I don't let myself think that it is in the least certain.' That particular letter ends: 'All my love darling. Will the Senior Scholarships be in *The Times*? I will be a good and careful wife.' On 7 November her anxiety is clearly mounting: 'I

40

wish the House would hurry up and decide. Do you think it's fairly certain they'll give you £200?' A week later, however, it was apparently confirmed that he had got a research Scholarship that would take him to Vienna to work in the Archives of the Holy Roman Empire, and an announcement that their marriage was to take place on 20 December 1930, appeared in *The Times*.

From then on Patience's letters become concerned with clothes, wedding presents, birth control, obtaining a passport and opening a bank account. William and Phoebe Lloyd had opened an account with Coutts when they married, beginning a benevolent relationship that was to become central to McElwee life. Bill would have undoubtedly insisted that Patience open her account with them, but would have been equally insistent that her account was separate from his, an idea that I was to welcome later. Their subsequent relationship with the bank must have tried Coutts' benevolence high, but it survived even at times when the exchanges of letters had become particularly acrimonious. It was during one such period that Coutts wrote to Bill in the following terms:

Sir,
  We note that your daughter, Miss Harriet Mary Arden McElwee, has now attained her seventeenth year. We also note that your Grandparents Inspector General and Mrs William Lloyd opened an account with us in 1870.
  We trust that this connection will continue in the future.
  We remain, Sir, Ever your obedient servants,
  Coutts & Co.

It always delighted Bill that however cross the tone of a Coutts letter, it invariably ended with the statement that they were ever his obedient servants. In response to their letter, he increased his overdraft by £20 so that I could have a bank account, and I enjoyed the cachet and paternalistic support they provided for many years. This included delightful handwritten letters sent on the birth of my own daughters, which conjured up visions of a Dickensian clerk sitting in some eyrie in their old, mahogany-panelled Strand offices, labouriously scanning *The Times* for such announcements before penning a formal letter of congratulation and good wishes. Alas, in the eighties they succumbed to Thatcherism and, when I complained about their massive charges, only avoided by having a balance that vastly exceeded my monthly pay cheque, they as good as said that their services were not for the likes of modestly paid public servants, and in spite of fears about family grave-turning I regretfully closed my account.

With her bank account sorted, Patience's thoughts turned to birth control. In one letter to Bill she writes: 'I had a talk with Anne about birth control but she wasn't in the least helpful though very kind.' Anne was presumably a friend and must initially have seemed a more likely source of helpful information than Maudie, whom Patience never forgave for failing to tell her about menstruation, which started for her at the early age of ten, giving her a tremendous shock. Indeed, another letter says: 'As to birth control, I think the information I shall get from my parent will be primitive, so please don't send me any Stopes devices. Get me a medium sized cap and you'll have to do your bit on the first night. You don't know how thankful I am to you for embarrassing me so little. I couldn't be happy marrying anyone else.'

However, it later seemed that she had wronged Maudie: 'Mummy is writing you a terrific letter. She is so afraid you won't like her for doing it, but I must say I am thankful to her. We discussed the matter last night. I don't know quite what she is saying to you, but her own method seems very safe and simple, and one of my married friends advised me to use exactly the same thing. I don't feel in the least frightened or worried now, so don't be afraid for me.' Open though she was about such things, I do not remember her mentioning this 'safe and simple' method. Since it involved Maudie writing to Bill about it, I can only think it was coitus interruptus.

Patience was ambivalent about future parenthood. In one letter she remarks that they could surely have a baby as soon as they have set up house properly and in another describes her dreams about having children, but after visiting a friend with a new daughter, she was thoroughly put off. 'I went to see Sylvia's baby yesterday. Oh it is a tragedy. I couldn't eat any tea. I was so depressed. It is exactly like Alec and very red, with a horrid little damp head. All the way home I vowed I wouldn't have a baby, but I guess I shall because I know I am going to have a son.'

Because of Syd's position as Bursar at Lancing, they were able to be married in the dramatic, Victorian Gothic school chapel. The wedding party seems to have consisted mainly of family, who were given lunch prepared by the school chef. The night before their wedding, Maudie had become particularly exasperated with Syd and stormed in the room, saying: 'Whatever you do, Patience, never marry a man.'

Maudie's expressed view had always been that the only reason for marrying was to have someone around to look up trains and open tins. In spite of the future vicissitudes of their relationship, Patience was never so extreme in her statements about marriage, holding that whatever the quality of the relationship, for a woman almost any marriage was better than none. Her own began with a skiing honeymoon during which she remained wedded to the nursery slopes and destroyed their hotel's elaborate heating system by insisting on having a window open at night.

They seemed to have had fun and there exist happy photographs of them on the slopes, but sex was not the success Patience had clearly hoped it would be. She always maintained that her supposedly thickened hymen, which apparently proved an impenetrable barrier, was a condition which, according to one biographer, she shared with Elizabeth I. I have since wondered about the accuracy of the diagnosis, but it was lent some credence by the fact that my conception followed an operation. However, it is somewhat contradicted by Bill telling me after her death that while they reached a reasonably happy compromise following my birth, they were unable to achieve penetrative sex ever again. Patience was also apt to extol the virtues of men being 'educated' sexually by older, experienced women before they married their virgin brides, which suggests that she thought that their problems might have been solved had Bill gone through this thoroughly Edwardian process. Bill did later have at least two affairs where sex seems to have been entirely satisfactory, and I suspect that Patience actually suffered from vaginismus, a condition not much understood before the advent of Masters and Johnson. Maudie's fears of what might happen during the operation compounded her delay, but the outbreak of war and Bill going off to fight was a catalyst. He had apparently said that were he to find himself dying on a battlefield, his greatest regret would be the fact that he had not fathered a child. My conception was apparently a riot, fuelled by champagne and the fact that the bed broke only added to the fun. Tragic that they were unable to recapture that fun.

Married life in Vienna was something of a struggle for Patience, who spoke no German and who had entirely failed to learn to cook. She would say dramatically that she was unable to boil an egg when she married, but in fact, armed with a 1920s *Mrs Beeton*, she learnt fast. Her initial determination to do things thoroughly precipitated an event that was to provide a major piece of family lore. Mrs Beeton having stated that a stockpot was essential to good cooking, Patience began one. It was most successful until the day she forgot to boil it up. One day stretched to a number of days, with Patience becoming increasingly apprehensive about telling Bill. Finally, she could bear it no longer, burst into floods of tears and confessed. Bill's description of taking the evil-smelling pot down from their third-floor flat to the dustbins in the area at the dead of night, was graphic. Ever afterwards, the unwritten, difficult letter or the pile of papers in which one knows something needing urgent attention lurks, has been known in the family as a 'Stockpot'.

They seemed to have liked their flat in the Nineteenth District of the city, and to have acquired a Siamese cat called Evans, referred to by their much-loved landlady as 'Der Efans'. Bill found his research hampered by the fact that the Archives of the Empire were in 13 different languages. However, he managed to use his French and German to reasonable effect, emerging with a set of lecture notes, sufficient material for a book on the Emperor Charles V, and a knowledge of nineteenth-century Germany and Austria which was also put to use in a book.

They apparently had a rich social and cultural life, hearing a magical *Rosenkavalier* sung by Lotte Lehmann and Elizabeth Schumann, and being bedewed by Furtwängler's sweat during a spectacular concert. They also attended a performance of *Meistersinger* that caused Patience to stand up in the stalls and keel over in a faint. The distinguished classical scholar Denys Page, who had signed his congratulatory note to Bill so elegantly and who had accompanied them to the opera, was heard to say loudly as she was carried out, 'How pleased Wagner would have been to know that he had bludgeoned someone into insensibility.' Patience was prone to faint when kept waiting for food, and I can well imagine that the length of a Wagner opera would have been far too much of a good thing.

Denys Page was also at Patience's twenty-first birthday party, which would have taken place on 12 July 1931. A chaste invitation card exists signed by those attending, Kitty McElwee included. Alan (A.J.P.) Taylor does not appear to have been among those present, but it was in Vienna that he first met Bill and Patience. In his *Personal History*, Alan gives brief, vivid descriptions of them both:

'At Easter 1931 I went to Vienna, where we got to know Bill McElwee, a former pupil of Ernest's. Bill was cut out to be a good historian. Unlike me he longed to return to Oxford and, again unlike me, failed to do so. He became a lecturer at Liverpool University and could not stand it. He disliked the place and still more the professor, Veitch, of whom Ted Hughes said, "The higher the monkey climbs the tree, the more you see of his arse." So Bill became senior history master at Stowe where he lived in a house that had been built for Capability Brown.' Of Patience, Taylor wrote: 'Patience McElwee, Bill's wife, was an extraordinary character. She wrote fourteen novels all of which were rejected. Undeterred she succeeded with her fifteenth and poured out many more. They were inferior Wodehouse or Angela Thirkell, with no merits maybe but monuments of industry. Patience disliked Vienna and foreign ways ... but instead of lapsing into unhappiness she became aggressively English and welcomed us on our first visit to their flat with the cry, "Only English people admitted here". Nor was it surprising that she served roast beef even at lunchtime.'

I think Taylor's judgement of Patience's novels is too harsh, but in spite of their diametrically opposed political views, they remained devoted to each other. Taylor referred to Bill as his closest friend, and he mourned both Bill and Patience deeply.

Patience was unable to escape all 'foreign' contact, and she would recall one grand diplomatic dinner party with a mixture of horror and relish. On one side of her was an English musician of growing distinction, who asked her in fruity tones 'Don't you think that pity is the death of love?' while on the other, the opening gambit of an Austrian Count of impeccable lineage was ''Ave you ever been to Brighton at ze weekend?' Later in the meal, not knowing that in German an unadorned 'thank you' means a refusal, she failed to get any port, a drink she adored, and having taken her tightly fitting shoes off under the table, she had a severe struggle to get them back on when the ladies rose to leave the table.

Such grandeur did not of course extend across much of the city, which was suffering appallingly from galloping inflation. They were deeply concerned for the struggles of their landlady to survive, but seemed themselves to have managed on the £200 a year provided by Christ Church and the £100 that Patience, remarkably, received from her father. However, when England came off the Gold Standard in September 1931, they were suddenly without any resources at all, so bequeathing Evans to their landlady, they came swiftly home, arriving, so they always said, with ninepence between them. Once safely back on English soil, Patience declared that she loathed abroad, hated foreigners and had no intention of ever setting foot outside

England again – a vow to which she remained constant for the rest of her life.

In fact she did remember a number of things about Vienna with great affection, though these were mostly connected with food. Italian water ices and enormous meals at the Rathaus Keller, where the waiters offered to pack up any food left on diner's plates, were among the things she recalled happily when I was on my way to the city in 1960. However, immediately, in the winter of 1931–2, life, even on familiar soil, remained unsatisfactory. As Alan Taylor notes, Bill swiftly succeeded in getting a post at Liverpool, but Patience seems to have disliked academic life in Liverpool quite as much if not more than Bill, never talking about 15 Montpelier Terrace, where they lived for a time, and only giving a general impression of antipathy to her fellow academic wives. There are no letters to document this period, so Alan Taylor's description is all that remains. In 1961 Bill wrote a lucid account of England between the wars, which, quoting Churchill, he called *Britain's Locust Years*, but it recounts none of his personal experiences. Their unhappiness in Liverpool led to their moving to an attractive rented house in the Berkshire village of North Moreton where they tried, unsuccessfully, to start a pig farm.

It was while they were failing to farm pigs in the autumn of 1933 that Patience seems to have heard on some grapevine that J. F. Roxburgh wanted a history tutor. Before he became the founding headmaster of Stowe in 1923, Roxburgh had been a housemaster at Lancing and was clearly well-known to the Kenningtons, as the following letter reveals:

Dear Mr Roxburgh,

I am being brought over to Stowe by some cousins of one of your boys on Saturday. I should like just to clap eyes on you if you aren't too desperately busy.

It must be twelve years since you brought Dumpy some codliver oil and walked about the garden on stilts.

The boy we are coming to see is called Tony and has a grandmother – more than that I do not know.

Yours very sincerely,
Patience McElwee.

The picture of the immensely dignified Roxburgh on stilts is one to treasure.

The lift to Stowe was no accident. Phoebe Ames, who was one of the cousins concerned, remembers vividly that Patience asked them if she could go with them, but was mysterious about why she wanted to go. Though no hint of her purpose appeared in her first letter to Roxburgh, the following would appear to have been written the night after she saw him:

Dear JF,

I have been talking to Bill, and he would give up all idea of Oxford if there were to be a chance of your taking him at Stowe. I feel so excited about it, and yet don't want to worry you about it.

He is the sort of person who likes to dig in roots, and we should be able to feel that Stowe was final. It would be wonderful for me to anchor in a school again.

I suppose you won't be able to say anything definite for a long time, but of course it would be just like life if he were offered the Ch.Ch. job and fell between two stools. Still, he would throw it up if you found you could have him.

We could get as far as Oxford any Friday, Saturday or Sunday.

I did so enjoy myself today.

Yours very sincerely,

Patience McElwee.

Until I found that letter recently in Bill's personal file, still kept at Stowe, I had no idea that there was a possibility of an Oxford job. The letter suggests that Patience passionately wanted him to go to Stowe. What is unknown is whether Bill really wanted to go to Oxford, which Alan Taylor implied that he did, but took the Stowe job to please her. If he did, he never mentioned it, and I find it hard to believe that he would have shown the same enthusiasm for the job had it not been his own choice to take it. Patience need not have worried that J. F. would have to keep them waiting for an answer since he wrote to Bill on 30 October 1933 in the following terms:

Dear Mr McElwee,

I write to confirm the result of our conversation yesterday and to invite you definitely to join the staff here in January. I shall be glad to hear from you that you can accept my offer of a post.

The work I shall ask you to undertake will be concerned almost entirely with the History Specialists in the Upper School and you will have control of these as 'History Tutor'. In addition it may be necessary to give you a small number of periods with other boys. I shall in any case wish you to take charge of the School Fencing arrangements – for which the History Tutor has always been responsible here.

The letter goes on to detail Bill's salary which, including various allowances, came to a grand total of £450 a year, and what the school could offer by way of accommodation and pension arrangements.

The formal letter was accompanied by another typed letter which said:

Dear McElwee,

Here is my formal offer. I much hope that you will come to us and that you will enjoy the work. There is a real chance here not only to get results but also to see them. The History department has been given a fine start by MacLaughlin and it ought to have a distinguished future.

Vancouver will be available to you and I find that we last offered it to a Master at a rent of £60 p.a. excluding rates – although we lose heavily on the deal. Let me know when you and Patience feel inclined to come over and see the place.

Yours very sincerely,

J. F. Roxburgh

The post was duly accepted and Bill became History Tutor at Stowe in January 1934.

6

Stowe and Vancouver Lodge

When Bill joined the staff, Stowe had been going for ten years and had just come through a period of financial upheaval. In his life of J. F. Roxburgh, Noel Annan describes how the school, along with several others, had been started on somewhat shaky financial foundations, by an evangelical group wishing to counteract what they saw as a growing threat of Anglo-Catholicism in the country. Roxburgh, on the other hand, had wished to create an institution that, while not challenging existing social conventions and structures, nonetheless allowed boys much greater freedom to explore ideas and interests than was usual in public schools at that time. As Bill wrote in his *Times* obituary of Roxburgh, 'There was nothing cranky or modernistic about Roxburgh's approach to the problems of education and, though he disliked the self-consciousness of school "traditions" as such, he maintained the traditional organisation, methods, and ideals of the English Public School, seeking only to offer a greatly increased freedom within that framework and to develop boys much more as individuals rather than parts of a system.' He seems to have been anxious that the importance of sporting prowess should be modified, with games other than rugby and cricket being encouraged. Good teaching of the major subjects were important to him, though science did not get the same backing as arts subjects. He also felt that boys should have leisure to read and to pursue a variety of interests.

In his autobiography, Professor Roland Oliver, who went to Stowe in 1936, paints a vivid picture of J.F.

'The great treat of the week was to be taught by the headmaster, J. F. Roxburgh, who somehow managed to teach every boy in the school once a week and to know each of them unerringly by both Christian and surname... He was a magnificent, vital figure, immaculately tailored in Savile Row, with one gorgeous handkerchief in his breast pocket and another in his cuff, not a hair out of place, a spring in his step, and an unmistakeable whiff of some very discreet, very exotic scent as he swept past one into chapel or paced untiringly round a classroom. He drove, at reckless speeds, a maroon Daimler coupé accompanied when occasion demanded it by a chauffeur in breeches and leather gaiters. As the obituaries say, "he never married", but nor did he ever put a foot wrong. "Hilton Young" he would say musingly as he strode into the classroom, "What is the French for hairbrush?" When someone gratingly pushed back a chair, he would wince and exclaim "Oh, my dear man, *please* don't throw the furniture about."'

The comment on J.F.'s unmarried state implies that he was a repressed homosexual, but in his book, Noel Annan describes J.F.'s passionate attachment to a Russian girl while he was at the Sorbonne, a relationship doomed by their mutual lack of material resources. Though this seems to have been his most serious relationship, he did not totally abandon the idea of marriage. In March 1942 he wrote to Bill, who was then stationed at Dornoch, 'Years ago I used to play golf at Dornoch and very nearly became engaged to be married there. The lady is now the wife of a Major-General, and I think he has done better for her than I should have. But the Dornoch Golf Course still has a kind of golden glow over it in my memory.'

Noel Annan feels that J.F. greatly regretted his failure to marry and that though a legend of misogyny grew round him, he remained a warm and affectionate man towards both sexes. I once, when very young, accompanied Patience, who was apparently paying a call on him. I remember only being told to be very quiet and fulfilling this injunction by lying stretched out on the carpet. I suspect Patience had a serious reason for going to see him, but nothing remains. I do not think he paid me any attention at all.

As Noel Annan stresses, given J.F.'s ambitions to produce rounded individuals, the house and grounds of Stowe provided the ideal setting for such a school. The Stowe estate, built on prosperous sheep farming, had belonged to the Temple family since the sixteenth century. It was Sir Richard Temple, later Lord Cobham, a successful General in Marlborough's army and a Whig politician who, prudently marrying an heiress, began the transformation of Stowe into a ravishingly beautiful park and garden. The house in its present form was created by his succeeding nephew and great-nephew. These men, through some wangle beginning with Lord Cobham's sister being created Countess of Temple, inherited through the female line adding a succession of heiresses' surnames, the first and most used being Grenville. Stowe became the home of 'Grand Whiggery' and continuing political success resulted in Lady Temple's grandson being created Marquess of Buckingham and, finally, in 1824, the family being granted a Dukedom.

Everyone who was then anyone in architecture and landscape design, including Adam, Borra, Vanburgh, Bridgeman, Kent and Capability Brown, who was head gardener at Stowe for ten years, had a hand in the creation of the imposing and elegant north and south facades of the house, the lavish state rooms and the grounds which were packed with temples and follies placed in such a way that fresh vistas constantly presented themselves. I was told in my youth that our village had once been clustered round its church, but had been removed to make way for Kent's delightful Elysian Fields, permission to move the church having been refused by the bishop. Whatever the truth of this story, the church remains, incorporated into the landscape design, and situated a mile or more from the village. This left villagers a considerable trek on ordinary Sundays, a coach only being provided once a month and on special occasions.

Inevitably the escalating grandeur of the grounds, the house and its fittings took an enormous financial toll. In 1848 the second Duke was forced to sell much of the contents of the house. This enabled the third Duke to hold things together for a time, but as well as money, heirs to most of the titles or ways of fiddling a male successor had also run out. Lady Kinloss, daughter of the third Duke and able to inherit the Scottish Barony, had little stomach for maintaining the estate. She let it for a time to the Comte de Paris, but when her eldest son was killed in the First World War, she decided to sell the place, Allied Schools being the successful purchasers in the 1921 sale. The spectacular avenue that ran from Stowe to the town of Buckingham had been sold separately, but was subsequently purchased by Eton and presented to the new school as a goodwill gesture.

Converting the vast and, as is now only too clear, shabbily built house into a school was a mammoth task. In his obituary of J.F., Bill writes: 'The difficulties, financial, technical, and architectural, involved in the adaptation of the house and grounds of Stowe to the needs of a great public school, Roxburgh had to meet almost single-handed.' Much of it apparently had to take place with the boys in situ. In doing this, it would seem that J.F. was hampered by the machinations of the Reverend Percy Warrington, a man who had been a moving spirit behind the creation of the school. However, he had also undertaken some pretty shady financial dealings. By 1933 these had been curtailed, matters were on a more even keel and Stowe was about to embark on a highly successful period. It remained part of the Allied Schools Group, however, and as late as 1939 Bill was expressing concern to J.F. about the possibility that profits accrued by Stowe were being used to bolster shortfalls in the finances of other schools in the group. J.F. was reassuring, but Warrington had clearly created an atmosphere of mistrust.

There were inevitable conflicts. As Roland Oliver notes, one of Roxburgh's legendary strengths was his ability to remember not only the name of every boy in the school, but also their nicknames and birthdays. This was coupled with a desire to maintain a grasp on all that was happening in the place, which must have been the bane of housemasters hoping to run an autonomous ship. Housemasters did undertake a considerable amount of teaching, but once boys were in the upper school, they went onto 'Sides', which included the Classics, English, History, Modern Languages, Mathematics and the Sciences. French and English continued to be studied alongside their core subjects, these often being taught to non-specialists by housemasters, while other modern languages, art and music were taken up by choice. Each Side was run by a Tutor who then assumed responsibility for the boys' academic prowess. This could be a fine recipe for major clashes when Housemaster and Tutor differed fundamentally over how adolescents should be treated.

In his book *Our Age*, Noel Annan cites the lack of a shared vision among the staff as the reason Roxburgh only partially succeeded in his aims. He writes: 'Only a few of his housemasters really understood him. There were as there always will be, clever rebellious boys who could not fit in and sensitive creatures who suffered at the hands of their insensitive tough contemporaries.' He goes on to single out T. H. White and George Rude as examples of lively young masters who were there during his time at Stowe between 1930 and 1935 and adds that 'My tutor, William McElwee, was one of the many gifted sixth form history teachers of the day.' In a recent letter he expands on this, describing how he and his fellow Historians 'dramatised the divisions among the staff', seeing on the one hand a group of young masters who were 'exemplars of the kind of liberal education J.F. stood for' as against an 'old guard who had totally failed to see what J.F. was about'. The appointment of both these groups must have been Roxburgh's own responsibility, and possibly he was unable to find men who combined, as he did, a belief in a conventional framework within which more liberal ideals could flourish. Or possibly he thought the system would work best if he appointed people from both ends of the spectrum.

It is likely that there was considerable rivalry between Bill and Tim White. Both were brought into the school as young heads of departments, both were charismatic teachers bent on making their mark, and both wrote books. White was, of course, already an established author and destined to be a much greater literary success, but at the time they were nearer level pegging. Noel Annan writes: 'Tim was then preaching that we should all try to be renaissance man, able to hunt in the morning, shoot game in the afternoon and fish at dusk, know how to paunch a rabbit or tie a fly; and after dinner read poetry and discuss whether it was direct or oblique.'

Lord Annan suggests that Bill felt he had to show that he too 'was devoted to country pursuits, the sort of things that his country-bred pupils knew instinctively how to do and had learnt as children.' Bill had, in fact, learnt many of these things as an adolescent in Devon. He was a reasonable shot, apparently able to perform respectably at grand house parties, and though it is unlikely that he could afford to hunt before the war, he could ride decently and was probably able to paunch a rabbit. He certainly could after the war, when we kept them for food. Bill himself undoubtedly subscribed to the renaissance man thesis, but he felt White to be an irritating poseur. He told stories of him coming to dinner with a hawk on his wrist and being boring about where the necessary newspaper was to be placed, and would relate the occasion when White had turned up at some local party and announced loudly: 'This party has no racial future. Parties should be like bird sanctuaries, people should come to them to mate.'

Peter Orde, who joined the History Side when Bill had been at Stowe for about a year, also provides an interesting view of T. H. White which suggests ample fuel for further rivalry. He writes: 'English was easily my best subject, and I had hopes of a literary career. The English tutor was T. H. White, an up and coming author with several works published and well reviewed. He was a picturesque character who kept snakes and a hawk in his room, drove an ancient Bentley, and was learning to fly. Unfortunately he was not a natural teacher – tough, impatient and, to my mind, obscure. I found myself floundering, unable to understand just what he expected from me and

53

too shy to ask. Tim White had few specialist pupils and not all of them survived. Early in my third term with him, no doubt bored with my inadequacy, he said in a tutorial "I'm getting rid of you, Orde; better leave the room and don't come back." Devastated, I left, and coming towards me down the passage came Bill, arms full of books. He stopped, concerned at my expression and asked what was wrong? Then he told me not to worry – the Historians would be glad to have me.'

Peter Orde struggled to learn history, of which he knew little, and, while Bill gave him sympathy and encouragement, he also presented him with a formidable reading list. Though he was only just 17, Bill decided to enter him for the scholarship examination at Oxford to give him 'valuable experience'. Though his History papers apparently revealed the expected shortcomings, he did exceptionally well in the English essay and was awarded a scholarship on the strength of it. Tim White's teaching had, after all, borne fruit, perhaps when combined with the confidence instilled by Bill, who would certainly have claimed it as a History Side success.

What put White ultimately beyond the pale in Bill's eyes, however, was his departure to Ireland at the outbreak of the war, telling people on his return to England that he had been unable to get out of the country. Bill would cite the hundreds of people who did leave Eire to join up and would tell a story about White, on his return to England, going into the bar of the White Hart in Buckingham, where the country friends he had made while at Stowe drank regularly. He arrived with a flourish, loudly proclaiming his return, only to be greeted by dead silence. After a moment, a quiet voice in one corner said: 'So 'e's decided England is to 'ave his bloody bones after all, 'as 'e?' Even if this story had been given a considerable amount of McElwee embroidery, there was probably an element of truth in it. Reading Sylvia Townsend-Warner's biography of Tim White, it is clear that he did make some attempt to get out of Ireland, but his efforts appear to have been halfhearted.

What is also clear though, is that, for all the drawbacks, Bill's upbringing and temperament left him much more psychologically grounded than Tim White, and while he did indeed project some of his ambitions on to his pupils, he nonetheless had sufficient confidence in himself to enjoy teaching and nurturing them. White seems to have been an exciting and, at times, passionate teacher, but did not apparently enjoy it and was given to bombast about his abilities. Townsend-

Warner thought that White's appalling upbringing had left him with little real self-confidence, hence his urgent desire to leave teaching after four years and his hesitant lingering in Ireland during the war.

Like J.F., Bill endorsed the traditional structure of the public school and indeed, Robert Skepper, a postwar historian, said that he felt Bill to be a conventional man who continually challenged conventions. To the old guard in 1934 it would have been the iconoclast that appeared uppermost, and to them Bill must have been anathema, compounded by the fact that he offered his pupils a 'package' that included Patience and a centre outside the school. At 27 and 24, they were not much older than the boys. Patience cared as passionately about the future of the Historians as Bill did, regarding herself as nearly one of them rather than seeing them as a rather tiresome race apart, as many schoolmasters' wives did then, and possibly still do. At that time there were few married masters, so she was unusual on almost every count. Noel Annan described her as being 'dynamite and as unlike a normal master's wife as it was possible to be', with 'a sharp tongue that gave rise to many stories'. He recalls meeting her for the first time, when he and others were being given a lift in what he describes as 'Bill's ancient car'. He was startled when she turned to him and asked: 'Have you got sharp buttocks or have I?'

The house they were allotted provided a splendid setting for their joint enterprise. Most young couples would probably have recoiled in horror from Vancouver Lodge, but Bill and Patience were delighted with it. It was in Dadford, the village created by the machinations of the second Duke of Buckingham. The house was quite large, damp and dark, with no electricity, and was set in some four acres of land. There were conflicting views as to its origins, one being that mentioned by Alan Taylor, that it had been built for Capability Brown; another being that it had been an inn. This latter theory was reinforced by the presence in the garden of a milestone dated 1776 and the fact that when, in one of the myriad attempts to do something about the drainage, part of the drive was dug up, a skeleton was discovered. Since the point where it was found could have been a crossroads in the past, Patience instantly decided that it was a highwayman, the remains of whom were usually buried at crossroads. A line of stones revealed when a nearby field was ploughed, suggested what could have been the old London road, and therefore Vancouver could have been a roadside pub. It could, of course, have been an inn that was later converted for Capability Brown. Whatever the origins of the house, it

55

had been considerably enlarged in the nineteenth century. I have yet to discover why it was called Vancouver.

The house had five bedrooms, an oak-panelled sitting-room with pleasing French windows, a gloomy dining room, which was screened from the rest of the house by heavy curtains, and a small study. The kitchen area was also dark, with stone floors that sweated when it rained. There were a china cupboard and a lamp room, small rooms rather than large cupboards, in which one got the sense of things lurking in unlit corners. Before the war, the lamp room must have been just that. After the war, when electricity had been installed, it became the home, among other things, of the little oil stoves that provided extra cooking power and could be placed at strategic points to stop the pipes freezing. The cooking arrangements were clearly primitive, and in January 1939 Bill was so frustrated by the Bursar refusing to make proper provision, he wrote directly to J.F. He said: 'I think you are familiar with the history of our kitchen stove and boiler. Both ought, by common consent, to have been scrapped two years ago.' He goes on to describe a bizarre situation by which a bucket of water had to be removed from the fireplace every morning before the kitchen fire could be laid and lit.

Three attic rooms completed the interior accommodation. Outside there were four stables with a loft over them and a garage which probably replaced a coach house. A further stable and a lean-to were situated on the other side of the garden. The lengthy drive between the village and the house was bordered with box hedges and various kinds of undergrowth. A dense, wooded area on one side led to open country. When I was a child, none of my village friends would walk up this drive alone after dark. For me it became a point of honour to do so, forcing myself never to run or to look back whatever terror was engendered by noises in the undergrowth. Before it became a school house, Vancouver had belonged to an amateur steeplechase jockey called Charlie Thompson, who was known locally as 'Bonnetty Bob' since his sister was a milliner. He was remembered affectionately, even by those who worked for him and who might have been expected to object to his habit of throwing all the harness out into the mud if it were not cleaned to his liking. He was reputed to haunt the house, and Patience would allege that she regularly saw him just nipping round a corner.

The garden had, from a child's point of view, a splendidly dense shrubbery down one side, in which snowdrops flourished in spring and secret camps could be constructed. Gnarled fruit trees in the neglected orchard still managed to produce a certain amount of fruit. Damsons were particularly abundant, as were gooseberry and currant bushes. These were heavily protected by nettles by the time I knew them and could enjoy eating quantities of unripe gooseberries illicitly. There was also an exciting, if faintly sinister, pond full of black mud and teeming with newts, sticklebacks and minnows. The village brook ran along the bottom of the orchard and flooded extensively whenever it rained heavily. I suspect the tennis court had deteriorated even before the war. Afterwards it became a paddock.

There was a reasonably respectable lawn and some flower beds, one of which Patience, aided by Stephen Whitwell, a thirties Historian, had tried to turn into a water garden with a centrepiece consisting of an elegant bust on a plinth, filched from the Art School. They were bent on mocking what they saw as the pomposity of Stephen's much-disliked housemaster who had placed a similar bust in front of Chatham, the House he ran. This enterprise added greatly to the difficulties of draining an area reputed to be home to 17 springs. Theoretically, drainage was assisted by a 'soakaway', the murky depths of which were a source of fear and fascination to me, but it never seemed to help. The rest of the grounds were woods and undergrowth. Alongside the garden was what had been a proper walled kitchen garden running down to a tangled osier bed and the brook. This now belonged to the neighbouring farmer. It was surrounded by a lovely red-brick wall with a narrow opening, ingress being permitted erratically according to the mood of Jack Davis, the irascible Welsh owner.

It was during a period when the gap was closed that Patience saw a far more dramatic ghost than Charlie Thompson. On a winter afternoon in the thirties, she had been standing on the lawn watching hounds draw the osier bed, and as she turned to go in, she became aware of a woman on a horse standing in the drive. Surprised by the fact that she had not heard the horse on the gravel, she went up to the woman and told her that there was no way through and that she would have to return down the drive. When the woman did not answer, she thought it was typical Grafton hunt snootiness and repeated her statement, whereupon horse and rider moved silently forwards and disappeared through the blocked-up gap. Patience's description was vivid. The woman was riding sidesaddle, was wearing a much lighter blue habit and shallower hat than were then worn, and bore, so Patience said, an exact resemblance to Winterhalter's portrait of Elizabeth,

Empress of Austria, a picture at which Patience had often gazed when she was in Vienna. Elizabeth had hunted regularly with the Grafton, it being one of the few activities she really enjoyed. On the possible principle, therefore, that ghosts are pictures that linger in the ether at sites where the extremes of emotion have been experienced, and can be 'logged into' by those with sufficiently sensitive antennae, Patience could just have been right. As a clincher, she always added that the dog with her had become hysterical with fear.

Before the war, in spite of Bill's rather meagre salary, they were able to employ a manservant, Pritchard, though quite what he did is unclear since everyone who knew them then described the house as spectacularly untidy and dirty. Bill used to tell stories about Pritchard, who would intone contemptuously through an aristocratic nose, 'I've waited on the Kaiser and I've waited on Queen Victoria and now I'm waiting on you.' It was also Pritchard who had worked in some army mess where an erratic General allegedly threw decanters of port at the waiters. 'He was a Gentleman, he was,' Pritchard would remark admiringly when recounting such stories.

Later there was Driver, but he seems to have been much less colourful. Touchingly, though, he sent me a prayer book when I was a baby. Bert Hutchins, who worked in the garden, survived until some time after the war. He was known to the boys rather cruelly as 'Groundsel' and was stone deaf, coming from a family who would seem to have suffered greatly from inbreeding. As war approached he became increasingly anxious, coming regularly to the house to say: ''e won't get me, Kaiser Bill, will'e?' He would accept reassurance on this point until one day Patience managed to set a small greenhouse on fire. Whereupon Bert came rushing into the house, shouting ''e's come, Kaiser Bill 'as. 'E's come.'

Besides the untidiness, the constant burning of candles and oil lamps rendered the ceilings in Vancouver black and once, with a dinner party looming, Patience was talking halfheartedly about cleaning them. Robert Kee, who was with her at the time, announced that he would make her do so, and leaping on some piece of furniture wrote, in large letters across the ceiling, 'fuck' according to Patience, or 'bugger' according to Robert. He was a legendary Historian, apparently full of wild inspiration. What must have been a Christmas card from him still exists in the shape of a folded piece of paper with, on the front in sepia-coloured capital letters: 'WORKERS LET THE BOURGEOIS BLOOD FLOW FAST THROUGHOUT THE COMING YEAR'.

58

Inked in in tiny writing is: '(blood by Kee)'. His Oxford tutor later wrote wistfully to Bill, asking if he could 'send us more like Kee'.

The urgent need for a History Tutor at Stowe had arisen because the original Tutor, Martin MacLaughlin, known as Cluffy, had gone sadly off the rails, succumbing to drink and, possibly, other delinquencies. The fort had been held temporarily by a young man called John Gough, and the transition from these two to Bill is vividly described by John Stoye, a History don at Magdalen College, Oxford. He was already on the History Side and therefore part of the first group of schoolboys, as opposed to University students, that Bill taught. John thinks that this may have made him more experimental and tentative than was the case later, but goes on, 'there we were – after the dottyish, bewildering McClaughlin, and gentle v. youthful John Gough – confronted by this new chap with bright eyes and smile who speedily turned out remarkable. For one thing he treated us as more grown up than we were, and for another – and most important – he treated us as a group. The "Historians" speedily became an entity, I think to the dissatisfaction of certain other teachers and boys, but this sense of membership helped in pushing us forward.'

John cites the activities jointly undertaken by the History Side: 'a little thing, the annual photograph, or, a big thing, the Historians' Shakespeare productions.' He also mentions 'the communal effort to write an amazing historical novel on the Dissolution of the Monasteries, in which we vied with each other in creating the characters of dissolute, dissolved monks.' Stephen Whitwell remembers the opening sentence as being: 'There was a nip in the air that belied the approach of spring.' This sentence also became part of the Historian's Cantata, of which snatches would be sung by old Historians during my childhood. For the annual photograph a different temple or part of the grounds would be chosen each time, with elements of fancy dress sometimes appearing. Above all, however, John Stoye stresses a recurring and important theme of Bill's pupils, the fact that he taught them to write fluent historical essays.

Another aspect of Bill mentioned by John Stoye was a 'romantic Tory – Old England of the Shires' attitude, which he later found distasteful. This was less of an issue for other Historians, but it was indeed a part of Bill, becoming modified by age and experience. However, his treatment of his pupils as adults and his determination to teach them to write remained constant. Some of his other enduring charac-

59

teristics were believing passionately that Historians could succeed – generally in getting a Scholarship or Exhibition to Oxford or Cambridge – and his 'rescuing' boys who, like Peter Orde, had fallen foul of other masters or the whole system.

Stephen Whitwell remembers surprise as being one of his first impressions of Vancouver. He was taken there by a friend in his first term some time before he was formally a member of the History Side, though he had been taught by Bill, who regularly took the lower forms containing bright boys. Coming from an austere and inhibited family background, he suddenly found himself 'surrounded by people who never stopped talking, throwing phrases and ideas at each other without pause, using first or nicknames. Of them, but only it seemed first among peers, were the history tutor and his wife. It was less a question of my feeling grown up as of wondering whether they were, for in my experience grown-ups, especially those put in authority over me, were, however kindly disposed, reserved and discreet to the point of numbing dullness. This, by contrast, was wonderful fun, even though at first I understood little. I was content to fetch plates of marmalade sandwiches and sit at the feet of Noel Annan or John Stoye. If I had sat at Robert Kee's feet I should have been kicked, less perhaps in malice than excitement. The greatest surprise of all was that I was in, totally accepted from the start as a member of this magic circle.' Stephen found the physical state of Vancouver part of the charm, but his formidable mother remarked, after meeting Bill and Patience at Vancouver for the first time, 'What a very Bohemian couple'.

Stephen, together with Iain Moncreiffe and Paul Johnstone, all later to be distinguished in different ways, were, as Stephen says 'refugees from our housemaster, Ivor Cross. I cannot explain the speed at which the enmity between him and Bill developed. Bill had after all only been at Stowe for two terms when I came, but already he and Patience stood, in Ivor's eyes, for subversion and disloyalty.' Stephen, regarded initially as 'sound' because he had been head of his prep school, was totally *persona non grata* once attached to Vancouver. He notes that this 'added spice' to his visits there. At about this time, a critic of Ivor Cross put the following rhyme into his mouth:

'I have made my house so clean
That there's nothing to be seen
But ME, and my ideas,

And my big stick,
And my dog, Mick,
And Dan, who cleans the rears.'

In a volume of reminiscences about Chatham, Ivor Cross's house, several Old Stoics speak warmly of him, but historians would always be subversives. He did in the end, however, forgive Stephen his disloyal attachment to Vancouver, giving him a birthday present in his final year and making him a monitor.

Peregrine Worsthorne, who went to Stowe in 1938, writes in his autobiography published in 1994, vividly and romantically of Bill, Patience and Vancouver. He details Bill's achievements and friends such as Alan Taylor and Wystan Auden, saying that: 'Nowadays Bill McElwee would unquestionably been awarded a fellowship on going down from Oxford with a first; and very probably a chair shortly thereafter, so distinguished were his published works.' Noting that 'sophisticated gossip' was much encouraged at Vancouver, Worsthorne writes: 'If at Stowe J. F. Roxburgh was king, then McElwee was Prince Regent and Vancouver Lodge a kind of alternative court where disaffection against the likes of Fritz (Worsthorne's much disliked Housemaster) was not so much encouraged as tolerated.' It was impossible to be at Stowe even for a term without noticing Bill and Patience. 'They would roar up to Chapel in a vintage Bentley, the back seat of which was either strewn with dogs, guns and sporting bric-a-brac, or filled with two or three Sixth Form swells who clambered out looking immensely pleased with themselves, having just attended the Vancouver Sunday gathering.' There is much disagreement about the make of car that Bill drove before the war, but it was certainly not a Bentley. A lesser car, however, would not fit so well in this extravagant description.

Peregrine Worsthorne was to invoke Bill's help in successfully getting him permission to hunt, something which had been forbidden by Fritz Clifford, who was a constant adversary of Bill's, and thereafter Peregrine began to visit Vancouver regularly. He gives a thorough description of Bill's views at the time:

'Bill was a conservative in the sense of being sceptical of all forms of Utopianism. At the time that meant doubting the efficacy of the League of Nations and being quite clear about the fact that nothing would stop Hitler except brute force. He was also contemptuous about Russian communism. How on earth, he asked, could anyone be so stupid as to believe that a group of Marxist intellectuals could possibly turn barbaric Mother Russia, which had proved resistant to the reforms of Peter the Great, into a New Jerusalem? Belief in communism made no more sense than belief in flat-earthism. It flew in the face of all the evidence, not of science but of history; of how people actually behaved. "Don't bother to read Marx," he advised. "It may or may not make sense in theory. But in practice it can't possibly work. Human nature, particularly Russian human nature, won't let it." As for dreaming about equality, that too was dismissed as impractical folly. "After turning society upside down in dreadful tumult and disorder, all they'll end up with is another form of inequality which may well be worse than the one which went before".'

Noting how new such scepticism was to him, Peregrine Worsthorne added that 'Bill was the first authority figure to suggest that socialism was not so much evil as stupid.'

Events in Russia would, of course, mostly prove Bill right. To the end of his life he believed that countries, like individuals, tended to produce recurring patterns of behaviour. Though his examples were in some ways dangerously general, I feel there were strong grains of truth in his theories. Thus, he said, in England any crisis was met by the formation of a committee, which then formed subcommittees to get the work done, Parliament, he pointed out, being a particularly good illustration of this. The Irish, he contended, could not bear to be united, witness the occasion when under Brian Boru they had, briefly, been a nation. The strain was too great and they ended up killing Boru. German vulnerability to authority figures was another belief which he found reinforced by his wartime experiences.

Peregrine Worsthorne found himself surprised that such conservative opinions emanated from such an 'unstuffy and unpompous' atmosphere as that generated by Vancouver. He notes that 'the house was filthy beyond belief' and says: 'Patience's appearance was also quite extraordinary – huge sack-like trousers and baggy jumpers, with a slash of lipstick pasted casually on. Nor was there a hint of Wildean cynicism and decadence about the scepticism. Both Bill and Patience were religious, patriotic, and, in a way, strait-laced, in spite of their love of gossip. Only tea was drunk; never so much as a glass of sherry.' Possibly he hit a period of near wartime austerity. He also felt the renaissance man ideal was much encouraged and recalls being rebuked for saying how boring and silly all the OTC drilling was.

"Not nearly so boring and silly as complaining about it," retorted Bill. "It's a duty to be endured, not whined about".'

Bill is also seen as not being 'an ideas man, any more than was his mentor, Namier, or his friend Alan Taylor. He believed that politics was about power and people. "Take Fritz," he would say. "Nobody talks more about leadership and backbone and service. But what will he do when the war comes? He'll do nothing." "It's not opinions but character that count. Don't waste your time studying the ideals of the men in power. Concentrate on their actions. History is deeds not words."' Peregrine Worsthorne regretted that he was never taught formally by Bill, but reckons that the 'Vancouver salon left an indelible impression.'

7

Historians and Grand Connections

Having provided a dramatic description of Roxburgh, Roland Oliver, like Peregrine Worsthorne, paints a romantic picture of Bill, his methods of recruiting to the History Side and teaching style. In appearance he describes him as: 'short, sallow, dark-haired, his brown eyes full of laughter, with wrinkles fanning out from their corners right across his cheeks. He dressed like a well-bred tramp, in very old suits, wore his cloth cap at a rakish angle and drove a huge, old, open Lagonda.' I suspect that he is actually recalling the postwar Bill. In the thirties the suits were comparatively new, but were still going strong after the war. His de-mob suit went on being 'new' well into the fifties. He also became more stooped as he aged.

Professor Oliver goes on: 'Bill McElwee did his scouting for talent in the second year Scholars' form called the Twenty. The School Certificate examination lay at the end of the course, but he paid it scant attention. Ceaselessly pacing the room, hands in pockets, shoulders hunched, he would present the personalities of kings and popes and ministers and royal mistresses rather in the style of the seventeenth century essayist John Aubrey, farts and all, yet without avoiding subjects of high seriousness where they existed. At the age of fourteen or fifteen, this opened new worlds to most of us. We knew his reputation as the most dashing and successful of the heads of departments. We knew that he was among us to fish, and that at the end of the year he would cast his net at those whom he judged the most promising for his purposes.'

Wayland Kennet (then the Hilton Young mentioned by Professor Oliver in J.F.'s French class), recalls an apparently arbitrary recruitment onto the History Side. He had started his public schooling at Winchester, but towards the end of his first term there, wrote to his father saying 'This place is a Mediaeval Madhouse. Please take me away.' Lord Kennet responded to this heartfelt plea by sending Wayland to Stowe where, being clever, he took the School Certificate at 14, obtaining almost full marks in Maths and a poor 48 in History. These marks made no difference to Bill, who met Wayland Kennet when walking through the school and told him that he should join the History Side. Kennet, who could summon up no enthusiasm for the elderly and boring Maths Tutor, happily complied. Possibly Bill had already heard his description of Winchester, since it was something he would quote with relish all his life, and had decided that it was essential to recruit a boy who, at 13, could write such a phrase. Wayland proceeded to get an Exhibition to Cambridge. Following his examination, he received a letter from G.M. Trevelyan which said: 'I have read your history papers with interest. They were very clever. Now you had better come up and learn some history.'

It was not however, only future winners of scholarships who were recruited onto the History Side. While some boys, including the captains of rugby and cricket, may well have been taken on because they would add to the prestige of the Historians, I doubt if Bill ever took anyone on solely for that reason. He would have spotted something in the boy which could respond to what was on offer or felt that there was potential that might be in danger of being missed by other staff. Whatever his motives, the less academic boys were not neglected. Michael Scholfield, who was on the side from 1936–39, felt that he was never 'one of the real Historians', since he spent much of his time playing 'hearty games, Rugger, Cricket and Athletics to name but a few', but he felt that he received as much attention as the more academic Historians and benefited from Bill's teaching skill.

Bill never apparently had any difficulty in keeping order, and later in his life would express his thankfulness that it had never occurred to him that he might not be obeyed in the classroom. He vividly remembered his first encounter with the History Side when one of them announced that someone had got jam on his chair. 'Then he will have to sit on the floor,' rejoined Bill without thinking; he only realised afterwards that had he allowed them loose to hunt for another chair, he would have lost them.

It is easy to see how deeply irritating the formation of this tight-knit group whose members could not all be dismissed as rebels, must have been to traditional housemasters anxious that loyalty should be to the House and the school as a whole. Noel Annan describes

Vancouver as: 'a hive of gossip, and its existence made housemasters wary and critical. But there were limits as to how far you could go. Bill never allowed gossip about romantic and sexual relationships between boys to be discussed. He knew he would be in an equivocal position vis-à-vis a boy's housemaster if he knew of an illicit relationship and had not reported it. Still there were unbridled stories about the dimmer or reactionary masters; and an alphabet in verse about the masters worth several thousand pounds in libel damages, was circulated.'

Stephen Whitwell too, recalls the diehards who were totally opposed to Bill, and the junior masters who 'were mercilessly ragged by Patience and the Historians'. He mentions 'Jethro Miracle Todd', surely a name invented by Historians, and the master who asked Bill and Patience out to dinner and enquired: 'Are you partial to the hare when jugged?' This, naturally, became a Historian and family catch-phrase.

There were, however, strong allies on the staff: Humphrey Playford, an immensely tall parson who would appear at Henley as a Steward with the absurd pink cap of the Leander rowing club perched on his head, Edward Capel Cure, a gentle man whose performance in class of the Erl King in German, was legendary and who was to die early of leukaemia, Leslie Huggins, Director of Music and Master of the Grafton foxhounds, given to taking choir practice with spurs sticking out beneath his cassock, and Robin and Dodie Watt. Robin, who was Canadian, ran the Art School and, with Dodie, provided an alternative centre to Vancouver. The two couples were not, I think, rivals, but rather agreed on the importance of encouraging boys, building on success rather than harping on failure. Both Art and History happily nurtured a number of boys. Stephen painted a portrait of Patience, Christopher Cash and others produced a number of pictures for the walls of Vancouver, and Robin Watt painted an attractive portrait of Bill in fencing kit which he took with him when he returned to Canada after the war, as the centrepiece for the exhibition with which he hoped to establish himself as a full-time artist.

The importance of Bill being combined with Patience and Vancouver is continually emphasised by old Historians. Another prewar description of Vancouver conversation contrasts with that of Noel Annan: 'We were invited (almost commanded) to come to Vancouver Lodge on Sundays for tea. Here there were often friends of theirs from outside, often from Oxford. Conversation was adult, stimulating and often opened our minds to new ideas and horizons beyond school. Vancouver was the most unkempt house I ever entered. Patience believed that dusting and cleaning were a waste of valuable time, and most of the furniture was worn and not comfortable, but what did that matter? Bill was a genial host of these occasions; Patience stayed in the background.'

John Stoye is rather more critical of the conversation, though he concurs about the state of Vancouver, which he found: 'quite unlike any house I had ever been in; much less tidy, shabbier, in general *darker*, but tremendously *interesting*; with Patience not a housekeeper, but the lady novelist somehow feeding quite large numbers; with talk, talk, talk about persons. Perhaps we later said (some of us did) that that talk was snobbish and narrowing to an extraordinary degree; but we did love it then. Why, we had acquired membership of a wonderful clan.'

Noel Annan confirms the snobbery, but qualifies it, feeling that it was 'difficult for a Christ Church man not to be.' He remembers Bill maintaining his Oxford contacts, apparently calling on ex-Historians now up at Oxford, including some of MacLaughlin's vintage, and keeping in touch with influential dons to whom he could 'write a glowing letter about his own Stowe Historians.' He describes Bill regaling his pupils with stories of the parties he had attended: 'at which everyone got "bottled" and names were dropped such as Lord Normanby and Osy Darell. Not all of us were impressed. Adolescents are cruel and swift to mock someone who shows off.' Noel Annan goes on: 'He liked the upper classes and the romance of ancient country houses and old families. But this never influenced his relations with members of the school. He was as courteous and solicitous to those palpably not of the upper middle classes as to the few sprigs of the aristocracy who graced Stowe. You might have expected him to have made much of his friendship with Auden. But he hardly ever mentioned him. He was not the kind of schoolmaster who oiled to wellborn parents in the hope of being invited to stay for a weekend. When I look back I realise how desperately poor he and Patience were and how generous they were to us, his pupils.'

Namier has been cited as a particularly powerful influence on Bill, affecting his view of the aristocracy and his teaching of history. Namier figured strongly at Liverpool and was referred to by Bill and Alan Taylor as 'Uncle Lewis'. Noel Annan points out that Namier was: 'in love with the whole of the English aristocracy and ruling class, regarding their contempt for general ideas and political theory as the salvation of Britain, unafflicted by a Continental intelligentsia that bred revolutionaries, marxists and anarchists.' He goes on: 'Bill taught us Namierism, namely that eighteenth-century Tories and Whigs were fragments of the imagination of liberal historians: parties with ideologies did not then exist: all that existed were individuals striving in Parliament for power and influence, most influential of whom was the King himself. History, Bill taught us, was about individuals and shifting political power between nations. Hardly a word about the impersonal forces of history, e.g. climate, demography, trade cycles and economic factors, social structure, e.g. social classes.' These shortcomings were compensated Noel felt, by the fact that Bill 'was almost unique among schoolmasters in writing books himself.' He cites the translation of Friedjung's *The Struggle for Supremacy in Germany 1859–1866*, which Bill had undertaken with Alan Taylor, and recalls his teaching not from the abridged published version, but from the full text, using his German to enhance the 'marvellous stories about the battle of Koeniggraetz'.

The snobbery, like the high Toryism, did modify after the war though a strong element always remained. Pondering this, two immediately postwar Historians decided it was a 'romantic snobbery', which feels accurate, though Patience could condemn someone for their accent alone unless she came to know and like them, in which case it did not matter at all. Ideas and wider horizons were always part of the teatime discussions, but so was gossip. There were limits though, as Noel Annan notes, and the breaking of school rules was never condoned and nor were boys forced to choose if they did show loyalty to a master not approved of at Vancouver. Brian Stephan, a housemaster who knew Bill after the war, felt that Bill's success as a Tutor not only aroused strong envy, but also made it difficult for other masters to confront him about behaviour that angered them. He also told me that it was widely believed in the school that boys were encouraged to smoke at Vancouver and on their first visit there were subjected to initiation rites such as having their heads shoved under the flush of a lavatory. The first was only marginally true in that Sixth Formers asked to dinner would be allowed a cigarette afterwards, and the second would have been total anathema to Bill and Patience.

Perhaps the possibility of such rites was first generated by the Viveur Club, which ran for a time when Bill first arrived at Stowe, and had strong links with Vancouver. George Rude was the moving spirit behind the club, aided and abetted by two Historians who were, to start with, the only boy members. One of these still possesses the record of the club, which shows that the first meeting elected George Rude as President, with Tim White, Charles Robinson and Anthony Ireland, also known as the Baron von Simonitch, as vice-presidents, all these being masters. Other boys quickly joined in. It was agreed that the group should be limited to ten members, elected unanimously, should meet once a week with optional attendance, and that the group 'should take nothing seriously'. Later it was agreed that the proceedings of the group be kept confidential, which is unsurprising. Mostly the 'Group' gathered in Masters' rooms to read plays or short stories, tell ghost stories and play card games. A line from a Saki short story became the Group's 'unofficial motto': 'You can't expect a boy to be vicious until he has been to a good school.'

Bill and Patience were jointly elected vice-presidents at the eleventh meeting of the Group, the tenth having been at Vancouver, when a treasure hunt was won by Bill and Noel Annan. Lurid initiation ceremonies taking place at Vancouver possibly account for later rumours. Vancouver was described as 'the spiritual womb of "Viveur"'. The Group survived from January 1934 until May 1935, the departures of Charles Robinson and George Rude clearly precipitating its demise. From the record of the Group, it appears to have combined a mixture of adolescent high jinks with some sophisticated wit and, in spite of the motto, serious play-reading. Once involved, Bill and Patience apparently never missed a meeting.

Mouse Vickers, one of the first Historians, and therefore only with Bill for a year, was a moving spirit behind the Viveur Group. He felt that he benefited not only academically from Bill's teaching, but also from the sense of family life he got at Vancouver. His father having been killed in the First World War, he did not get on with his stepfather, so found at Vancouver support and appreciation for what seems to have been a talent for benign mischief, for which the Viveur Group must have been an excellent vehicle. Mouse's mother was appalled by his apparent lack of ambition and wailed to J.F.: 'But he wants to be a *teacher*, Mr Roxburgh, *a teacher*', a comment much treasured by both J.F. and Bill. Mouse recounts with some glee that it was even worse for her when he became a senior Trades Union official.

The discomfort of Vancouver is a constant theme of old Historians. One prewar Head of School commented that he was given the honour of sitting on the 'bacon settle', a piece of furniture I remember vividly as an entirely genuine article with a narrow bench to sit on, which had all the worst attributes of a church pew. However, the conversation and the food went a long way towards making up for the lack of comfort. Patience had come on as a cook since Vienna, and though she was described as having more interest 'in books than housekeeping', her teas were hugely enjoyed. After the war, she no longer bothered with recipe books or with weighing anything, cooking entirely 'by eye'. Her chocolate cakes tended to sag in the middle, but they were delicious. Michael Scholfield remembers going to Vancouver for dinner, and has 'a clear recollection of total darkness apart from a few candles and some excellent brandy snaps full of whipped cream'.

Noel Annan mentioned Oswald Normanby and Osy Darell as being names regularly dropped by Bill and Patience. How they met either of them is unknown, though Oswald, the Marquess of Normanby, they probably got to know when he was up at Oxford. Now, Bill and Patience would clearly be labelled middle class; then, they certainly thought of themselves as at least on the edge of the upper classes and were sufficiently socially adroit to mix in aristocratic circles with reasonable comfort. Their lack of money and the lowly status of Bill's profession were offset by their wit, their charm and their skills as bridge players.

They stayed several times at Mulgrave, Oswald's grand country house in Yorkshire, where his mother maintained a rigid formality. There were picnics that were only marginally less formal than dinner, with the butler changing into a tweed jacket and cloth cap for the occasion, and expeditions to look at the grounds. Patience recalled one such outing to see primroses when one of Oswald's more irrepressible friends suddenly exclaimed, 'Oh my God, they're worse here.' Once Lady Normanby was in bed, Oswald's friends could let rip playing charades and the sort of games that strike terror into some hearts, but stimulated Bill and Patience. An example they often quoted was one where a poem had to be composed bringing in a particular word, a name and an object. Oswald also stayed at Vancouver some five times before the war and would, I imagine, have found the informal discomfort enjoyable in contrast to the pomp at Mulgrave.

Osy Darell, heir to a baronetcy and extremely rich, seems to have been much more rackety than Oswald Normanby. His parents apparently had not spoken to one another in private for 30 years, but maintained a perfect façade in public. Bill and Patience stayed with them too, and Osy seems to have been a very close friend for a time. He was a homosexual and a highly talented pianist who was apparently not allowed by his family to exploit his ability publicly. Instead he was sent to Sandhurst, where he and an equally recalcitrant friend discovered that going cub-hunting allowed them off early parades. They had breeches designed to hold hot water bottles over their stomachs in order to combat the early morning autumnal chill. Patience fell seriously in love with Osy, and while there was little sexual future in the relationship they appear to have been enormously close friends. She may even have cherished hopes of his returning her love. In one of the few letters to Bill written after their marriage, she writes: 'Do angel, do the insurance – be brave over it and take the plunge of writing to them. You see, if you did die, I couldn't bear it if your affairs weren't in order and the trustees were vile. Because though I should prob marry Osy I couldn't bear to have mud slung at my little dead pooshums.' This self-conscious letter, which I trust, her older self would have repudiated with loathing, was signed with a roughly drawn cat. I think though, that she did not fundamentally want to change Osy, and I imagine her acceptance of him was balm to his soul – in contrast to the expectations of his parents. He was wildly amusing and coped with the pressures on him by becoming an alcoholic.

Bill and Patience may have visited other country houses. They certainly had regular contact with other scions of the aristocracy. Patience was photographed for the *Tatler* at a race meeting with Simon Ramsey, later Lord Dalhousie, and had him to stay at Vancouver regularly when he was supposed to be working for Oxford exams. He struggled badly with this and generally ended up echoing the cry that 'work was the ruin of the drinking classes'. She was also pictured at a Hunt Ball with the severe-looking Lord Haig, son of the Field Marshal, who was at Stowe, but not on the History Side. He did an attractive drawing of Bill, though, which appeared alongside one of the reviews of *The House*. The dirt and untidiness of Vancouver seems to have deterred no one from staying there, though the collapse of the kitchen range, so eloquently described by Bill in his letter to J.F., seems to have threatened to hamper their attending the Grafton Hunt Ball in the company of the Earl and Countess Cadogan. Again, it is unclear as to how they got to know these two, but they seem to have been intermittently part of their world for a time.

The Vancouver visitors' book reveals a constant stream of moderately grand guests as well as old Stoics who had left the school.

71

Quintin Hogg, now Lord Hailsham, and his then wife, stayed (a letter from him suggests that Bill had been an usher at their wedding), as did Christabel Ampthill, heroine of the famous Russell divorce case, whose son, Geoffrey, was on the History Side. Michael Crichton-Stuart, later a well-known member of the Long Range Desert Group, was there several times and had them to stay at Falkland Palace, of which he was the hereditary keeper. They gave him a spaniel as a birthday present, but the wretched dog refused to go into the house, evidence, said Patience, that the place was seriously haunted.

Michael's sister, Ismay Tiverton, also stayed regularly, continuing to do so after the war. She was a beautiful woman who had been photographed as Europa when a debutante. Bill had a most happy affair with her during the war, about which Patience knew. She always maintained that she did not mind in the least, and indeed Ismay remained one of Patience's few close women friends. The other affair to which Bill admitted was with Ismay's sister Claudia. Patience apparently condoned this relationship as well. Hamish St Clair Erskine, who had been engaged to Nancy Mitford for a time, also stayed at Vancouver and once visited again after the war. On that later occasion I remember him giving a brilliantly camp and funny description of his part in the fall of Tobruk. Gavin Maxwell became a more frequent visitor for a period after the war, but did stay a couple of times in the thirties. He had been at Stowe before Bill arrived there, leaving early when he became seriously ill. Gavin and Simon Ramsey apparently went on a ghost hunt, commemorating this event with the word 'Ghosts' in the visitors' book. The numbers staying averaged about 40 a year.

8

Extra-Curricular Activities

The Historians' Shakespeare productions mentioned by John Stoye began in 1935 with *Richard II* Apart from three, one preceding and two following the war, they were all staged out of doors on the steps of the classical Queen's Temple. Built at the top of an incline and of golden stone, it was framed by beech trees and had a space in front that could be adapted to form a natural auditorium. After the war this was bulldozed into an appropriate shape, but in the early days, audiences had to contend with it sloping the wrong way. The Temple itself had deep steps, an elegant portico, a central door and balustrades behind which electricians and the orchestra could be concealed. They also provided a balcony from which Mark Anthony could harangue the crowd in *Julius Caesar* or from which Richard ll was able to descend 'like glistering Phaeton'. It would have done nicely for Juliet, but Bill always said that he had never found a younger boy with the emotional range to play her; and if he had, it would have placed the boy at enormous risk from more senior predators. Inside, the Temple had a large room generally used for orchestral rehearsals, but also most suitable for after-play parties, and underneath it were a collection of musicians' practice rooms, which were ideal for changing and for Patience to set up camp as wardrobe mistress.

The idea for putting on a Shakespeare play came from Noel Annan. A staging of the masque *Comus* on another of the Stowe Temples gave him the initial idea, and seeing a production of *Richard of Bordeaux* put on by the impresario Bronson Albery, with Gielgud in the main part, inspired the choice of play. Albery's son was one of Noel's best friends at Stowe, and he thought his father would be prepared to lend the costumes for a Stowe production. Lord Annan says: 'I asked Tim White if he would produce it. He contemptuously refused. Not for him schoolboys aping West End stars. When Bill heard this, he offered to do so. True to form, he insisted that it became a "Historians" production.' Noel was unhappy with this, being resistant to the separate 'Historian' identity, which had also happened under MacLaughlin and created an even greater resentment among other staff members than was true under Bill's rule. He accepted the situation, however, jointly producing the play with Bill and taking the part of Bolingbroke.

John Stoye, who played Gaunt, wrote of the play: '*We* thought the producer (Bill) and the actors (ourselves) were all wonderful' and the review in *The Stoic* was enthusiastic about the enterprise, but also highlights some of the hazards of such outdoor performances. 'The production of *Richard II* on the steps of the Queen's Temple in July, was a reckless venture. The unfamiliarity of a flight of steps as a stage; the difficulty of diction in such a theatre; the seating problem in an auditorium that sloped inconveniently in the wrong direction; a dozen such questions were discounted by good luck or constant rehearsal. Without the kindness of the Headmaster who bribed an audience of parents by allowing their sons home two days early, the Historians' "Merchant Adventure" might easily have become a "South Sea Bubble".' The review goes on to note the one hazard of outdoor productions that could not be predicted, the weather. For that first production, the night was apparently cold, but dry and calm.

The annual Shakespeare play became the most powerful of the Historian traditions, and probably this was the last occasion on which J.F. had to bribe an audience. The play would be produced on a Friday and Saturday towards the end of July, the Saturday coinciding with the School Speech Day. While the productions inevitably added to the prestige of Bill and the glamour of the History Side, they were particularly intended to be a means of giving a wide variety of boys an educational experience, an aim in which they largely succeeded. Historians mostly took the major male roles, with Bill often spotting next years' potential star when they were performing a lesser part in the current production. When there was no obvious actor on which to build a production, but a number of useful performers, he would put on *Julius Caesar*. Boys with unbroken voices almost invariably took the female parts, though a more senior boy in the role of the Duchess of York in a postwar production of *Richard II*, added some light relief.

Such scenery as was required would be designed, made and painted by boys, a Stoic sometimes composed incidental music, and, of course, the School Orchestra played it. Lighting provided a particular challenge, since much of it had to be suspended in the surrounding trees while a trench was dug for the footlights. The play began at eight o'clock so there was a subtle shading from daylight, through dusk to total darkness. This was highly effective for *Macbeth* and the 'Night thickens' speech, but also added an extra romance to *Twelfth Night* or *A Midsummer Night's Dream*. The fully lit temple, framed by beech trees and the night sky, was magical. In the fifties, a particularly ingenious band of electricians built a massive 'Dimmer' which worked a treat, but was wildly dangerous and would have been instantly condemned by any health and safety inspection. Bill was horrified one night, when it had been raining, to discover the boys operating the switches with screwdrivers as the whole thing was alive, but he did not call a halt to the production. Patience loved it since one of its apparent foibles was to produce too much power so that a small electric ring was run off it to absorb the extra current, thus ensuring a constant supply of the incredibly strong tea that she favoured.

Programmes were always designed by a boy, though not necessarily a Historian; so, frequently, were the costumes. For the second production, which was *Henry IV Part II*, they were designed by Christopher Cash, who also played Doll Tearsheet. He was a talented artist who later never quite lived up to the enormous promise he showed when at Stowe, but who became a much-loved art teacher at Bedales. A local dressmaker would be found to make up the costumes since Patience, though always designated 'Wardrobe Mistress', had no talent for making clothes and saw her role as providing running repairs, aspirin, soothing words for the stage-frightened and constructing breasts for the female characters. These were based on a pair of spectacular undergarments known as 'Mrs Purefoy's bust bodices'. These constricting, padded garments must have been wildly uncomfortable and generally produced the effect of Edwardian bosoms rather than breasts. The Purefoys had once been a rather grand local family, and how the underwear of one of its members fell into theatrical hands is unknown.

Patience was apt to become quite stressed herself during the play productions which, combined with the end of the long summer term, could produce emotional tension and dramas with which she would strongly identify. Vancouver would fill up with old Stoics who wished to be part of it all. Their need for food and beds must have made enormous demands on her. Gin, added to the tea and aspirin, helped, and in one postwar year, an old Historian was designated to keep her going by repeating at regular intervals: 'Patience, I don't know how you do it.'

Henry IV was the first of the Historians' productions to be mentioned in *The Times*, though on this occasion only as part of a report on the Speech Day. The piece included a complaint from J.F. that: 'in spite of his wish expressed at successive Speech Days, that the school might be kept within the limits of what one man could be expected to keep personal touch with, the numbers still went up. They would be up next term by a further 30, to 570.' Later the Chairman of the Governors noted that the school had been subjected to its first full inspection by the Board of Education, which revealed Stowe to be 'up to the standards of the rest of the public schools in all respects and more than ordinarily good in History. The year's successes showed three Firsts taken by former members of the History Side at Oxford and Cambridge'. The final paragraph details matches, a concert that included madrigals and an exhibition in the new art school, mentioning the 'decorative work of C.B. Cash who also designed the costumes and posters for Mr W. McElwee's fine production of *Henry IV Part II* with good lighting effects, on the steps of the Queen's Temple'. The distinguished Oxford don, Neville Coghill, wrote enthusiastically to Bill after seeing this performance, saying that he thought Bill was doing 'fine work at Stowe bringing out so much talent'. He was impressed by Christopher Cash's performance and loved his costumes, but thought that 'he should have rolled his low-life characters (in their costumes) down a muddy slope, just to make their clothes look *soiled* as well ragged.' At the end of the letter Coghill wrote: 'I wish Wystan could have been there.'

Paul Johnstone, who was to play the Third Witch in *Macbeth* the following year and a distinguished Lear in 1939, livened up Speech Days after the war when he was staying at Vancouver for the current production. Meeting Bill after the speeches, he announced that 'the Johnstone Cup for Cliché had been awarded on the strength of the afternoon's performances'. Ever after on Speech Day, Historians could be spotted scribbling notes during the inevitably boring speeches. The Chairman of the Governors won outright one year with 'Facts are facts and we must face them.'

The *Macbeth* of 1937 was the first production to have a full review in *The Times*, something that continued with only the one wartime play being excluded, presumably because other matters claimed attention. On some occasions a correspondent came to see the plays, and on others an old Historian would do the review. The write-up of *Macbeth* was complimentary, commending the way in which Bill had cut the play and his choosing to set it in the eighteenth century, noting the surprise of the audience when the wounded sergeant staggered on in a kilt. Bill justified his choice in a programme note:

'The production of any Shakespeare play, and of *Macbeth* in particular, presents so many insoluble problems for the producer, that we feel bound to offer some sort of apology for our treatment. When it is necessary to shorten a play, no two critics will agree as to what should be cut and what left in. We have eliminated those passages which are generally agreed not to be the work of Shakespeare; and we have cut out the murder of Lady Macduff and her son because, quite frankly, we felt unable to produce it effectively. We have also considerably shortened the scene between Malcolm and Macduff at the English court which is apt to be tedious when it is no longer necessary to relieve the tension caused by the Lady Macduff scene. The main problem however with *Macbeth* is dress. We were not convinced by the O.U.D.S. producer's argument that only the Viking or the Baroque Russian periods really suit the play; nor would either have harmonised with our setting. Absolute historical accuracy was impossible, anyway, if only because the Highlander of Macbeth's day went into battle stark naked. Besides we dislike cross-gartering. Modern dress for Shakespeare is still such a novelty that it is apt to obscure from the audience any other qualities or defects in the production. We therefore decided to match the costumes to the setting. The eighteenth century was one in which usurpers, dictators and assassinations flourished and it is near enough to the age of witchcraft to make the weird sisters not wholly incredible.'

The 'we' he has used in this piece is not an attempt to be royal, but because he always made two senior Historians joint producers. A further programme note states that 'Most of the dresses were made for the recent film production of the *Ghost Goes West*.' No record exists of how he managed to lay hands on these.

Interestingly, Bill had changed his tune somewhat when writing a programme note about *Julius Caesar* the following year. He said: 'In these days it has become almost necessary to justify a decision not to produce Shakespeare in modern dress. At the same time there is a tendency abroad to interpret everything, art, literature, morals, and politics, in terms of a world struggle between Communism and Fascism. We believe that the lessons of history, ancient or modern, are less obvious and less easily underlined. We do not feel that great poetry should be subordinated to propaganda, nor that the comparative accuracy of Shakespeare's history should be distorted by irrelevantly modern associations. So we have tried not to be too clever with *Julius Caesar*.' After the war, though, he always said that he would love to produce the play with the crowd in black shirts shouting 'Duce, Duce', but though he did it twice more, he never took the risk.

Togas did look good against the Queen's Temple and they must have been well designed as, again, he managed to borrow some made for a production of the play by Sir Herbert Tree and some from a projected film version of *I, Claudius*. The remainder came from Blundells, presumably via his brother Patrick, who was by then teaching there. For the production he put on in 1957, he made the togas according to a pattern found in my copy of *Everyday Life in Roman Britain*, using the sewing machine bought by his mother before his birth in 1907. In the programme notes for both the postwar productions he does not address the issue of dress, but cites the universality of the play, the relevance to modern states hoping to improve their lot by political violence, and the complexity of the central characters.

The Times review of the 1939 *Lear* highlights some of the advantages and limitations of producing Shakespeare with a schoolboy cast. Bill acknowledges in his notes that while it is the greatest of plays it is almost impossible to stage. He then goes on to justify his decision to do so. *The Times* picks up on this: 'Courage should have its meed, and for that and to suggest other adventures of the sort elsewhere, it may be recorded that on Friday and Saturday of last week the Historians at Stowe School played *King Lear*, and played it in a way which justified their daring. Sincerity, discipline and a touch of poetic imagination in the producers, who were two boys and a master, achieved the all but impossible, and carried the prodigious play across to the audience, in spite of the immaturity of the actors.'

Noting the beauty of the setting and the happy addition of genuine owls, the reviewer continued: 'There was beauty in the performance itself. The actors had been so well trained in speech that their words were easily audible without microphones; they had been taught to be still, unless significant gesture or movement was required; and it seemed that they had been trained to seek to express as much and no more of the emotions of the play as they could be expected to understand. In the result the performance was a contribution to the understanding of Lear. One felt that at any rate no veil of misapprehension had been interposed between audience and poet.' There exists a delightful photograph of the present Lord Kennet being made up for his part as Regan.

Though *The Times* was absent from the 1940 production of *Twelfth Night*, staged in the School Gym just before Bill left to join the army, the faithful local paper, the *Buckingham Advertiser*, did the play full justice as it had for three of the previous productions. The paper invariably made sure that every name in the programme was recorded and was always wonderfully fulsome, as is shown by this paragraph in its review of *Macbeth*: 'The treatment of the play and of the setting must form the theme of our opening commendations. To see *Macbeth*, or, for that matter, any production of Shakespearean drama or comedy in such surroundings is an experience to be treasured in the mind. It was simplicity itself and yet it might be described appropriately, if somewhat garishly, as Shakespeare de luxe.'

The same splendid convoluted style opens the 1938 review: '*Julius Caesar* has probably enjoyed a more liberal share of the attention of the schools than any other of the works of Shakespeare and while it would be deemed by some to be akin to irreverence vulgarly to describe any one of these immortal works as "hackneyed", we should pervert the truth, were we to allude under normal circumstances, to a school production of *Julius Caesar* as anything partaking of the nature of a novelty.' It then, of course, goes on to demonstrate the uniqueness of this particular production. *Lear* drove the reviewer to ever greater flights of eloquence, while *Twelfth Night* was hailed as providing a welcome change from all the drama.

The other extracurricular activity available to the Historians was the annual 'Culture Tour'. Possibly it was his own early European travels that inspired Bill to initiate these, with his parents' bicycle tours of France also being an influence. The title 'Culture Tour' was undoubtedly coined with tongue in cheek, but it stuck. The first Tour took place in early September 1936, visiting France and going no further south than the Loire Valley. The Tours were not only concerned with seeing French architecture, but also with food, wine and the general sense of 'being abroad' which, judging by the feelings expressed in his war novel, Bill felt to be enormously important.

On this first occasion it was a small group, consisting of four current Historians, Brooks Richards, Peter Orde, Norman Brown and Iain Moncreiffe, and two who had already left: Eric Hanrott, who was a recent Historian, and Christopher Barlow, who had been among the original 1923 Stoics. A diary was invariably kept, generally by more than one person. The final paragraph of the 1936 diary which must have been written by Peter Orde, is a summary of the tour:

'We had seen eight Cathedrals, eight Chateaux, and twenty-two Churches. We had travelled by 'bus and motorcar and train; we had slept the sleep of a tourist and eaten the breakfast of a Frenchman; we had drunk the wines of Champagne and Burgundy and Bordeaux and Anjou; we had imbibed culture and atmosphere, and if we grew to dislike the French, we intended to return to them one day. We had spent two-hundred and eighty-eight consecutive hours of glorious, and covered goodness knows how many miles in praiseworthy endeavour. It is probable that the tour's successor will be better, but only because of experience derived from this. Bill is, as usual, looking into the future. Long may he do so.'

Throughout the diary there are footnote comments from Bill, two of which illustrate the dual inspiration for the whole enterprise. In the first, the writer is unenthusiastic about the Gothic when describing the party's reaction to Chartres. Bill writes at the bottom of the page, 'The diarist here is expressing a highly personal point of view. The party was wholly and properly moved by the Gothic. – Tutor'. Later an evening is summarised briefly: 'we settled down in peace to sole and four wines'. Below comes the comment: 'A specially cooked Sole Dieppoise – some more of the 23 Burgundies and an excellent Vouvray just to show what the Pays could do. It is to be regretted that this diarist had a soul beneath food and drink'.

Wine figured later, when Bill celebrated his twenty-ninth birthday. Dinner was 'the Tutor's present yet also in his honour'. Before they sat down, apparently Bill had 'taught the Patron to know his own cellar' and had 'snatched in triumph from a dusty corner, the last two bottles of Nuits St. George 1923, and an excellent Aloxe Corton of the same year'. The diarist noted that 'the wine was like velvet and smelt of decay'. Bill handwrote the menu, which consisted of Melon Frappe au Porto, Omelette aux Champignons, Tournedos Sautes au Boeuf with a Sauce Madere, Pommes à l'Anglaise and Petit Pois, Salade, Crêpes Suzette, Fromages, Fruits and Café. The Crêpes Suzette apparently let the side down slightly.

On their arrival back in England, Iain Moncreiffe, later of that Ilk and a distinguished, colourful genealogist, arrived at the Customs desk, perused the list of forbidden items and announced that he had brought in half a pound of hashish. This unlikely statement resulted in his being gone over with a fine toothcomb while Bill worried about missing their train. He was reassured by the Customs Officer that they were simply bent on teaching Iain not to make that kind of joke and would keep an eye on the time. A chastened Iain was at last released with the valediction: 'And if your Grandmother didn't pay duty on that camera, she was a very naughty old lady.'

In April 1937 a party of ten went to Italy. Christopher Barlow was again with them. Possibly he was there to help Bill manage the group. Christopher Cash, who had just left, was also with them, as were Robert Kee and Stephen Whitwell. They went to Verona and to Venice, where Mussolini was visiting at the same time and where they were photographed having tea on the expensive side of the Piazza San Marco wearing their very formal hats, and having the same meal on the cheap side bareheaded. After Venice, they clearly feared that Padua would be an anticlimax, but seem to have cheered up after seeing Giotto's frescos and a number of architectural delights. There were mixed feelings about Ravenna and a lightning visit to Bologna, followed by Florence, Siena and, finally, Pisa.

The diarists, three of them this time, clearly prided themselves on playing down any enthusiasm and on being wittily rude about Bill and each other. In spite of the superior adolescent manner, though, Venice clearly overwhelmed them. It is mouthwatering to read a casual remark about spending 'an hour in the Uffizi' when now it takes at least that to get in, and a vivid picture, probably written by Robert Kee, was painted of the party being forced to walk to Santa Croce 'Led doggedly by an unkindly light in a panama hat'. That hat lasted Bill all his life and was probably quite smart still in 1937. Another enjoyable piece of diary runs: 'The Pitti is a very large Palace; and there you have it really. Nothing could be more tempting than the reproductions in the handbooks, the two stars in Baedeker. But inside are only the declamations of guides, the angry glint of monstrous picture frames, comehither saints, strip-teasing Magdalenes.' After this trying experience, the party 'revived itself with tea in a shoppe that had all the Italian equivalents of handwoven linen, Jacobean chairs and so-sorry-but-we've-no-change-for-a-pound'. Bill firmly maintained that the Pitti was the worst hung gallery in Europe, one of the few things that he would find unchanged in present-day Florence.

Apart from one visit to Spain in 1957, the tours stuck to France and Italy, travelling greater distances once Bill acquired his sizable Lancia and had joined up with his colleague Humphrey Playford, who was also a Lancia fancier. I have no diaries for the 1938 tour, but Stephen Whitwell wrote a detailed account of a trip to France in April 1939. There is no mention of the political situation and they appear, as before, to have enjoyed some memorable wine. Patience stuck to the vow she made on returning from Vienna and never went with them. When travel generally was limited, these tours provided an unusual inspiration for Bill's pupils, and nearly all those who went with him found them a starting point in learning about European culture. Right at the end of his Stowe career, it soured slightly, with many of the boys taken on his final tour having already experienced European travel and in rather grander circumstances. They resented staying in cheap pensions geared to the pockets of Bill and the poorer members of the party, and were unimpressed by the sights that had wrought such magic for earlier generations.

Prewar, Bill undertook excursions in England as well. Wayland Kennet recalls enjoyable visits lasting a day, to Oxford and to Tewkesbury, when architecture was examined and photographed. I believe Ely was another destination of these mini-tours. Possibly a more intense curriculum prevented such excursions taking place after the war.

The plays and the Culture Tours were particularly geared to the Historians, and the Vancouver gatherings fostered some rebel elements. However, the other activities with which Bill became involved and the contribution he made to them demonstrated that the more conventional leanings that he had noted in Roxburgh were also a strong part of him. From early on until he left Stowe he was President of the Debating Society, the formality of which provided a framework for encouraging experimentation if not actual rebellion. Descriptions of the meetings appeared regularly in *The Stoic*, and the report of a debate in December 1935 is interesting. It was a Visitors' Debate held to celebrate the hundredth meeting of the Society. The motion was 'That Western Civilization is Doomed'. J. C. Dundas proposed the motion, declaring that 'there was a Gresham's Law of civilisation; bad things and bad taste were driving out good things and good taste. Advertisement debased art, and propaganda was withering poetry. The lack of manners of the American civilisation and the absence of individualism in German Culture were infecting and debasing the virtues of our way of life.' He was opposed by the Hon. Mrs F. A. Pakenham, who 'deprecated such blind and useless pessimism, while admiring the subtlety of the Hon. Proposer's sarcasm. A civilisation which admitted of such daily improvements as were ours was not yet doomed. Doubt, our modern crown of thorns, was the cause of many delays and much vexation. But she maintained that a pure and undiluted Socialism would pull our civilisation through at last.'

Philip Toynbee, subsequently a highly distinguished journalist, 'heartily detested his pretended ally, the Hon. Proposer. After a lengthy attack on that gentleman, he finally veered towards the point at issue, contending that Socialism would succeed, and not uphold, our polluted and inequitable Western Civilisation, and that here alone did he disagree with the Hon. Opposer.'

The Hon. F. A. Pakenham 'disarmingly suggested that when he and his wife agreed upon any one thing it must be true. For many centuries, he reminded the house, the general level of culture had been rising. He warmly advocated the Collective System, claiming that the vitality of our civilisation was proved by its vigorous resistance to ever-increasing dangers.'

Other motions debated during the thirties provide an interesting insight into what were then current preoccupations. The motion debated in March 1936, 'That this House would rather fight with than against Germany', was carried by one vote in the Upper House and 44 in the Lower, while in the same term the motion 'That the True Peril is not yellow but Red' was lost in both Houses. A year later the motion. 'This House has no further use for Politicians' was also lost in both Houses, and 'That this House would rather send an Expeditionary Force to Spain than a Cricket Team to Australia' was carried in the Upper House and lost in the Lower. World affairs continued to come to the fore with 'That alliances by the British Empire can do more to secure World Peace than can the League of Nations', which was also carried in the Upper House and lost in the Lower, while on a more frivolous note, 'In the opinion of this House, a man is in general better pleased when he hath a good dinner upon his table than when his wife talks Greek' was, pleasingly, lost in both Houses. Other motions were: 'That this House would rather have written Gray's Elegy than taken Quebec', 'That this House has more confidence in Mae West than Mr Lloyd-George', and 'That this House is in sympathy with the "Old man of Themopylae/Who never did anything properly".' This last was proposed by Peter Orde, who was then charged with being a hypocrite by the Opposer, since he 'had gone to Oxford to fail an examination and had returned a Senior Scholar of Hertford College'.

Bill knew the Pakenhams, now the Longfords, slightly when they were all up at Oxford together. It would have been a considerable coup getting them to come to Stowe for the debate. They remember little about the occasion, apart from staying at Vancouver and sleeping in a double bed much decorated with carved oak containing deathwatch beetle, their sleep being somewhat disturbed by the clicking. Bill's ability to attract outsiders on such occasions and for the Sunday tea parties is something frequently cited by Old Stoics as a particular joy of the History Side and Vancouver.

Being Master in charge of the School Library was another task Bill undertook in his early days at Stowe. Reports on the library in *The Stoic* were limited to lists of books given and purchased, and the entry in the Edition of April 1936 is interesting. Besides John Boyd-Carpenter giving £5 'for the purchase of books', Major Haworth, a highly traditional and much-loved Master, presented *Kelly's Handbook to the Titled, Landed and Official Classes of Great Britain*, and Prince Yuri Galitzine gave them *Vols CLXVIII* and *CLXIX* of the *Illustrated Sporting and Dramatic News*. There were a large number of books bought that term, no doubt with the help of the £5, including Bill's own *Life* of the Emperor Charles V, Auden and Isherwood's *The Dog Beneath the Skin*, two novels each by E. F. Benson and Eric Linklater, together with a Saki novel, Lowes Dickenson's *The Modern Symposium*, *The Wind in the Willows* and all eight volumes of the Barchester novels, all of which reflect Bill's personal taste. There were books on various historical periods, a couple of sporting volumes, one each on opera and music, and several works on poets and poetry, but though there is one book on pure mathematics and Bertrand Russell's *Introduction to Mathematical Philosophy*, there is nothing specifically scientific.

Another school activity with which Bill became involved was the 'Twelve Club'. This was a group of twelve prominent and senior boys who would meet in the evening, to listen to a paper read by one of their number. The club met about three times a term and had a splendidly varied collection of papers presented. In one term they had Noel Annan on the Battle of Sadowa, a Mr Maurice Dobb on the Anti-War Movement, Eric Hanrott on Peru and Bill himself on 'His Utopia'. In a later term, the club was informed about Genghis Khan, about relativity, and heard from a member who 'alternatively read and sang a paper on Elizabethan Song'. Wayland Kennet remembers presenting a paper on the Siege of La Rochelle, which required him to undertake a considerable amount of research, something otherwise lacking in his history teaching. After the war the variety of Twelve Club papers continued, with papers on everything from Bee-Keeping to Modern Art, this last being presented by Reg Gadney.

It was to the Twelve Club that Noel Annan and Patience presented a joint paper on the Public School Novel. It appears largely written by Patience, though the knowledge and tastes of them both went into the text. Naturally, it begins with Rugby and *Tom Brown's Schooldays*. This is put in the context of the period which was, she notes, 'still the age of cockfighting, of long, icy journeys in stage coaches, of hard drinking, child labour, and of great wealth contrasting with utter poverty, and so necessarily a time of great brutality.' The paper goes on: 'Public Schools were hotbeds of bullying and the manlier vices, gin at twopence a quart being a consolation to schoolboys no less than to the starving labourer in the towns.' Delicately, it is stated that, 'what one might call the social evil in school life was dismissed by the author of Tom Brown as many a noble friendship between large boys and small.' The other book of this period cited, is *Fathers of Men* by E. W. Hornung, creator of Raffles, which describes the other great nineteenth-century headmaster, Thring of Uppingham. *Stalky & Co* is covered, along with a variety of authors long since forgotten in most circles. *Eric or Litle by Little* is, of course, featured, as is *The Fifth Form at St Dominic's*, written by Talbot Baines Read, of whom she and Noel approved. 'He was a schoolmaster himself and turned to writing without the cloudy nostalgia of so many of his contemporaries. His books simply fizz along. No conflict between good and evil here, but naked hate in which we can all share, between hero and villain.'

Mr Perrin and Mr Traill is noted as a 'haunting, terrible book' and about *Goodbye Mr Chips*, she writes: 'The end brings the same lump into the throat we experience when we read of the death of some favourite old horse or dog, the sentimental, purely English attitude towards the useless that stands us in such bad stead in a workaday world.' Alec Waugh's *Loom of Youth* brought some uncomfortable realities about real public school life to the fore, and the central character of his brother Evelyn's novel, *Decline and Fall*, is noted as having been at 'a small school of ecclesiastical temperament on the South Downs'. Patience goes on: 'This school was described, oddly enough, by a Russian, Leonid Bely, in a fairly neat book called *Destination*. I am perhaps biased in favour of this book in that nearly all the characters were either personal friends or personal enemies of my own, and because the description of my father, the Bursar, as a hawk-nosed man liable to uncertain fits of bad temper was so particularly apt.'

The paper ends by saying that public schools are no longer of much interest to the public, citing as evidence a play about a friendship between 'a large boy and a small' which had 'slipped easily past the censor'. The final sentence reads: 'Public schools are no longer news. They are the subject of a White Paper.'

In his letter of appointment, J.F. had told Bill that as History Tutor, he would be expected to take charge of fencing at Stowe. This seems a trifle arbitrary, but given J.F.'s wish to encourage sports other than cricket and rugger, a number of teaching staff would probably have had to take on such responsibilities. It was in fact through fencing that Peter Orde first met Bill. He writes that, having arrived at Stowe in 1932, he was 'quite soon persuaded to take up Fencing. More Fencers had to be recruited, I imagine to justify the cost of an instructor and the overheads and I had no great gifts for Cricket or Rugger. Lessons took place in the agreeable location of the Temple of Concord overlooking the Grecian Valley and the atmosphere was informal – no heartiness!' He thought that Bill had no 'great experience of Fencing, but he conscientiously paid visits, got to know us and generally took an interest. We came to expect his sudden genial appearances on Fencing afternoons, his sleek black hair, flashing smile and rather sallow complexion, his tweed suits from Oxford and invariable suede shoes. When matches took place against other public schools, he was there to support us, to greet our opponents and to spread charm and good will. When matches were away, he accompanied the bus which took the team, driving his rather shabby two-seater café-au-lait car and generally took with him the team captain. Those journeys were memorable for the stimulating talk – instructive, entertaining often about novel subjects. As a high-class teacher he took the opportunity to stretch one's mind and assess one's character.'

Bill in fact knew more about fencing than it appeared to Peter Orde. He had been an 'Assassin' when he was up at Oxford, and in the portrait painted by Robin Watt he was wearing the club uniform. When he again took charge of the sport after the war, he would regularly referee matches, but from the contemporary descriptions of the youthful Bill, clearly his fencing skills were largely irrelevant. It was his interest and his charm that mattered. The other aspect that comes across powerfully, is his style. The 'shabby, café-au-lait two-seater' must have competed satisfactorily with Tim White's Bentley, though whether it was a Lancia or a Lagonda is disputed. I could have sworn that Bill used to lament the unknown fate of a Chrysler, which somehow disappeared while he was away fighting in the war.

The tradition of elderly but spectacular cars continued, though. After the war, he certainly had an elderly Lancia, which was built like a tank with battleship steel. It had lovely, shabby, soft leather seats, consumed horrendous amounts of petrol, and had to go to London for repairs and servicing, while spare parts could only be got from Milan. Never having any capital, Bill was always unable to afford new cars, so landed himself with machines that were a steady drain on his current income. Of course, he liked the style too. He occasionally ended up with an absurdity, like the ancient Baby Austin which looked as if it were made of papier-mâché and did not survive being turned over on ice when Bill was driving home from celebrating their Silver Wedding.

His last spectacular car was a vast Delage into which a Bedford truck engine had been inserted, which resulted in a juddering clutch, which made it hell to get moving. This car packed up in Italy, when it broke the crown wheel and pinion and had to be broken up under the suspicious eye of the Italian Government. Following this disaster, a splendid cartoon appeared in the Stowe satirical magazine, *The Epicurean*. It showed Bill pulling the car along on a rope and had the caption: 'Après moi le Delage'.

9

Authorship

Throughout their lives Bill and Patience wrote. Patience invariably wrote novels, but Bill's output included history books, novels, articles, plays and reviews. It may have been reaction to the fact that Bill got into print long before she did, that caused Patience to say of him in an interview with a local Sussex paper, given in 1946 when her second novel was published, 'He is a historian really, but he caught it from us, I think, we were always writing about the house so he had to write too.' She describes her own need to write as a 'fever' and the 'we' she refers to are herself and her brother Alan. There may have been some truth in her assertion, but it is likely that Bill would have seen writing history as something expected of him as part of his academic career.

Whatever the spur, his first publication was the work of translation mentioned by Noel Annan and undertaken with Alan Taylor. Their researches in Vienna inspired them to collaborate on *The Struggle for Supremacy in Germany 1859–1866* by Heinrich Friedjung. In his introduction, Alan Taylor described Friedjung as 'perhaps the greatest of Austrian historians', outlining how he had produced this detailed documentation of the struggle between Austria and Prussia for the domination of Germany and also his involvement in their politics. He describes how, with two others, Friedjung designed the 'Linz Programme' as a way forward, a proposal that was then adopted by the new German Nationalist Party in 1822, who then promptly stated that no Jew could be a member of their party. This excluded Friedjung, who nonetheless continued to cooperate with the Party, a fact that Alan Taylor would probably have emphasised had he been writing the introduction after the Second World War.

The original book had been in two volumes, but was successfully reduced to one by Alan and Bill. Reviews were few, but were complimentary. They included the *Manchester Guardian*, *The Times Literary Supplement* and *Time and Tide*, who all welcomed the translation as long overdue. One review did note, however, that the delay meant that additional material, that had come to light during the translators' own researches into the Austrian Archives, could be included. Alan Taylor's introduction was particularly commended. It was never a book that was going to sell widely, but was clearly immensely relevant to that period between the wars when, before long, Austria, together with Central and Eastern Europe, were again to prove vulnerable to Germany's covetous ambitions. Bill continued to receive small amounts of royalties from the book, and in 1966 it was reissued in America. After Bill died, Alan Taylor sent me a cheque for a little over £2 with a note expressing the hope that 'it made me feel rich'.

In Bill's press-cutting album, between the reviews of Friedjung and his book on the Emperor Charles V, there is pasted a copy of a short story entitled *The Harp*, which appeared in the *Evening Star* in January 1935. It is a taut if rather conventional piece, describing the unmasking of a murderer with the aid of a ghostly harp. The influence of his brother-in-law Alan can be detected in it, and I imagine that while it brought in a small amount of cash, it was not a genre he found comfortable. There is no trace of his writing any other short stories.

The Reign of Charles V, 1516–1558 was published at the end of 1935, being widely reviewed throughout the early part of the following year. Clearly, the publishing world was then infinitely more leisurely, and books that failed to get written up immediately following publication would not be swept away by avalanches of further literary output. Bill therefore got a steady trickle of mentions from February to August, though the later ones were mostly from America, Australia and the *Calcutta Statesman*. It was a book that set the pattern of Bill's historical writing in that it was a short, readable summary rather than a scholarly tome. In his introduction Bill writes: 'This book has grown out of the notes made for a detailed course of lectures delivered at Liverpool University in 1931 and 1932 on "The Age of Charles V". It does not claim to be a work of original research, in that it is based entirely on printed sources and contains little or no information which is not to be found in other secondary authorities. Equally it does not attempt the picturesque biography which is so much the fashion. It is rather an attempt to present, very shortly, the main problems and events in the life and reign of Charles V.' The book gives a highly readable and comprehensible overview of an immensely complex period, but it was a utilitarian volume without frills which would have been cheered up by at least one portrait of Charles and greatly helped by some maps and a genealogical table.

Reviewers were unaffected by these absences and hailed the book as a clear and useful introduction to an important period of history. In some reviews it is specifically commended for not being a 'picturesque biography'. That Bill almost certainly got his coverage of the complex religious conflicts of the time about right is demonstrated by two reviews. The first, in the *Church Times*, summarises the general response to the book when it says: 'Mr McElwee has written a very short and very competent summary of one of the most crowded and critical reigns in European history. Although it makes no great pretensions to originality, and is, in fact, written expressly for students who are not specialising in this period and have no time to read a more detailed survey, yet it is a considerably more distinguished piece of work than the average textbook.' The writer then ends by saying: 'Mr McElwee has some sense of style. True, he shows little understanding of the creative religious genius and the titanic stature of Doctor Martin Luther; but the same may be said of at least ninety-nine Englishmen in a hundred. The Church of England herself has yet to discover the significance of Luther for Anglo-Catholic theology.'

This statement is balanced by the review in the *Irish Independent*, which noted in conclusion that: 'It has been said that this book is impartial. Nevertheless we should have wished that a more generous tone had been adopted in reference to Pope Adrian VI, a great and saintly Pontiff who was more conscious of his religious responsibilities than of his political commitments. Mr McElwee is not harsh in his judgement of Adrian, but one feels that he might well have been more lavish in his tribute.'

It was not until after the war that Bill produced another historical work. Instead, in the autumn of 1936, a play called *Time and the Hour*, written jointly with Alan Kennington, was tried out in London. By this time, Alan was also teaching, at St Aubyn's, a prep school near Brighton. They would both, therefore, have had lengthy holidays in which to pursue their collaboration. Bill could provide the necessary structure within which Alan's flow of jokes and effective dialogue could be fitted. It was put on by an enterprise called The New Shop Window, which was apparently run by Anne Kennington, a cousin of Alan's, in conjunction with the Arts Theatre Club, and which existed to put on new plays on Sunday evenings. Sadly, the manuscript of the play has disappeared, but the plot was thoroughly described in the many reviews it received. It was set in 1945, following a successful Socialist revolution which resulted in England becoming a Republic. One of the newly governing comrades descends on a Devon village, intending to take over from the local squire. The *Morning Post* describes the outcome: 'But although Milton Peverell Church is now "The Temple of Reason" and its Inn "The Hammer and Sickle", and although Godiva Jones (played by Anne Kennington) brings down the latest idea from Leningrad, Milton Peverell refuses to accept the red dawn, and for a time Comrade Saunderson (played by Jack Livesey) finds life uncomfortable. The end is Gilbertian with Sir Thomas Vallence (the squire, played by Alan Napier) of all people, accepting a post as Superintendent of the district and Saunderson, now his prospective son-in-law, proceeding to Exeter as Vice-Commissary.'

The review in *The Times* said that: 'The authors have an exceedingly pretty wit, which gurgles and bubbles through two acts as if the supply of jokes was likely to overflow. It does overflow, and the last act is treated as a receptacle for a surplus they cannot bring themselves to throw away.' The review notes that 'the production is rough and ready, even by Sunday night standards', but goes on: 'The play, therefore, needs drastic revision, but is already full of delightful entertainment and good humoured enough to please all but the most desperately earnest among its political butts.' A number of the actor's performances are singled out for particular praise. The two-night run was widely publicised, and the reviews all agreed that this was an under-rehearsed production of great promise that needed polishing and tidying-up before being given a proper run. It did get a run of a week in the Richmond Theatre, with the distinguished actors Majorie Fielding and Ronald Shiner in the cast, but this was in November 1939, and while it was again well reviewed, it was clearly not robust enough to compete in wartime. Once the war was over, the theme would have been too painfully close to home. It was a continuing disappointment to Bill that the major success that seemed almost within their grasp slipped away. Sadly, he and Alan never worked together again. Postwar preoccupations were more serious.

Bill's first novel also suffered from being published close to the outbreak of war. *The House* came out in October 1938 and was widely praised, but failed to sell particularly well. The book was the compelling story of a tramp who has come a long way down in the world and who, on a wet night, comes across a house with an open window and a cat begging to be let in and fed. He climbs in, intending to feed the cat and go, his one remaining source of pride being his resistance to criminal behaviour. Warmth and the discovery of tinned food seduce him into staying the night, and in the morning an overheard conversation, the only dialogue in the book, tells him the occupants of the house are away for a week. The tramp is enchanted by the house and decides to stay and explore, but comes to dislike the family who live in it, feeling them to be unworthy of the place. He begins to arrange the pictures and furniture to his own satisfaction. In the one room that he finds instantly congenial, he discovers a collection of sonnets, apparently written by the son of the family, and telling the story of an illness and a love affair. An exploration of the tramp's history takes place alongside his probing into the family, and the sonnets trigger important memories for him. The process serves to strip away the cozening illusions by which he has kept himself going, and he is able to complete two missing lines of one sonnet. The family return early from their holiday and are furious to find him in the house. The author of the sonnets, however, feels a rapport with the tramp and enables him to leave before the police arrive. The final implication is that the experience has so changed the tramp that he will forsake the road for a more constructive way of life.

The sonnets, Shakespearean in style, were Bill's own work and were well received. The *Manchester Guardian* had some reservations about the book, but called it 'a charming study' and 'the work of a man who deserves the name of poet'. The *New Statesman* wrote that it was 'a sensitive and unusual novel', while the *Birmingham Sunday Mercury* called it 'a little novel of rare quality'. The *Evening Star* told its readers that this was 'A first novel which no reader must on any account miss' and *Truth* went to town, giving the plot in detail including an extensive quotation, and ending by saying 'Mr McElwee has packed so much, so clearly, into such a small space, that it gives his work a quite peculiar force and originality. And, high praise indeed, the sonnets he quotes as the work of his imaginary young poet are as deeply felt and as well expressed as the prose, a most unusual occurrence with poetic interpolations'. Finally, *John O'London's Weekly* gives *The House* a wide spread at the head of a list of books for Christmas, beginning the write-up: 'During the autumn rush of books, I have missed a work of rare quality. I now hasten to repair that omission, and to urge upon my readers a little story which they might well buy as a Christmas present to themselves. For it is a book to keep and re-read at leisure, since it is written by a poet who uses words deliberately and with a consciousness of their full value. In can be bought for five shillings.' Roxburgh wrote to Bill, saying: 'I have just finished *The House* and before its subtle flavour becomes overlaid in my memory by coarser things, I must write to thank you for the pleasure you have given me.' The letter goes on to make detailed and insightful comments.

The conclusion of the book is rather too pat, but the emotional charge is a powerful one. Bill once said that the initial inspiration had been a shaft of sunlight shining into the dining room at Vancouver, and there is much that is familiar in the house he describes. The idea of the tramp may possibly have come from his predecessor at Stowe, Martin MacLaughlin, who did eventually take to the road. More of Bill himself went into the young man who wrote the sonnets. Evidence is revealed of a time spent in an Alpine sanatorium, and the early sonnets in the sequence express mixed feelings at the possible approach of death. The first sonnet illustrates this:

> No fortune but the air I hardly breathe
> Nor name, nor fame have I to leave; no wealth,
> Nor ancestry, nor acres to bequeath;
> Only sick fears, regrets and failing health.
> Yet choked ambition struggles for release
> That, of my body, only half alive
> In this sad place, devoured by disease,
> Where all are dying, something may survive.
> If rotten flesh I would perpetuate
> Against all reason, how much more the need
> For new born hope a new life to create,
> Lest flowers I dare not dream of now lack seed.
> > So either way I look the truth is one:
> > Living, or dying, I most need a son.

Apparently recovered from his illness, the young man charts a love affair from uncertainties to reproaches, to fulfilment and peace followed by destructive doubts and an apparent ending of the relationship.

Bill never spoke in detail about what lay behind the emotions depicted in *The House*, but if this poem is a personal statement, a

93

possible conclusion to be drawn from it is that he is expressing regret for his still unconsummated marriage. Further speculation about his relationship with Patience is aroused by the poem he wrote at the start of the book as a dedication to her:

TO PATIENCE – JULY 12, 1937 (Her 27th birthday)

Seek not to flush a world-wide fame,
But nearer home a nobler game,
An honour more sincere;
Lest covetous and vain, you throw
The captives of your finer bow
To sate the hounds of fear

And all the love whereby you live
For some remoter contact give;
And realise too late
No vulgar fortune can atone
The loss of that which you alone
Intangibly create.

For value is not set by price
And cheap success will not suffice
For immortality.
Seek first the good, eschew the bad
And leave to God perchance to add
Material reality.

So at your death, though newsboys cry
Lesser events to passers-by,
There will remain a few
Who see the world a poorer place,
Yet, graceful themselves by your loved grace,
Live on inspired by you.

The warning may be aimed at Patience, exhorting her not to chase some kind of material success, and emphasising her value to him and to those around her, even if she was failing to get a book published, or, possibly, counselling against a hankering after money. It could, on the other hand, be attacking a weakness he senses in himself. Perhaps one element was a feeling that their regular contact with the grander

94

and more affluent worlds of the Normanbys and the Darells engendered some dissatisfaction which needed to be countered.

Patience finally got into print in 1939 with a novel called *Roman Holiday*. She had never stopped trying, in spite of the pain when a manuscript was returned. Even when she was reasonably established it still happened, and I well remember the misery occasioned by the rejection slips. The acceptance of *Roman Holiday*, her happiest book, must therefore have been a huge relief. It is the lighthearted story of a debutante whose mother has a steely determination that she should marry well, but whose campaign is temporarily flouted by her husband's diplomatic posting to somewhere with an insalubrious climate. Virginia is sent to stay with her upper-class cousins in the country. Their lives are equally ruled by their widowed mother, but her iron rule is achieved by her infinite capacity to suffer pain. Clearly based on Maudie, Lady Chariot dresses in layers of clothing acquired at jumble sales, employs staff because she is sorry for them and is determined that her eldest son shall marry one of her particular lame dogs. Her three sons, now joined by Virginia, lead a life of continual subterfuge mainly to spare her the pain of their growing independence. Naturally, Virginia falls in love with her cousin Charles and their attempts to outwit their respective mothers form the plot. All, of course, ends happily.

The book was widely and enthusiastically reviewed, the general tone of the comments being that it was a delightful book to read when recovering from flu or to: 'find an escape as far away as possible from the more realistic columns of the newspapers'. There was a particularly enjoyable final paragraph in a review headed: 'A Delightful First Novel': 'As a whole the novel is well written and is full of witty remarks, observations and reflections, which make any book worth the reading. The style is light and feminine. The prose dances gaily through the country air and away over the wooded slopes of the Downs; it saunters lazily through the old world atmosphere of village fetes and treads gently among the flowers of manor gardens. There is no psychological or mystery fiction here; for a change we have something delightful, fragrant and refreshing.'

Two other reviews are more perceptive and highlight what was to become a dilemma central to Patience's work. The *Sketch* dismissed the plot as 'of the most trivial kind', but goes on to praise the amusing characterisation and ends by saying: 'Miss McElwee's neat and economical prose style seems wasted on a theme as frivolous as this.'

In the *Observer*, L. P. Hartley finishes his review with the sentence: 'I think the author's real gift (and she certainly has talent) is for comedy: she could work on finer lines than these.' The difficulty of coming up with plots that were worthy of her prose and her ability to write funny dialogue continued to undermine Patience's novels. She further hampered herself by always wanting to write a serious book that would be a success with reviewers while also continuing to please what she called her 'faithful library public'.

There was no hint of criticism in the write-up of the ever-enthusiastic *Buckingham Advertiser*. Heading their article, 'NOVEL BY STOWE MASTER'S WIFE', it had a subheading, 'Husband and Wife are both Novelists' and began by writing about Bill and *The House*. It then proceeded: 'In the charming, sylvan neighbourhood of Dadford, where Mr. and Mrs. McElwee live, are to be found therefore, a husband and a wife who both write novels. The discovery is not phenomenal, but it is unusual enough to be interesting. In the realm of poetry the Brownings inevitably spring to mind when we set out to think of other husbands and wives who have contributed individually to our English literature; and in the world of fiction we are not without examples.' This promising theme is not developed further, probably because the writer could not think of any other couples. Instead, the article notes that Patience completed *Roman Holiday* in six weeks and comments: 'This we think, accounts in some measure for its spontaneity.' Before describing the plot in detail, the article quotes Patience as hoping that from now on she will produce a novel every year. Events were against this, however, and it would be seven years before either Bill or Patience published anything.

10

War

Patience kept her engagement diary for 1939, but there is nothing entered for 3 September. When I found it, I felt somehow cheated that the drama of war being declared had not been noted. Bill, however, had long foreseen the conflict and had been deeply troubled by the period of appeasement, so possibly it came as a relief when the waiting was finally over. His concern that in spite of events, the Historian's momentum and the Vancouver cohesion should be maintained, is illustrated by a letter he wrote to Paul Johnstone, who must have just left Stowe, some two weeks after war was declared. It is written on cheap lined paper and was returned to Bill by Paul's widow.

My Dear Paul,
    You are one of the few people I know well enough to write to on this paper; war has reduced us to straits even more degrading than usual. This really is only a plea for news; to lose touch with you all would be the one quite unbearable consequence of wartime. So write, and at length. Come and stay if you have a mind, before you go up to Oxford. For I devoutly hope that you are intending to go up. New College is to be open for undergraduates and I am told by the dons, that they hope that everyone who can come up will. I fear it won't be the Oxford career we had planned. It will be a queer place altogether – shortened degrees I expect, and most people waiting to be called up. But in some ways more of an opportunity than ever. Those who can keep sane and get educated will stand out head and shoulders when it is all over and we are left to remake a shifting world. Anyway, until your country wants you, there is no sense in hanging about.

97

I should begin to do a bit of work if I were you. I don't suppose you are much liable to worry, but it is better just now to have something to do. Also I feel that all you people, if I have done my job properly and you are as good as I think you all are, should stand out head and shoulders from your contemporaries when we come to face the much more serious crisis of the peace. (The next sentence is illegible) But you must make a start at it now, before the war sucks you into something less constructive – conning barnacles and scraping binnacles, or whatever it may be.

Forgive me for holding forth, specially if I am merely preaching to the converted. I have no time to tell you of our chaos here and of how we have all worked at the Bursar's job for him. Term starts on Tuesday – a week early. I suppose we shall all be alive and sane at the end of it. Patience sends love and give our loves to your mother. Write soon.

God bless you,

Bill.

Bill had also written to Stephen Whitwell, along similar lines but containing more about himself and expressing sentiments that are hard to reconcile with the postwar Bill who had apparently been determined to fight. In fairness, it was written a week after war was declared, when everyone must have been struggling to map their futures. Bill suggests that those flooding out the recruiting offices were merely creating problems for the authorities, and that it was better for individuals to supply details of what they could offer and then get on with some constructive activity. For Stephen he says, that should be continuing his education. He goes on:

'They [presumably the authorities] are quite right in thinking you unfit for military service just as I am. There are dozens of people better qualified to run searchlights and home defence who have been sent away and told to wait. I know that shining armour stuff with bitter clarity. But I know too the reality that I am valuable where I am and that I should be a nuisance, liable to break down, in the regular army. Of course if they want me, I shall go, but I don't think they will.'

Stephen had one leg shorter than the other, the legacy of childhood polio. Bill's expressed thesis to him, was that he should increase his value to society by getting his degree, stressing that Stephen would then have a head start on his contemporaries and the chance to be a great man. He writes:

'I feel quite passionately about all this. Please don't think I don't also mind enormously about winning this war. I long to cut loose and be a real soldier, instead of a joke in khaki once a week. But to save wastage of material just now is as important. Let us contribute what we can to winning the war. But the contribution which we can make is so desperately small and the contribution which we might make to the peace so desperately great, that we ought to do all we can to preserve both. It may mean some immediate and apparent sacrifice of the "what did you do in the Great War daddy" sort of pride. But that's a false pride, really, you know.'

This long and deeply felt letter seems to be Bill addressing himself rather than Stephen, perhaps because he felt he had no chance of being accepted for military service. Stephen ignored Bill's exhortations, wangled his way into the Coldsteam Guards and won a Military Cross in Italy.

It is not clear at what point Bill changed his mind, or whether he had it changed for him. Later, he always gave the impression that he had joined the Territorial Army in 1934 because he wanted to be prepared for events he saw as inevitable. His service as a Second Lieutenant had been with the Stowe Officers Training Corps – hence his reference to 'a joke in khaki', but he may also have had some extra training. He had every excuse for staying put, being in a reserved profession from which J.F. was reluctant to let him go. He was now 32 and had only one functioning lung. There is a brief note in his Stowe file, typed and dated 5 February 1940: 'This Officer's state of health is such that he cannot undertake much physical exertion. In addition, as he is a Tutor and Head of Department, I regard him as a key man.' Whether that was written with Bill's consent is unknown, but for the time being they remained at Vancouver and continued to have large numbers of people to stay, apparently trying to keep daily lives as normal as possible.

In October 1939, Bill wrote to J.F. suggesting that the boys should be strongly discouraged from listening to the news and speculating about what was happening with the war. He wrote:

'I have been doing my best to discourage any Historians from listening to wireless news. They waste not only the time they spend listening, but much more time afterwards in futile speculation. But I find that in all houses the rule against wireless during prep is specifically relaxed for the 9 PM news bulletin. I should have thought we were encouraging boys to do something education- ally harmful while preventing them from tuning in even to a sym- phony concert which might be valuable.'

J.F. sympathised and said he entirely agreed, but refused to ban the 9 o'clock news. That the boys should be actively discouraged from keeping in touch in such an important situation feels alien to those of us now conditioned to an inescapable flow of worldwide communica- tion, but perhaps fails to take account of a very different culture, together with the confusion and futility of those early months of the war. Stephen Whitwell thinks that in fact the boys quickly became bored with the news. It was their parents who listened avidly.

Bill and Patience's lives during the first year of the war can only be glimpsed in patches. In many ways life at Vancouver must have gone on as before, but with Bill experiencing a growing resolve to go off and fight, apparently encouraged by J.F., according to a letter Bill wrote to him as the war was ending. After the war he was contemp- tuous of those like Fritz, who, as Bill had told Peregrine Worsthorne, made intensely warlike noises and were physically fit, but chose to remain in their reserved profession, but he did respect real conscien- tious objectors who, like one of his pupils, engaged in hard and diffi- cult work in a factory producing artificial limbs.

By the time he had his medical, Bill's ambivalence about joining up had apparently vanished. He always said that he got himself passed fit by making the examining doctor angry. Asked what he did in the afternoons by a man who clearly admired sporting activity, he replied insouciantly, 'nothing'. Enraged by this flippancy, the doctor passed him A1 to teach him a lesson, and the die was cast. He left at the end of the summer term, and in August 1940 J.F. wrote to him, saying,

'I am writing to tell you that although I have filled your place on the staff, we shall of course look forward to having you back here when the war is over, provided that the school is then able to carry a staff of its present size. One cannot of course foresee what is in store for schools of this kind. But if it is possible to take you

100

back, you may be very sure that we shall do so gladly and thank-fully.'

The letter ends with an enquiry about his finances, which implies that there was an allowance for staff serving in the army.

Bill's reply notes that the school wanted Vancouver left furnished and goes on to reveal something of how much his decision cost him:

'I understand that you have already been very kind and helpful over Patience's move. Keep a kindly eye on her if you will. I anticipate that I shall be very remote and preoccupied and even worse at writing letters than usual. I didn't come to say goodbye. You do hate such things as much as I do, don't you? I can't even write what I feel about leaving you all. I'm sure you'll pull Stowe through all right and I shall love to think of you doing it.'

Peregrine Worsthorne noted that the outbreak of war brought some exciting new masters, but lamented the fact that Bill had departed just when he was about to join the History Side. The Side under Bill had, he said, become 'not only the school's intellectual powerhouse but also its most exclusive social club, neither of which roles survived his departure by so much as a week.'

Patience must in fact have stayed at Vancouver until October 1940, coping with an influx of evacuees. I imagine these six adults and two children must have arrived in late August or September. One of them, Winifred Teague, the mother of the two children, stayed in Dadford after Patience left, becoming a permanent resident in the village and a much-loved babysitter for me. She and Patience would tell lurid stories of the other five: Miss Edwards, who would insist on sleeping with a candlestick under her pillow, and a couple called Nicholls, who loathed and feared the countryside, quickly deciding that the East End and the Blitz were infinitely preferable.

Bill must have been granted leave in September, because there is a lyrical vignette in Alan Taylor's autobiography when he is writing of the possibility of German invasion and of his friendship with Count Michael Karolyi, the Hungarian aristocrat originally of enormous wealth, who had now ended up a refugee, apparently living, along with much of the exiled Czech Government, with the Taylors in Oxford. Alan wrote: 'I was in Michael's company when I first realised that the Germans were not coming. On 15th September [1940] I took him to see Bill and Patience McElwee at Stowe, one of the greatest eighteenth century houses in England. We sat on the steps overlooking the park. Michael said it reminded him of one of his smaller palaces. The sun shone. Aircraft flew over. Suddenly Michael said, 'On this day Hitler lost the Second World War.' He was right. We were very gay, especially from the conviction that the British governing classes were unavoidably condemned to alliance with Soviet Russia in the comparatively near future.'

It would have been an interlude of hopefulness before their lives became subject to enormous upheaval. On 24 September Bill wrote to J.F. complaining about the difficulties of getting the Army to tell him anything about his future pay, there not even being any of the necessary application forms available. For the time being, he was to receive 13/- and Patience 6/- per day. This, he says, 'is our total visible means of support.' He goes on to paint a vivid picture of life for him in an Officer's Training Unit in Aldershot.

'I am back at school and very much in the early stages. Life is a frightened rush again, as it was at first at Sedbergh, and the comparison holds almost everywhere. Cold water in the early hours for a scrambling shave and a fairly tough physical existence supported on bad and inadequate food which, maddeningly enough, yet seems very good for one. And rude, apparently heartless instructors very like the schoolmasters of my youth, who hold one up to the ridicule of the class and drive one through indigestible masses of fact and theory for nine hours a day. And that, too, I suspect, is very good for all of us. They are cramming a 7 week course into less than 4 weeks; hence the rush. And what happens then we don't know. The best of us – captains already mostly – will get companies in new battalions. For the rest almost anything may happen. I have turned down a chance to instruct here. It may be unpatriotic, but I don't think so. Plenty can do that, and if I am not allowed to teach history I'd rather do something quite different.'

With other billets found for the remaining evacuees, Patience went to live with her parents, Syd and Maudie. She kept up a regular correspondence with J.F. throughout the war, beginning with a letter saying that she had left Vancouver 'rather unsettled', which probably means it was a complete tip. All their belongings were left for a couple called Cooper, who moved in for a time. Patience regretted that Mrs Cooper had failed to call before she left, since that meant she would 'have to send a correspondence course about how to run the kitchen range.' It must have been an enormous wrench leaving Vancouver, her final act being to go and say goodbye to the rooks who inhabited some vast elms opposite the house. She always alleged that they promptly deserted their rookery, remaining absent until our return in 1947, thus confirming one of her many superstitions.

In November she wrote to J.F., asking for a reference for a job as a 'lady resident' at a hostel for evacuated grammar schoolboys. She writes:

'By the time I've paid for my keep there isn't much left of my 6/- a day and after a most terrifying time last night and this morning (presumably referring to air raids) I think my family would be glad if I took myself off to somewhere safer.'

It seems that this job did not come off and by December 1940, life was clearly even more difficult for her, with Stowe needing to come to her rescue. She wrote:

'Stowe's generosity will be the most enormous help, and removes a very real worry. I am stupidly not at all well at the moment and was rather dreading the prospect of having to take a job. It is difficult to live on £2 a week and I am naturally paying my extremely impoverished parents while I am with them and doctors and dentists are an expensive firm to visit so thank you very much.'

However, the letter also illustrates how much she kept in touch with old Historians:

'I have a message for you from Dawyck Haig [Earl Haig], A.D.C. in the Western Desert, who wrote to say they were shortly going to be very busy. I have just been staying with the Richards – Brooks still in plaster of Paris, but very gay considering his ship turned turtle with him when he crawled down with a broken leg to get the ships papers. I hear Robin Hastings is a captain and being what Dawyck calls very intelligent – I only hope being Intelligence Officer means a little degree of safety.'

Robin Hastings was someone to whom Patience was strongly attracted for a time. She comments on the Oxford prospects of two other old Historians and ends by saying:

'I think he [presumably Bill] is being a good soldier, but the uprooting from Stowe has been terrible for us both – I never thought, much as I loved being there, that absence would send me into a real Victorian decline.'

Bill joined the Argyll and Sutherland Highlanders, probably being accepted because the McElwees had Campbell connections. His choice is also likely to have been inspired by the romance of the legendary 'Thin Red Line', when the 93rd Argylls held firm in a dodgy situation when fighting at Balaklava. So, having finished his training in Aldershot, where he had refused to take on a training role, he was promptly posted to an Officer Cadet Training Unit (OCTU) in Dunbar as an instructor, where he stayed for just over a year. It was, I think, a comparatively happy period, though judging by his letters to J.F., he continued to miss Stowe terribly. In March 1941 he wrote about two ex-pupils and their scholastic achievements, also commenting on what had clearly been a flying visit to the school. He acknowledges the problems J.F. was facing managing the school in wartime and goes on:

'It was all too short a visit and yet just right. I left feeling home-sick for it all and before anybody had time to tell me of changes in my own little world which might have irritated me. I long to be back with you; yet I am sure that this, just now, is much the easier life. They've just made me Unit Librarian so it's more of a busman's holiday than ever.'

J.F.'s reply included the paragraph:

'Our total bag this year is now 10 – 8 scholarships and 2 exhibitions – and the Historians have contributed 6 of these. Comment is needless.'

During the following summer, Patience joined Bill in Dunbar after doing a stint in an unspecified 'Canteen' which had apparently, as Bill wrote to J.F., left her run down. She stayed with him and his brother officers in the Craig-en-Gelt Hotel. Mr MacDonald, the proprietor, had greeted their arrival with the words: 'This is a Temperance Hotel, but I'll no see ye want' in which, it seems, he was as good as his word. The Commanding Officer, 'Baby' Alexander, who was the youngest of a clutch of clever and successful Irishmen, was apparently delightful, given to saying before their regular visits to the local cinema with its ever changing programmes, 'I'm sick with excitement'. There was a country house to escape to, which was where her aristocratic hostess made a pass at Patience while they were making goats' cheese in the still-room. Their social relationship seems to have survived Patience's rejection of such advances, and she busily recruited a grandson as a future Stoic. She maintained contact with Old Historians, relaying news to J.F., noting that some were enjoying leave 'after sinking the *Bismarck*' and that another, who had apparently been showing signs of incipient pacifism, was, to everyone's delight, joining the Welsh Guards. Patience was also allowed to play the part of a beautiful spy during a major exercise and managed to extract full details of Edinburgh's defences from members of the Loretto OTC who were also taking part.

It was at Dunbar that Bill and Patience met a spectacular couple who were to become lifelong friends. Men arrived at the OCTU from a variety of regiments, and Norris Kennard, son of the last British Ambassador in Warsaw before the war, was also in the process of being commissioned into the Welsh Guards. At the time, this body had a ludicrous practice of ignoring newly joined subalterns in the mess for a specified period. However, Norris was so clearly a comparatively senior and distinguished individual that his Commanding Officer felt impelled to break this tradition of ostracism. He therefore politely asked Norris what he had been doing before the war started. Norris, who stammered and looked like a handsome, aristocratic camel, screwed his monocle into his eye and stuttered, 'Aaactually, I waaas in a Museum.' He was, in fact, an expert on arms and armour, ending up a Deputy Keeper of the Armoury at the Tower of London.

His wife Lee, born Helena Lee Washington, was six foot tall, slender, very dark and quite beautiful. She was also rich and would probably have been regarded as wild by her aristocratic American family. Their marriage was recent, and they seem to have enjoyed wartime rootlessness. This was epitomised for me by their story of the occasion just after their wedding, when they persuaded Fortnums to exchange a beautiful tea-service, which had been given to them as a wedding present, for a vast quantity of caviar. Certainly their postwar life resembled the plot of an Evelyn Waugh novel. Disapproved of by the adjutant's wife at Dunbar, who always referred to her as 'that little Mrs Kennard, as she calls herself', Lee became one of Patience's few close women friends, becoming my godmother and providing the biggest possible contrast to poor Mary McClelland, who had become a rather prim Devon spinster by the time I was born. Both Kennards adored vintage cars and drove them professionally after the war. Later in the war, once Norris was trained and serving properly, Lee joined up and chauffeured grand Generals round London, being wined and dined by them when off duty.

Bill wrote again to J.F. in September 1941, describing his life at Dunbar. 'We work very hard since we are now the only infantry OCTU left apart from Sandhurst; and our pleasures are curiously undergraduate, dinners and drinks in Edinburgh, innumerable cinemas and so forth. Its the kind of life I suppose, which will run itself, pending the resumption of real life when it's all over.' He feels he has had a good summer, particularly enjoying a period when being without a company, he was put onto 'some baby staff work for the Sector Commander and allowed to play about with the whole of the County defences. They have discovered my weakness for expressing myself at length on paper and when memoranda are required, I am turned on. I think I should enjoy staff work. It is fun sorting out the mind and ideas of an able senior officer and reducing them to coherence on paper; and quite fun jockeying a stupid one into a policy of which he has already expressed profound disapproval.' Otherwise he is bored by the instructing, but 'I gather rather good at it, since I alone of my generation am being kept on for another spell. I could get away if I made a scene. But the implied compliment keeps me here.' He is irritated that a blockage on promotion is keeping him from his Captaincy, but notes that if he does get it, it will be taken away from him again if he is posted to a Battalion. Wartime promotion was frequently of the 'Acting' kind and was removed when the posting changed. The constant loss of loved Stoics is demonstrated when he says: 'Robert Kee, writing the morning after his 20th raid over Germany, tells me Malcolm Bolton has been killed in a Blenheim daylight attack on Brest. It must be true I suppose. But I didn't know he'd got so far and vaguely thought he was still training to fly. Could you spare the time to let me know what happened and let me have his mother's address?'

Mourning such losses and responding to requests for news took an enormously heavy toll of J.F. Noel Annan describes how he had made

106

a resolution at the beginning of the war, 'to keep in touch with all the Old Stoics who take part in it', and on top of his work he spent untold hours in the writing of personal letters to congratulate, condole or fortify those of whose honours, losses and misfortunes he came to hear. This exchange of letters threw a stupendous burden on him; but it did a great deal for the community of Stoics. The effect on those taken prisoner was electrifying. 'The first ray of light and my first letter was from J.F. Two pages of interest, comment, good cheer with an offer to send me any books I might want.' J.F. duly confirmed the news of Malcolm Bolton's death to Bill, commenting, 'This is one of the more difficult losses to endure'. He regularly kept Bill informed about staff movements, writing in July 1941 that 'Saunders, Gilling-Lax and Negus, are going to the war. Snowden remains till Christmas but probably goes then. If David Brown can be guaranteed active service in spite of his knee, he will also go at Christmas. We have got two more women coming next term, one to do Chemistry and one to do maths. We have had a poor little Austrian Jew doing the Maths, but he couldn't get on with anybody and was always having soul storms. When he had soaked my hearth-rug with his tears for the third time I thought it better to suggest a move to a day-school!' Hard to know from this comment whether J.F. was aware of what might have happened to the man before he reached Stowe.

In a later letter he gave further news, describing Gilling as 'leaving to train as Radio-location man in a Night Fighter. He seems to have chosen that job because it was the nastiest he could find and the one for which he was least suited for by nature. But I have no doubt that he will do it well.' J.F. goes on: 'We picked up a few good men – some of them quite interesting – and we have got three women now. The real trouble, however, is not masters but boys. The Income-Tax combined with the reputed expensiveness of Stowe keeps parents away. Another trouble is that Stowe was made by the motor car and must suffer temporary eclipse while the motor car is no more. However, we are not doing so badly in reality.' An added problem was the youth of the boys since, as they reached the age of 17, they were heading off to get in a period at University before being called up. J.F. wrote in December 1941, 'The school is extremely young and next term there will be only three boys in it over eighteen.' Noel Annan notes that J.F. had initially been critical of boys leaving early, but had later started encouraging them to do so, 'believing as he did that the university strengthened the judgment of those who would have to run the country after the war if they survived.' The balance of the place became distorted, with the boys so young and many of the masters so old.

11

Parenthood and the Normandy Campaign

The constant seesawing between ranks continued. At Dunbar Bill had been an 'Acting' Captain, his permanent rank being that of a 'War Substantive' Lieutenant. Mysteriously, 'Temporary' was moderately permanent, while 'Acting' was removable. Stephen Whitwell recalls that when serving in home-service units, orders might be received signed by someone designated '2/Lt A/Brigadier'. Once away from Dunbar Bill apparently moved rapidly between units, ranks and, consequently, pay. It was from a Battalion stationed at Dornoch, when he was back to being a Lieutenant, that he next wrote to J.F. in March 1942. Having detailed his demotion and expressed his hopes of getting a Company, he goes on:

'No more news really. Patience is back in Oxford, with the Taylors at Holywell Ford. They are trying hard to lug me out of the army temporarily (1) To be seconded to the historical section of the War Office. (2) To help Alan Taylor with the MoI (Ministry of Information) broadcast to the forces on Tuesday evenings, which they are taking away from Vernon Bartlett. But I'm not playing. Patience, by the way is likely if all goes well to have a baby, rather remotely, next September. She appears fully' [I think – it is difficult to read] 'contented about it; and I am delighted. Odd that a thing one has desperately wanted for ten years should bounce out at one irrelevantly in the middle of a war when there was plenty else to do and think about. But it is a nice gesture of faith in the future if nothing else.'

J.F. wrote back expressing his pleasure at the prospect of a 'small Bill'. At some point during my gestation, Bill had one of his regular bouts of pneumonia and had to go into hospital. Here he discovered that the occupational therapy department had supplies of really good-quality white wool as opposed to the dreary, grey stuff that was available elsewhere. The skill his father had insisted on his acquiring coming into its own at last, he promptly set about knitting my layette. The hospital was about to be transported overseas and was therefore subject to constant inspection. 'You must come and see our officer who is having a baby,' the Matron would say to each grand, red-tabbed figure when they arrived.

Patience's description of life at Holywell Ford was one of her best sagas. Having waited so long, she was determined to make the most of her pregnancy and to take great care. Told that reaching up could cause a miscarriage, she refrained from pulling lavatory plugs and, suffering greatly from morning sickness, spent much time lying on a sofa with a rug to protect her from the Arctic conditions apparently prevailing in the house, and with a basin strategically placed. Here one day she was discovered by Countess Karolyi, who enquired as to why she was lying down. 'Actually, I'm having a baby,' said Patience, sounding fragile. 'You are giving birth now, this very minute, under the blanket?' asked the Countess severely. Patience had to confess that her confinement was sometime in the future, and later discovered that the Countess had bicycled to hospital to give birth to her last child, returning shortly afterwards with the baby in the basket.

Along with the entertainment provided by the stream of distinguished refugees from Eastern Europe and the Taylors' varied circle of British friends, there was the constant drama of Margaret Taylor's passionate infatuation with Robert Kee. In his autobiography, Alan vividly describes the enormous pain this caused him; Patience of course, was apt to make it into a good story. She would describe with relish the layers of black clothing assumed by Margaret when the news arrived that Robert's plane had been shot down. They next heard that the carrier pigeon, a bird which was apparently regularly carried in bombers, had made its way home, whereupon a few layers were removed. Colour was resumed once the news was received that Robert was alive and a prisoner of war.

Patience eventually left Holywell Ford and returned to Shadwells, booking herself into Worthing Maternity Home for my birth. She was playing bridge when she went into labour, and in spite of my being a breech presentation, does not seem to have had a particularly difficult time. J.F. had clearly been swiftly informed and had written warmly.

Patience wrote to thank him when I was five days old, saying: 'I am happy to have a daughter now she's here. Being as you know, incurably boy-minded, it simply never occurred to me that it would be a girl, but on being shown Harriet I find it was really a good idea.' She went on: 'We were happy before, blissfully happy, but it must really be the ultimate state of happiness always to put someone else before oneself.' She regularly told me that she had cried for three days because of my gender, but I think she refrained from saying this until she was convinced that she had in fact got a better deal with a girl.

When first pregnant, she had asked Osy Darell to be a godfather.

He had willingly accepted and put the McElwee infant down for Eton, saying that he would pay the fees. In the event, he once sent me £5, with which I bought a pig, gave me a copy of *Barchester Towers* on what was almost the only occasion on which we met, and left me £100 in his will, which I sensibly spent on a Swan's Hellenic Cruise. My other godfather was Oswald Normanby, who ignored me until he married, whereupon his kind wife, Grania, saw to it that I received regular, and, what were to me given our straitened circumstances, luxurious and exciting presents. Mary McClelland had a tendency to give me devotional books, but Lee Kennard was a wonderful and interested godmother.

Bill continued to move around the North, by now securely a Captain and at intervals being granted, and deprived, of the rank of Acting Major. In the spring of 1943 he was appointed GSO 2 Sheffield Sub-District with the rank of Acting Major and Brigade Major. His boss was the delightful Colonel 'Woolly' Alstom, about whom Bill would tell some of his best war stories. The poor man had a cleft palate, and Bill's imitation was both cruel and impossible to reproduce on paper. There were two particularly favoured stories. The first was of the occasion when they had all taken part in such a thoroughly successful exercise that Woolly took all his staff officers for a celebratory dinner at the Queen's Hotel in Leeds. Such a good evening did they have that Woolly was determined to reward the waiters properly. He lined them all up and solemnly tipped them threepence each. Bill's description of the head waiter's face was graphic. They were all used to black-market largesse and had seen nothing less than paper notes for years.

The other story concerned a paper exercise where Woolly came up with an entirely sensible, workable solution, only to be told, 'But the book says...' 'In that case,' said Woolly, drawing himself up, 'it's a bloody bad book.' I suspect that Woolly may have underlined his contempt by screwing a monocle into his eye and that this gesture inspired Bill to use one when his sight began to lengthen. He swore by it for looking up telephone numbers, but also found it effective in depressing the more pretentious statements made by his tutees. Bill clearly got on well with Woolly Alstom, whom he regarded with great affection, and there exists a splendid cutting from the *Sheffield Star*, dated July 1943, of Woolly inspecting the 69 (West Riding) Battalion of the Home Guard, accompanied by Bill adding colour to the unrelenting khaki in his kilt and gorgeous badger sporran. Guarding Sheffield District was a worry given that there was a dam just above the city which, had it been successfully bombed, would have caused total devastation. Much of Bill's energy seems to have been given over to attempts to persuade the War Office to take the danger seriously.

Though he apparently enjoyed some aspects of his time with Woolly in Sheffield Sub-District, Bill's frustration with administration, together with a surprising ambition, is revealed in a letter to J.F. written in March 1944. He begins by saying that he is thinking seriously of applying for the Headmastership of Loretto and asks for J.F.'s help with this, acknowledging that his position makes it difficult to arrange appropriate support for his attempt. He follows this by writing:

'You will see from my address that I have managed to work my way back into the real army. A year of super-bureaucracy in the back areas nearly broke my heart and I felt that I couldn't let the war come to an end and watch all our beloved Stoics fight it and not take a hand. It was very difficult to escape. The back areas are full of soldiers of my sort of age, rank and qualifications eating their hearts out at office desks. But I managed it just in time, in January, at the price of temporary reversion to Captain, and rather to my own surprise I think I am going to make good.'

He describes the Battalion he is with and goes on:

'so I may see some real war at last. To consider the Headmastership of Loretto in the midst of all this may seem to you odd. But one has to assume some sort of ordered future or go mad.'

It does seem odd, but making a commitment to a possible future must have seemed important and at least it would keep his name circulating in the public school world. Impossible now to know whether he

112

was proposing that if he got the post, they should hold it open for him until the war was over, or whether he would give up his apparent determination to go and fight.

What became of his application is unknown. J.F. wrote back, saying:

'I think you will be wise to apply for Loretto, but I also think that you are quite likely not to get it. It is always said that the Loretto Governors require an international rugger player with a large private income. What about Uppingham? You will have a much better chance at Uppingham than Loretto or so it seems to me.'

A testimonial was duly enclosed and Bill wrote belatedly, in May, to thank him. He said:

'It was probably silly even to think of trying to open such a negotiation at this juncture, but I was in a mood of bravado and although I agree that my chance is almost negligible, it is good for morale to have an iron in a civilian fire just now.'

He was, however, 'too busy to bother much about it'. Bill goes on to acknowledge that Stowe had reached its twenty-first birthday:

'That birthday should have been the subject of a separate and proper letter. But you will get so many essays telling you what a magnificent success you have made of Stowe in so short a time that I funk the competition. The war will have deprived you of the comfort and serenity which ought to have been your personal share. There is neither the time nor the mood for satisfaction and a sense of achievement. But as some compensation I think the war has given you even more to be proud of. Your personal achievement is not to be assessed in words at all. But I would like to record my own gratitude for having been allowed a hand in the job even for a few of those 21 years.'

The posting, in December 1943, about which Bill was so pleased, was to the 2nd Battalion of the Argylls, a body that had been 'resuscitated' as the 93rd Highlanders and was about to embark on strenuous training in preparation for the Normandy landings. In the short paperback history of the Argylls that Bill wrote for the *Men-at-Arms* series in 1972, he charted the origins and progress of the 91st Argyllshire Highlanders and the 93rd Sutherland Highlanders, describing their amalgamation during the reorganisation of the British Army that took place in 1881. This seems to have been a success, though both units retained some of their individualities and tended to go off in different directions. The 93rd had achieved legendary success during the Crimean War, when they had formed the 'Thin Red Line' at the battle of Balaklava, and, according to Bill, managed a heroic last-ditch stand when Malaya was overrun by the Japanese early in 1942. The Battalion was annhilated, with only two officers and 50 men surviving to go into captivity. On 28 May 1942, one of the Territorial Battalions formed before the war was suddenly informed on a ceremonial parade by the Colonel of the Regiment that it had ceased to exist and was to be immediately reconstituted as the 93rd, to take over 'the name, the honours, and the traditions of that celebrated battalion'. In tribute to the Malayan tragedy the chaplain said a prayer, the buglers sounded the Last Post, and the pipers played the 'Flowers of the Forest'. But then they sounded Reveille as a defiant assertion that the old 93rd still lived, and marched off parade to 'Hielan Laddie', a tune that had long been the Regimental quick march.

Bill went on: 'It is not easy to understand how and why this unusually imaginative gesture by the War Office succeeded so brilliantly', but it seems to have worked, and when Bill subsequently wrote the history of the Battalion, General MacMillan, who had commanded the 15th Scottish Division of which it was part, wrote in the foreword, 'that the training given by the commanding officer and his devoted cadre of N.C.O.s, infused into the unit the old spirit of the 93rd. The foundation which he laid was carried on nobly by his successors, and it was plain indeed for me to see during the time I had the honour to be their Divisional Commander that they were indeed the 93rd and not a new wartime unit with no background in history.' This romantic Celtic ethos that was so successful in persuading men to die bravely for their country appealed to Bill enormously, but he never allowed it to undermine his strong practical streak that eschewed unnecessary risks and husbanded the resources of himself and the men he came to command. He must though, have been delighted to be part of the 93rd.

Before he arrived, it had been training in the Orkneys, thereafter being moved around various training camps as it prepared for the invasion of Europe. This seems to have taken a long time and to have been intense for many months before they actually went. In the history, Bill writes: 'From Christmas onwards it became increasingly difficult to get transport for any purpose, as the Transport Officer became more and more immersed in the intricacies of water-proofing vehicles. Ever-varying scales were issued for loading the hundred odd vehicles with which a modern battalion goes to war with its multifarious equipment, and everybody wrestled with loading-tables which seemed to demand either that, in defiance of Euclid, the greater should go into the less, or that some apparently essential piece of battalion equipment should be left behind.' He goes on to describe the new drills learnt, the still remaining peace-time habits dropped and the Commanding Officer's determination to travel with 'the Battalion's secret weapon, the paint sprayer', so that vehicles could be given a final coating before departing overseas. They also took their band instruments 'carefully disguised as Quartermaster's stores, and quite illegal arrangements were made for a store of officer's and warrant officers' kilts to be carried abroad' in the hope that they would get a chance to impress the liberated populations of Europe.

In April they moved to a concentration area, which turned out to be on the Sussex Downs quite close to Lancing and Shadwells. Here they went in for intensive last-minute training, interspersed with parties, Beatings of Retreat, games of football and a visit from Eisenhower. Lengthy marches with all their kit, in preparation for occasions when they would be separated from their transport, were balanced by the fact that 'Worthing and the surrounding country of Sussex took the 15th Scottish division to its heart.' The Division was to sail to France once the D-Day landings had established a beach-head, and Bill describes the nerve-racking week they spent following the landings, when there were 'top secret conferences in the Commanding Officer's room, where a good deal more could be gleaned than was in the newspapers, and the first rough plans for the employment of the Division were becoming known, so that the Intelligence staff began to work overtime with strange bundles of maps and air photographs.' What they did not know was which day they would actually depart, but I, apparently, had a premonition. Some of their carriers were stationed in a quarry very close to Shadwells and I, aged just over 18 months, had become deeply attached to what I rather nauseatingly called 'Pussy choo choos', the 'pussy' being the red Scottish lion emblazoned on their sides. Patience said that one afternoon when I had, as usual, insisted on walking up to see the group, I announced as we were

115

leaving, 'Goodbye Pussy choo choos, you won't be here tomorrow', being proved right when they departed that night. I did seem to possess an element of second sight as a small child, being a successful though unexploited picker of winners on the racecourse or from a list of runners read out to me. Alas, it was a short-lived talent, and the hardened gamblers by whom I was surrounded clearly thought this was too easy a way to back winners, as very little money seems to have been made from my choices.

In fact the Battalion probably only got as far as the 'marshalling area', where 'life turned out to be on the whole, very pleasant'. Bill described the 'first pay out in francs which lent a sort of holiday tone to the whole proceedings, as if it was a weekend at Boulogne instead of a European campaign which was contemplated.' At last they were packed into their Naval transports at Newhaven on a perfect June evening, were piped out of the harbour, and lay at anchor watching Spitfires chasing flying bombs 'while the anti-aircraft tracer from the ships in the Channel and from batteries on shore were better than any free firework display.'

This euphoria was short-lived. Before leaving, they had been warned about the 'disappointment and disillusionment' of war, and their Channel crossing swiftly bore this out. Bill wrote: 'The troops who left Newhaven in the calm of that lovely summer evening found themselves the next morning rolling about in the grey of a Channel gale, unable to land; and there for two days and two nights they remained at anchor, except during the occasional enterprising attempts by the captains to enter the Mulberry harbour – operations which involved a great deal more rolling about and were a nightmare to the seasick.' This seems to have applied to the majority of the troops and certainly to Bill, who, though not in Patience's league as a traveller, nonetheless suffered particularly badly on the sea. The heart bleeds for him on reading that: 'conditions in the troop spaces were like something out of a particularly sordid Hogarth print, with weapons, equipment and men all rolling about together, while a few hearty and unaffected souls made matters worse for the others by eating tins of no doubt delicious greasy soup.'

In a swift reversal, once ashore over the 'long, heaving pontoons', the march to the beach-head was shorter than expected, and they were able to settle down briefly in a place that had 'an air of activity and some noise to the south; but the whole atmosphere was somehow more reminiscent of a big army exercise than a fulfilment of the untried

116

soldier's imaginings of total war'. There was a river to bathe in and 'everyone bargained for eggs – an activity at which, for some reason, Canadians seemed much more efficient than Scotsmen.' This break, which lasted no more than a few days, enabled all the different elements of the Division to assemble, and once this was completed by 26 June, the Battalion went into battle with Bill commanding a company.

Throughout the fifties and sixties, the ensuing battle which created the first break-out from the beach-head and the 'Scottish Corridor' which allowed further troops to penetrate into Normandy, was one studied by students at the Staff College. Bill was a regular guest lecturer with the task of describing what actually happened on the ground when the start-line is delayed and you are shelled by your own guns, when carefully laid battle plans go awry or when what was supposed to be nice firm ground becomes a sea of mud and all the vehicles get bogged down. In the Battalion history, he wrote: 'As far as the 2nd Argylls were concerned, nothing could have been less like the carefully laid plans for carrying the Odon bridges than the operations of June 26th and 27th that led to their capture.' He described the plans and then detailed the mud, the strength of the opposition, which had tanks lurking in unexpected places, and the difficulty of finding the way through a village when the instructions had been to 'leave the Church on the left'. This instruction failed to take account of the fact that the entire village was a heap of rubble, leaving troops 'searching for any fragment of Gothic architecture which would identify the building they sought'. Such hazards combined to hamper the hoped-for advance.

Bill's descriptions of his own Company's achievements are coolly and factually described, and though he gives proper credit to people other than himself, he merely adds his own name to the list of those who received medals. The citation for his Military Cross says it was for the way in which he managed his Company and other elements of the Battalion when under heavy attack on 28 and 29 June. It goes on to note the way in which he frustrated enemy attacks on two of his platoons, saying that: 'In this operation Major McElwee personally found time to direct a Piat stalk, which resulted in the destruction of a Tiger tank.' (The Piat was an anti-tank weapon with which Bill presumably tracked down the Tiger.) Later it says: 'Repeated attacks were made by the enemy, and each time Major McElwee, though holding a necessarily large area, ordered the move of guns and troops to the right spot to meet each situation as it occurred, the very thick woods making this most difficult. He inspired both officers and men by his calmness and his obvious control of the situation.' Noting that he had had to cope with more of the same on the following day, with the added handicap of his wireless having broken down, the citation ends: 'In the Battalion's first major engagement he gave a splendid example to be followed by all and especially less experienced sub-unit commanders.'

After the war, Bill would lightheartedly admit to having taken out a tank single-handed, but his chief story of the battle was of becoming holed up in the thick woods and resisting attempts to get him out. The bridges having been safely captured in spite of the difficulties, it was decided that it was no longer necessary to hold onto Bill's particular wood at Gavrus, in which he was commanding most of the Battalion. However, the orders he received were unclear, and of course his wireless was out of action. Two officers came up, saying that there were tanks waiting to get everyone out, but, as he wrote in the Battalion History: 'they had only the rather vague word of a tank subaltern as authority for the withdrawal and Major McElwee refused to move without a direct order. Captain Mackenzie was sent back with the other two to find Brigade H.Q. and get something more definite one way or the other; and he got back at seven with the necessary direct order to withdraw. By half past nine the remnants of the three companies were safely out, without having suffered any further casualties; and the heaviest mortar attacks of the entire day opened up on the wood just the as the last man left it.'

A more colourful account is given by Charles Alexander, an ex-Historian who was a liaison officer at Brigade. He says he was 'briefed more or less as follows, "Bill McElwee refuses to withdraw without written orders. We can't have people galloping about the battlefield with written orders, but there is a scout car and driver to take you to Gavrus by the direct route. You know Bill; make sure he is in no doubt about the Brigadier's plan." I am sure that I set off thinking that this is what comes of reading too many colourful histories. The journey was uneventful apart from a futile attempt to speak to a tank that was closed down and deaf. At Gavrus Bill was in good humour and very much in control of the situation. Mugs of tea appeared at once. I told him bluntly that it was not a time for dramatic gestures and that he must get out of this wretched wood tonight. Caught off guard by such presumptuous directness from his erstwhile tutee, he indicated that he would forthwith make plans for a move; though he ventured an aside

118

to the effect that he felt safer in this wood than meandering aimlessly about the countryside. I left hoping all would go well.' Bill always said that Charles' actual words were: 'Bill, do stop being a pompous ass and come out of this bloody wood', and that he felt entirely happy about responding to such an order.

The sequel to this event was also an episode that Bill enjoyed recounting. John Tweedie, the Commanding Officer, and his Second-in-Command, Russell Morgan, were unaware that the wood had been successfully evacuated and set out to look for Bill. The relationship between these two men was occasionally hampered by the fact that John Tweedie had a tendency to comprehensive loss of temper and Russell Morgan found his rages funny. Now while they were crawling up a ditch with the Germans close by, according to Russell, pathetically calling out to Bill, the alarm clock Russell had in a pack on his back went off. This caused a major explosion of rage from John Tweedie which sent Russell off into helpless giggles, it apparently being impossible to get the pack off and stop the clock. Luckily they survived to tell the tale.

Russell remained a close friend of Bill's, and when John Tweedie was posted elsewhere, Russell took over the command and was highly efficient, I suspect being the model for the Commanding Officer in *Final Objective*. He was a glamorous man who dressed immaculately – during an exercise in Scotland, someone captured his instructions to his batman which said, 'The pink pyjamas not the blue, and put the *Tatler* on top'. Like most of those in Scottish regiments, his language was colourful, something that once caused me trouble. After the war Russell, who remained a professional soldier, came down to inspect the Stowe OTC, which Bill was then running. He stayed at Vancouver, and it was following this that one of my village friends filed up to Patience and said in a shocked voice, 'Mrs McElwee, Harriet swore.' 'Oh dear, Mildred,' said my mother, 'what did she say?' 'She said "Mildred, you bugger".' Taxed with this, which in those days, of course, was serious, I replied indignantly that it was 'only what Brigadier Morgan called Daddy'. When he left the army, Russell went to work for J. Arthur Rank, but was sacked when he took the after-noon off to go to the Derby.

After their successful capture of the Odon bridges, something that earned the Battalion a great deal of kudos and the nickname 'The Crossing-Sweepers', they were pulled back for a brief rest. Bill described the immediate aftermath in a later letter to J.F.:

119

'And the next morning, after a vile night of disengagement and withdrawal, finished off with a few hours sleep in a ditch, I was wandering round, dirty, hungry, unshaven for three days and wrapped in a blanket against the cold, my morale at its lowest ebb, and I was hailed by Rollo Spencer [an old Stoic] out of a neighbouring ditch. "I say Bill, do you think Noel Annan really planned this very well?" He had some tea boiling and a flask and was very kind and completely restored me.'

Noel had indeed been involved with the planning of the European campaign, but Rollo Spencer was sadly killed shortly after this encounter.

Bill constantly praised the beneficial effects of tea on getting himself and the troops through the rigours of battle, and became canny in his use of the ration of rum issued during the fighting. While some used it to give themselves courage before going into battle, he reckoned that a good night's sleep was infinitely more valuable, particularly as the start of a battle was often delayed, resulting in the alcohol going cold in you before anything got going. So he used his ration as a nightcap, and, discovering that warm feet spread warmth to the rest of the body, would thrust his feet into the arms of his greatcoat before settling down. He pursued this self-preserving policy fighting across Normandy during the month of July, until some heavy fire during a night-time encounter with the enemy caused him to leap injudiciously into a slit trench, severely spraining his ankle in the process. This gave him a month's sick leave back at Shadwells.

12

The Home Front and a Return to Germany

Meanwhile, life for Patience had not been easy. A year earlier, in September 1943, she had written to J.F. asking if there were any list he could send her of those Stoics who had been killed. She says:

> 'Practically all our Historians are overseas now and it would be so dreadful if anyone were killed and we didn't know. I can't get *The Times* here and so have no way of finding out. I did ask Mr Hunter [Senior Tutor at Stowe] if I could have the *Stoic* sent me – it's heartbreaking to lose touch with Stowe – but he seems to have forgotten.'

She goes on:

> 'Bill is still Brigade-Major at Doncaster, but is chafing to be away. I know you will be sorry to hear my father died very suddenly about three months ago – this leaves me as man of the family except when Dumpy gets home, which is very exhausting with this huge garden and no labour of any sort. Harriet is very gay and well in spite of having been in the front line rather a lot lately, but small babies are far more exhausting than the most difficult of boys, and I feel very care-worn. But it's better not to have too much time to think in – we are losing all our friends.'

There seems to be a touch of impatience in J.F.'s answer. He does send her some form of list, but no *Stoic* on account of the shortage of paper. Surprisingly, he makes no comment on the death of her father and merely ends,

121

'I am glad that there is good news of Bill and that the small princess continues to give satisfaction.'

After writing such a miserable letter, she must have found this response something of a slap in the face. Clearly, I was as much a burden as a satisfaction, and indeed, though she was an appreciative and stimulating parent once I was adolescent, small children were not Patience's forte. Though she proudly breastfed me for nine months, my babyhood was ordered along the rigid lines laid down by Truby King, the contemporary equivalent of Dr Benjamin Spock, and I was later assured that I was a very good baby. 'Your mother always kept you so beautifully,' said Bill gazing disapprovingly at my eldest daughter, who was happily whizzing round the floor on her stomach wearing a grubby baby-gro. I had in fact been mostly dressed in gorgeous Irish linen dresses that Bill had worn during his infancy and presumably kept firmly off the Shadwells floors, which Maudie's Pekes regularly used as a lavatory. The 'front line' in which I had been, referred to the frequent bombing raids across the coast. My earliest memory is of the air raid warning going off and Patience snatching me from my bed to take me to the shelter, which was in the cellar of the next door house. Our neighbours had a delightful Siamese cat called Meltis which entirely reconciled me to this gloomy incarceration, but I dislike sirens even now.

The loss of Syd must have resulted in considerable pain and ambivalence for Maudie, Patience and, probably, Alan who, unlike Bill, had not managed to get a patch on a lung past a medical. It also produced one of the better family legends. Syd had always been determined to pull off 'the Spring Double', a feat apparently much prized by gamblers. His excitement was such when he finally did achieve this ambition, that he had a stroke and died without regaining consciousness. The great irony was that, having promised Maudie for the umpteenth time that he had stopped betting, he was doing so through an accommodation address with a tobacconist's in Worthing. No one ever discovered the address, so the one big killing that Syd had ever managed was entirely lost to his family. Bill always said ruthlessly that it served Maudie right, but she apparently forgave Syd sufficiently to allow his ashes to be scattered on Brighton Racecourse. I regret knowing so little about Syd and recall that almost all the information I do have about him came from Bill and not Patience.

The next letter Bill wrote to J.F. also lacks enthusiasm. Though he acknowledges that a month 'in the bosom of my family was absolute heaven', he then found that instead of being sent back to his Battalion, he was 'suddenly and incomprehensibly posted to Lockerbie to a training and draft-finding unit, not even of my own regiment, to do a dull but strenuous job in the wettest climate imaginable, and I am feeling very ill-used.' He ends this letter by asking about his future at Stowe, wanting to know if J.F. would like him back as soon as possible after the war, or whether he should try to hang on in the army for a time. He writes: 'There may be some good jobs going administering Germany, but I don't want to get involved in anything that may be hard to get out of if there is a chance of getting back quickly to Stowe.'

J.F. wrote back saying that while teachers, along with bricklayers apparently, were in a priority section for release, employers were not allowed to ask for individuals. He goes on: 'So far as we are concerned I think Ben Fawcett [who had taken Bill's place] would like to get back to his classics and you know well enough that we should all for personal reasons like to have you here again. We don't know where Bill Snowden will sleep (he is in Vancouver now), but with a little notice he will be able to find somewhere I am sure. But I don't think that there is any good trying to do anything just now. For one thing I have still to be convinced that the German war is nearly over. It looks to me as if it was only just beginning. However, you are better informed than I am about that.' It was Patience who replied to that letter, following Bill's further visit to Shadwells on embarkation leave. She is clearly displeased, writing: 'I wish he'd rest on his laurels and take the home job he was offered, but he has pulled all his strings and is off again.' I can well understand how she must have felt, and yet my gut sympathy is all with Bill.

As he later recorded, presumably with the aid of war diaries and gossip, the Battalion had continued in his absence to battle across Normandy and into Belgium and Holland. He had missed being present for an episode which would have delighted him. In August, with the Corridor firmly established, John Tweedie was sent off to command elsewhere and 'casualties were beginning to make the shortage of officers felt, though the situation was partially eased by the highly illegal arrival of Major S. C. D. Fergusson who "borrowed" a car and broke out of a Reinforcement Holding Unit to get to the Battalion.' Bill must have appreciated this behaviour enormously, and would have been further pleased by the fact that the Black Watch to whom he should actually have gone, promptly posted him as a deserter. He was

123

allowed to get away with it, but his behaviour prompted a 'Special Army Order' forbidding anyone to emulate him.

Major Fergusson also featured when the Battalion crossed into Belgium and were given a rapturous welcome by the inhabitants. They had, of course, been well-received in France, but the enthusiasm of the Normandy farmers had been severely tempered by the appalling damage done to their land by the fighting. However, 'wild though they had sometimes been, French rejoicings were almost nothing compared with the delirious joy of the Belgians when the Brigade crossed the frontier at Moucron on September 7th.' Progress was hampered by enthusiastic crowds, and the troops 'were loaded with apples and pears, plums, tomatoes, eggs, wine and coffee; and there was an orgy of kissing in which everyone, from three-year old children to grey-beards did their best to seize and embrace every Argyll they could get hold of. Some of the troops were lucky enough to be kissed by pretty girls; others, notably Major Fergusson, were less so. He, when he hopefully thrust his head from the window of his car, was vigorously hugged by the Mayor whose two-day growth of beard effectually discouraged him from any further experiments.' For a time Major Fergusson commanded the Battalion, cheering his subordinates enormously by providing port and cigars for meetings. He had, though, to take second placce when Russell Morgan returned from a stint with the Highland Light Infantry.

Bill rejoined the Battalion on 1 November in time to spend what must have been a hellishly uncomfortable winter clearing the way slowly through Belgium and Holland. He describes 'one of the dullest and most uncomfortable periods of the war', based in an area where, 'the country was flat and boggy and intersected with waterways.' The villages had been badly battered by the fighting and it rained all the time, which, combined with thickly strewn 'Shumines', made it impossible for any vehicles, including tanks, to move around. Here they stayed for three months 'stabilising the situation' before clearing the 'Enemy Bridgehead up to the banks of the Maas.' Their lives were lightened by periods when they could stop in towns, Beat the Retreat, making use of their illegally transported kilts and band instruments, give parties and take leave in Brussels, where 'though prices were exorbitant, there was plenty to buy'. Christmas and, more importantly to the Scots, Hogmanay were celebrated, albeit in a somewhat hand-to-mouth fashion, the Maas was crossed, and they began preparations to breach the Siegfried Line.

Bill quotes General Horrocks as leading them to expect a major battle with the idea that not only was the Siegfried Line to be breached, but also that large numbers of the Germans should be engaged in order to weaken their defence of the Rhine. This was the first 'set-piece battle' that the Battalion had encountered since Normandy, but they were without Russell Morgan, who was on leave, and the ebullient Major Fergusson had been sent on a course after 'a colossal farewell party', so Bill found himself Second-in-Command during the planning stage, reverting to being a Company Commander when the fighting actually started. I suspect he used this battle as a model for one he describes in his war novel. The reality was that companies, though not apparently his, kept getting in the wrong place, minefields abounded, and the ground was boggy making it difficult for the vehicles known as 'funnies', which were supposed to clear them. There was always the race to keep ahead of the artillery barrage timed to move just in front of the troops and assuming that there would be no delays. They got there, however, and 'by last light all companies were reorganised and solidly dug in on their final objectives'.

A passage in the novel possibly illustrates what Bill felt at this moment. With his Company preening itself on having arrived successfully with comparatively few casualties, McCann ponders that, 'only he knew clearly how narrow the margin had been between complete success and complete failure, and he knew that he was always inclined to dwell too much on that. He always found it incredible that victory could emerge from the chaos of battle and the incompetence of everyone concerned, including himself, and he attributed his long run of successes to a phenomenal good fortune.' Another passage also reveals self-doubt. Returning to his quarters after receiving orders for the next day's attack, McCann finds his Sergeant-Major waiting up for him with a mug of tea. 'It was on the Sergeant-Major that McCann really depended to keep the company going from day to day. He was a tower of strength both in and out of battle and McCann sometimes wondered whether he did not owe everything – his reputation for efficiency and his company's fine fighting record and even his own Military Cross – to this one man who was always just there when one wanted him.'

Possibly it was during this muddy battle that an incident occurred that was to provide Bill with one of his favourite examples of effective communication. When the last of their Company Carriers broke down, Bill found the driver with his head under the bonnet, gloomily peering into the entrails of the engine. When he asked what was wrong, the driver raised his head and announced laconically, 'The fucking fucker's fucked.' Bill said he would inform Headquarters immediately. When he got through, an aristocratic voice asked what was thought to be wrong. Bill, enunciating with great care, repeated exactly what the driver had said. 'I quite understand' said the voice and proceeded to provide succour. Many years later Bill would use this piece of dialogue in a course he set up at the Royal Military Academy, Sandhurst, designed to teach cadets to communicate briefly and effectively.

The Battalion was prevented from following up this latest success by Higher Command. In 1965, Bill wrote a brief history of D-Day, ending the book with an analysis of the further campaigning. In this he argued that the fighting could have been ended by Christmas given that, following the successes in Northern Europe, the French and the Americans combined to land a fresh army in the South of France which drove the German Divisions there back to Strasbourg and the Upper Rhine. In addition, Patton had swept round Paris and got to the German frontier. Bill wrote: 'Unfortunately, however, this advance on so wide a front began to outrun its supplies, especially of petrol.'

He went on to describe how Patton and Montgomery each wanted to take all the fuel for themselves in order to pursue their own plans, one across the Siegfried Line and the Rhine to Berlin, the other north-eastward to outflank the German forces. Eisenhower would allow neither plan. 'His conception – typically American – was to line all his armies up along the Rhine and, when he had built up the necessary supplies, assault along the whole front. He achieved this in the end, but in the worst possible way. He let both Patton and Montgomery go when it was impossible to keep up a full flow of supplies to both. Montgomery's brilliantly conceived thrust, when he dropped the 1st Airborne Division far ahead of him at Arnhem, failed because his armour could not fight its way through in time to save it from destruction; and a last, despairing Christmas counter-attack by the remaining mass of German Panzers brought the Americans to a halt.

There is only the faintest hint of all this in the history of the 93rd which, having described the part the Battalion played in breaching the Siegfried Line, goes on to depict the Rhine crossing. It was now February,and presumably by this time the problems of supply had been worked out and Eisenhower had his troops where he wanted them. For the Battalion, however, there seems to have been much to-ing and fro-ing before the Brigade of which they were part was pulled back to become part of the Corps reserve. This meant that they were 'kept constantly working out hypothetical operations which might or might not become necessary, according to the fluctuations of the battle.' However improbable, plans had to be worked out to the last detail, so 'the Commanding Officer sat spinning out plan after plan, while the Intelligence Section issued and withdrew maps and air photographs in bewildering profusion, and harassed company commanders stood their companies to and packed up all their kit almost daily, only to stand them down and unpack again and start studying another change of plan.' Finally they got moving, battling their way forward under heavy bombardment since the Germans, knowing they had lost, were making no attempt to conserve their ammunition. Having achieved their objective, the 93rd were then pulled back for a rest in the Dutch town of Tilburg where, whenever they were not being royally entertained by the Dutch, Russell Morgan was bullying them into smartening up their clothes so that they could maintain their reputation as the 'best turned out unit in the British Army of Liberation'.

For the actual crossing of the Rhine, Bill acted as Second-in-Command. Before the crossing could take place, however, they had to practice. It seems that 'some members of the Battalion retained a dimming memory of exercises across the Wharfe and the Derwent', but 'this had taught few lessons that were directly relevant to the problems of a river that was five hundred yards wide and with a current moving at about four knots.' The Maas, though narrower, was faster, and was therefore felt to provide a useful testing ground for the curious 'Buffaloes' in which the crossing was to take place. These vehicles were in the hands of the Yeomanry Regiment, a group that clearly appealed greatly to Bill, who described them as: 'a delightful lot to work with, with a fine cavalry dash and a persistently horsy outlook, even in the water when squadron commanders might sometimes be heard urging their drivers to "get their whips out".' The practices helped, the Buffaloes were successfully whipped along and the Rhine was crossed, to be followed by heavy fighting the other side against well-dug-in Germans. The Brigade irritated the troops by urging speed without taking account of the difficulties they were encountering, and they suffered a bad period of being shelled by their own side in an area with almost no cover. This frayed nerves and tempers, but they apparently loved their Gunnery Officer dearly and so 'worked off their bad temper by quoting taller and taller stories of the language used by the Commanding Officer over the wireless when he was trying to get the shelling stopped.'

It was by now the end of March, and they were properly in Germany. In the history, Bill gives no hint of the complex feeling engendered by fighting across a country he had loved, but in the novel he wrote of McCann as 'going through a whole series of experiences which they [his fellow soldiers] could never share and never even understand; and, since he was not by nature reserved, he disliked the restraint imposed on him by the fact that he could never talk to anyone about what was, for nine-tenths of the time when he was not busy, uppermost in his mind.' Bill, unlike his hero, did not, as far as I am aware, fight across countryside that he knew, but he had felt close to German friends and was entirely unable to see the Germans as an alien race, so had to live with an immensely complex response to the irritating and highly dangerous determination of young Germans to hold out as long as possible against the invading forces, to the vast streams of refugees accumulating and to the devastation created across the country by the intense bombing.

Gerda, the heroine of *Final Objective*, is furiously accusing to McCann about the bombing after he has defended it as a necessary part of saving humanity and civilisation. She says: 'I wish I could believe in the future of a civilisation which marches behind a thousand bombers. You have smashed Europe, you and your precious allies; destroyed everything in it that was worth having: its homes and its people, its pictures and its churches. And now you say: "we have done it for freedom and humanity". Cant.' McCann, not entirely convincingly, holds to his line that there is truth behind the cant while he stresses his dislike of the methods used.

Bill, I think, was particularly torn by the destruction. Later in the same scene in the book, McCann makes a statement in response to further anger from Gerda that must have reflected what Bill felt. He wrote: 'it may be that you are right and the future lies with the people who can only see one side of a question and whose world is all blacks and whites – or blacks and reds. If that is true – if there is no room in the new world for people who honestly want, however they may fail, to see both sides of a question, to deal with life reasonably and – kindly – then one might as well be dead. It is too late now to start becoming a Fascist or a Communist, to start hating Germans because they are Germans, or to find any of those simple solutions. I've been brought up wrong and I couldn't do it even if I wanted to.'

The destructive bombing is also referred to in the Battalion History, and again it relates to the complexities encountered as they worked their way across Northern Germany. The policy of non-fraternisation with the German population sounded clear, but when such issues arose as the requisitioning of accommodation from the local people in order to billet troops, it was not so straightforward. Bill wrote: 'the natural kindliness of the Britisher and the shortness of his memory made such policies harder to carry out in practice than they sounded theoretically. Even hard bitten seniors, who belonged firmly and loudly to the "kick 'em around" school and expressed the most bloodcurdling intentions, tended to start rummaging in haversacks for chocolate the moment they were confronted by a small girl in tears.' He goes on: 'after the first flush of success had worn off, satisfaction at the evidence everywhere of the destructiveness of the RAF raids soon palled, the pleasure of knowing that the Germans were only getting some of their own medicine quickly staled, and the presence everywhere of innumerable German civilians in conditions of gross discomfort and often of real hardship became a perpetual irritation which took away some, at any rate, of the savour from victory.' He would later tell the story of a young Countess who was struggling to take care of 23 totally destitute people who were somehow crammed into a once-elegant ice-cream kiosk.

Bill describes the attitude of his fellow soldiers towards the Germans who held out against them as one of: 'acute annoyance with their stupidity in refusing to accept the obvious fact of their total defeat and stop fighting'. From the time they crossed into Germany, 'every casualty seemed more than ever a total waste, and the minor hardships of the future were to be more resented than the major hardships of the past had been because they were felt to be unnecessary.' They apparently gritted their teeth and pushed on over the Elbe, having 'by the Grace of God, been spared, though by the narrowest of margins, a sight of Belsen Camp.' The war ended for the Battalion in Ahrensberg where on the evening of 4 May, they 'celebrated the news that all the enemy forces in North-West Europe had laid down their arms.' A characteristic photograph appeared in the *Illustrated London News*, showing Bill in battledress with his stance and tin hat both slightly askew, and his hands in his pockets, taking part, no doubt as an interpreter, in local negotiations for surrender. Russell Morgan, standing beside him, is ramrod straight.

His survival and achievements must have meant a tremendous

amount to Bill. Apart from his sprained ankle, he received only a minor bullet wound in his shoulder and, remarkably, his health had held up. Being old enough to avoid unnecessary heroics, he would have been sensible about keeping warm and would religiously have cleared out his lungs every morning. The complexities of his response to Germany must have been a stress, but otherwise he may well again have been like his hero, whom he describes as having had a reputation 'for maintaining a sour sort of cheerfulness in adversity' and also as not suffering acute anxiety before going into battle. McCann woke with a 'slightly sickening, end of the holidays sinking of the stomach', but then 'found that the prospect of a fight did not worry him unduly until it was actually imminent.' Then, as the start line is neared, temper and irritation increased, particularly as there were nearly always delays. There is something heartfelt too, in his fictional descriptions of the time it takes to get soldiers on the move, and the Battalion fetish about leaving a place in which they had been billeted immaculately tidy, in the teeth of 'the ease and speed with which comparatively civilised men, the moment they were put into uniform and herded into masses, relapsed into brutishness and squalor.' McCann is described as having learnt what sort of filth could be left behind and where to look for it, while the Commanding Officer would go round unnoticed at the last moment and would 'triumphantly disinter some horror which everybody else had overlooked.'

From Ahrenberg the Battalion moved further north to Travemunde, which was right up on the Baltic, and here they settled down to begin the appalling task of administering a country in which the infrastructure had gone and where huge numbers of refugees swirled round, fuelled mainly by a grim determination to keep out of the hands of the Russians at all costs. When he got back to England, Bill wrote a pamphlet entitled 'We Were Never Nazis', in which he principally describes the attitudes he encountered among the German population and how he felt that governments should not repeat the mistakes made in the settlement following the First World War. However, he also described part of the process on which the Army of Liberation was now embarked and which highlighted many of the general themes of the pamphlet. He wrote that most of the Germans he met expressed no remorse and would take no responsibility for what had happened, but 'officially or unofficially, consciously or unconsciously, German talk constantly revealed that the only regret they felt was a wistful regret for the lost opportunities and mistakes that cost them the war'.

This inability to take responsibility extended into practical areas, he said. In trying to get daily living organised in the British zone, great difficulty was encountered in persuading the Germans to take on the most basic task. Most senior administrators had been reckoned to be tainted with Nazi-ism, so had been removed from their posts, and those lower down the scale were apparently unable to cope.

Bill felt that the British overcame these handicaps successfully, and while acknowledging that mistakes were made, appreciated 'the smoothness with which the whole place was taken over.' He described order being created out of chaos, the population being supplied with 'a surprisingly large amount to eat', epidemics being controlled, the bulk of the evacuees and refugees being found some sort of shelter before the cold weather set in, and 'a remarkable proportion of the essential services were restored, even before winter.' All this along with disbanding the million-strong defeated German army, repatriating the Allied prisoners of war and 'rounding up, organising and feeding hundreds of thousands of displaced persons.'

Bill found the local attitude towards these last particularly annoying. He wrote: 'nothing was more common during the early months of occupation than to see Germans marching into the offices of Military Government officials, or of the commanders of occupying troops, to protest with flashing, self-righteous indignation at the behaviour of some Displaced Persons, especially Poles, in their neighbourhood. Granted, a minority of these luckless folk, still penned in camps, often in shocking conditions, long after the war had ceased, uprooted from their homes and very uncertain if they would ever be able to return to them, without property, occupation or interest, behaved very badly.' He expressed surprise that, given this situation, more of them had not turned to crime, and acknowledged that the lawless minority were troublesome, but these were properly punished. What exasperated the Allies, though, was the German's inability to see that 'his own Government had, in most cases forcibly, transplanted these helpless civilians thousands of miles, depriving them in the process of their very few remaining decencies of life, and that, apart from his general responsibility for his Country's policy, he personally had been battening on their cheap labour for years.' While deploring this attitude, he also noted that 'for a thousand years the Slav, and especially the Pole, has been for the German the principal enemy, to be feared, hated and, whenever possibly exterminated.' He felt that such deep-rooted feelings were unlikely to be swiftly reversed.

131

Bill cites the greatest achievement of the period however, as being the establishment of Military Courts of Justice, something of which he had some direct experience as he was used as an interpreter. He wrote:

'Here alone we have earned unqualified and almost universal admiration from the Germans themselves though that is not really surprising. In all other departments we have had to compete, under very disadvantageous circumstances, against the things the Germans were best at. Even their enemies cannot deny that they had a long and very fine tradition of administration, and this the Nazis inherited. Though the good manners of our Military Government officers might impress folk who were used to being bullied and ordered about, they could not hope to function with the effortless smoothness of the German civil servants whom they replaced; and in Germany even the good manners were unimpressive and liable to be despised as weakness. Similarly on the military side, our soldiers were hard put to it to emulate the ruthless efficiency of the Wehrmacht in hunting out concealed enemies or dumps of arms. But justice was a commodity unknown in Nazi Germany, even before the war, and the quality of ours impressed at once, almost as if it was something wholly new.'

He goes on to quote the 'joy' of lawyers who had become so disheartened by the almost total disappearance of 'Not Guilty' verdicts, that 'they had fallen into a fixed habit of delivering only pleas of mitigation of sentence even when they had advised their clients to plead Not Guilty.' On the other hand, when a case was proved, the sentences were harsh. Bill felt this combination gave a clear and important message to the Germans.

Bill's determination to write the pamphlet stemmed from his historical sense as much as from the denial he encountered in Germany. He feared that following the First World War, the Germans had been allowed 'in the immortal phrase of 1918, to "organise sympathy" for themselves', and that the mistakes of that period would be repeated and insufficient safeguards imposed. He describes the failure to discern an 'ambitious, enthusiastic opposition, which had been eagerly waiting underground for the chance to demonstrate a better Germany', and continues: 'If the first impression was that there was no large, worthwhile body of anti-Nazis, the second, equally significant, was that there were no Nazis. Those who were hopelessly identified with the regime, the members of the Gestapo and of the SS, and the known party officials and enthusiasts quickly vanished into prison or into hiding. After that it was impossible to meet a Nazi – even a lukewarm one, or one who had once believed and since seen the error of his ways. The entire population took on a strikingly uniform – and completely negative – political colour.' He further describes the attitude that it had all been Hitler's fault, they had all deplored it and there had been nothing anyone could have done to stop him.

The pamphlet was never published. Bill always said that when he presented it for publication in January 1946, the tide of sympathy had already turned and such views were unacceptable. It is strange now to read his eulogy of the settlement Churchill and Roosevelt negotiated with Stalin and his anger with the Germans for apparently creating rumours of possible Russian betrayal, but the 74 pages reflected the impressions and experiences he encountered during the summer of 1945. As far as I am aware, he remained entirely in the North, in Prussia, and it is not clear whether he was able to do any research in other parts of the country. His views have, of course, been overtaken by events, and a very different Germany emerged to the one he feared. Perhaps he failed to take account of the fact that, unlike the period following the First World War, Germany in 1945 had no remaining government at all and had to start from scratch. This may have been the factor that enabled the different Germany to evolve. Bill ended the pamphlet by expressing the hope that a sensible settlement would enable the Army of Occupation to be swiftly withdrawn. Ironic then that it remained for so long because of the agreement he admired so much. Meanwhile, however, Bill was demobbed in September 1945 and returned to England to begin the process of his personal resettlement.

13

Return to Stowe

Absorbed in the fighting and in German affairs, Bill apparently shelved his future teaching career during the summer of 1945. Following his grumble written from Lockerbie in September 1944, the next letter on his Stowe file is one from Germany sent in July 1945, containing what seems to have been something of a shock to J.F. He writes that he is to be demobbed in September, that he realises that this is an inconvenient time, but expresses the hope that J.F. will be able to use him 'in any capacity that suited you and on any reasonable terms, to get my hand in again.' He fears he may have forgotten most of his history, but says: 'my German is going from strength to strength and I am at present employed whole-time teaching the Battalion enough to fraternise effectively.' Bill apologises for this abrupt announcement coming after many months of silence and acknowledges the difficulty of catching up on all that has happened. He feels that 'the next few years will have to be spent in avoiding becoming a war bore' and goes on, 'I assume that you do not need to be told how much I look forward to getting out of uniform and back into a gown, or how I look forward to seeing you all again. The occupation of Schleswig-Holstein is a very tedious interim occupation of which I am heartily sick.'

J.F.'s reply seemed to lack enthusiasm. He wrote: 'This is a great surprise! As I had heard nothing from you I had to suppose that your release was not imminent. Of course it is excellent to hear that it is imminent after all. But we cannot, I am afraid, take you on in September.' He goes on to detail the difficulties with the Snowdens, who were living in Vancouver, finding somewhere else to live, and the term's notice required by the person currently filling Bill's shoes. He hopes that Bill 'will be able to fill up the time between September and January in some way that will be interesting and not too costly.'

Part of the reason for the lack of enthusiasm becomes clear from the following series of letters on the file. These were a recent revelation to me and leave an unpleasant taste in the mouth. On the day following his reply to Bill, J.F. wrote this to the secretary to the Governors, Kenneth Adams:

'I have just heard from Mr McElwee (now Major McElwee, M.C.) that he is being demobilised earlier than he had expected and would like to return to Stowe in September. I have told him that we cannot take him back at such short notice, but that we shall be very glad to see him in January.

It is quite true that I shall be glad to see him, but it would not be true to say that I shall be glad to see his wife. You will remember that under her slatternly management the pleasant little house, Vancouver Lodge, was turned into a slum dwelling, the state of which angered even the good-tempered Mr. Godwin.

Mr. McElwee is a very fine teacher and he was a great asset to the School, but his wife was from several points of view a serious liability.

I am not allowed by law to refuse to take Mr. McElwee back, but I should feel happier if his wife lived at a rather greater distance than Vancouver. I am wondering whether it would be possible for the Governors to say that, in view of the condition to which Vancouver Lodge was reduced by the occupation of the McElwees, it will not be possible for the school to let them live in Vancouver Lodge again or in any other house belonging to Stowe.

I do not want this said unless it can be fairly said on the facts. But if you think it can be fairly said on the facts I should certainly be glad to pass on the decision. It could perhaps be given in the form of a letter to me saying that the Governors are glad to hear of Mr. McElwee's return but regret etc. etc. I would take the correspondence on from that point, though knowing the lady I hardly expect that its tone will be amicable throughout. Naturally I should not wish the McElwees to know that I have raised this question with you at all. But it is of course quite right that I should inform you of their projected return and it is natural that the rest should follow from your own memories.'

Kenneth Adams baulked at tackling the matter head on, saying to J.F.:

'I think it would be a fair description of the facts to say that in view of the condition of Vancouver Lodge was reduced to after they had occupied it before, they could not occupy it again or any other house of ours, but on the whole I think it is better not to put such a thing into writing, but I should have thought that the reason why they would be unable to do so is fairly obvious.'

The letter to be passed to Bill duly expressed Adams' pleasure at his return and added that he was: 'afraid the Governors will not be able to allocate one of the houses for him and his wife to occupy'. He hopes they will be able to find something locally, but realises this will be difficult. J.F. passed this to Bill with a covering letter saying:

'When I reported your return to my Governors I received a reply which I think I must pass straight on to you. I think I know what is in the minds of my lords and masters and I am sure in any case that Bill Snowden doesn't come into the picture at all. We cannot turn him out of course as the law now stands, but he would make way for you as soon as he could if it all depended on him. The real trouble is the attitude of the Governors which whatever you think about it, you probably understand. Houses are certainly very difficult to get in this part of the world, but a chance one does sometime turn up.'

This naturally provoked outrage from Bill, who wrote at length saying that an earlier letter had given him a 'categorical assurance that Vancouver Lodge would be available, along with my job on my release from the service'. He stressed the importance he and Patience attached to the house, and noting that it was J.F. himself that had

'first approached me with the suggestion that it was time to make myself available for the army; and though I welcomed the suggestion, I do not feel that my absence for five years was in any way in defiance of the Governors, wishes or deserving of being penalised as it is being penalised, without any hint of changed circumstance since 1940 to justify such an action.'

He then gets to the nub of the matter:

'I have no doubt that the Governors believe themselves to have much reason to complain of me as an unsatisfactory tenant. I could have filled a volume in 1940 with my grievances against the Governors as landlords. I did not do so because I have always hated recrimination; and I still hope we may avoid a mutual slinging of reproaches.'

Bill also says that he turned down the offer of having his commission extended and 'thereby forfeited the opportunity of promotion and an interesting job in the administration of Germany, which would have been very much up my street' – this not being just because he wanted to be reunited with Patience, but also because Stowe had behaved generously to him and he felt it behoved him to repay this by getting back to the school as quickly as possible. In asking J.F. to do battle of his behalf, he ends with a real sting:

'For the next three weeks I shall be commanding this Battalion and shall have little time for thinking about my own affairs. But your letter left me with a whole series of new personal worries and anxieties which I cannot leave to stew until late in September. And since I am controlling a larger community than yours and with problems at least as complex, I have the less hesitation in asking you to deal with Adams on my behalf in spite of your many other preoccupations, and to try and persuade him to revise what seems to me as I read his letter a somewhat unimaginative and light-hearted dismissal of the matter as a triviality.'

In the letter he wrote to Bill early in 1944, J.F. did indeed imply that Vancouver would be his when he returned. Adams thinks it may not be binding and suggests they consult their solicitors. J.F. wrote again to Adams, thanking him for this opinion and saying:

'As I think you know we are very much attached to Major McElwee, but have not quite the same feelings towards his wife. My own personal feeling is that I would rather have neither of them back than both of them back. But Mr McElwee is both on moral and legal grounds entitled to return to his job if he wished to do so. If he would come as a bachelor or find a house at a considerable distance from the school, he would find himself most welcome.

That is the position from my point of view. The point of view of the Governors is doubtless that they do not wish Vancouver or any other house belonging to them to be turned again into a slum. It would be a pity however if they took a strong line now and were ultimately compelled to withdraw.'

He therefore endorsed the decision to take legal advice and wrote to Bill saying that the Governors did not necessarily feel legally bound and that Adams would be writing himself.

This correspondence, which had taken place throughout August and September, then abruptly ceased, and the next item is a comparatively cheerful letter from Bill written in October, saying that he has heard nothing from Adams, but that in the meantime he has taken a job tutoring somewhere unspecified, since 'Patience refused to have me idle about the house for four months and army pay won't last forever.' His pupils are 'two very backward and difficult boys for Common Entrance, who test my patience but do not otherwise strain my rusty faculties.' The main purpose of his letter though, is to say that his own old Headmaster, Weech, had told him that the Headmastership of Monmouth was going and that he thought Bill should apply.

Bill has also heard that a headmastership may also be going at Kings School Bruton. He asks for references and J.F.'s advice about applying. His final paragraph sounds cheerful:

'I had a fortnight at Lancing before coming down here, and found them all in tremendous form. Daughters, I know, are not in your line, but I truly believe mine is a remarkable one. And now, on a prosperous farm, with plenty of eggs and butter and a bit of riding and shooting to sweeten the job, I am once more the complete civilian. Many people told me that the transition would be difficult and not pleasant. I can't tell you how wrong they were. But I fear I was always a rather bogus soldier.'

J.F. replied blandly to this, saying that 'The storm about Vancouver has blown over and everything is amicably settled.' He advised that Bill should indeed apply to Kings School, Bruton, as well as Monmouth, and enclosed a glowing reference. He also asks Bill if he will take over what was shortly to be christened the 'Combined Cadet Force'. This was to relieve the warlike Fritz, who had been commanding the Corps throughout the war. Bill accepted happily, clearly relishing the task, but was pretty scathing about the complaints of over-work heard subsequently from Fritz.

Presumably the legal advice had counselled against excluding Bill and Patience from Vancouver. Given the comments from the History side, and indeed my own vivid memories of the limitations of Patience's housekeeping, I can understand the concern over the maintenance of Vancouver. Nevertheless, I also remember the difficulty of getting repairs organised after the war, and have no doubt that Bill's complaints were also entirely justified. What sticks in the gullet, though, is the lack of honesty and the fact that Patience got all the blame. J.F. fails to specify what else he had against her, though he strongly implies that it was not just her slatternly housekeeping that was at issue.

As far as I am aware, Bill and Patience never knew about J.F.'s underhand dealing with Adams, though the initial suggestion that they would not be allowed the house may well have been a factor in the difficulty Bill had in persuading Patience to go back to Stowe at all. The serene picture of his return painted in his October letter is belied by the stories he later told me about Patience's determination to stay at Shadwells with Maudie. She felt that they could never re-create the prewar Vancouver, that the pain of all the losses would be unbearable and that she would prefer to remain in what seemed a safe haven rather than risk trying to do it all again and failing.

The fact that Patience had managed to spend the best part of Bill's savings must have heightened the conflict between them. While fighting, spending much on himself had been difficult for him, so a considerable portion of his pay had accumulated in the bank. In spite of their separate bank accounts, the fact that Bill could have been killed at any time meant that Patience had to have access to his money, and she decided she would use it to try to make more. Her idea can only be seen as a manifestation of the fearful Kennington gambling tendency. She bought a Gordon setter bitch and proceeded to mate her, hoping to sell the resulting puppies for much gold. Of course it went wrong, with the puppies developing distemper, and such sales as there were barely covered the stud fee. Bill, thinking he had what was then the considerable sum of £200 to fall back on, was appalled to find that between the dogs and some shabby pieces of antique furniture, it was almost all gone. His reproaches no doubt added to Patience's determination not to resume married life with him. I, aged just four, have a dim memory of acute tension in the atmosphere and slammed doors.

However, Bill would not accept Patience's refusal to return to Stowe, just quietly making the assumption that she would go back there eventually. I have always been profoundly thankful that he won this battle. Living with the reclusive Maudie, Patience would have become increasingly fearful of the outside world and I would have been stuck with two anxious women, both prone to migraine and given to endless brewing of senna tea. I can still shudderingly recall the smell of this liquid left overnight in the bathroom to infuse. Maudie's brooding anxiety was epitomised by her attitude to my belts. A wiry child, I generally wore trousers with a belt over which she would agonise, convinced it was too tight.

The return to Vancouver must have been a nightmare, though, and took time to engineer. Late in January 1946, Bill wrote to J.F. detailing the plans he had to get their furniture dried out and repaired. In a swift reversal of complaints, Bill and Patience now had a major grievance. The furnishings they had been asked to leave for future tenants of Vancouver had subsequently been removed and stored in the loft above the stables, prey to damp and the attentions not only of 'the morth', but rats and mice. Furniture had come unglued, while upholstery and blankets were riddled with holes. I still possess a darned blanket as a souvenir. Bill was attempting to sort all this out while suffering from a heavy cold and, at the same time, trying to prepare for interviews at Bruton and Monmouth, for both of which he had been shortlisted.

Whether because of the state of Vancouver, or her continuing determination to stay with Maudie, Patience did not move back into Vancouver for another year. In the meantime, Bill Snowden moved out, though not without difficulty. Bill went to see him on the day of his move and found the pantechnicon stuck halfway up the drive and Snowden sitting in the kitchen, shaking and saying: 'It hates me, this house. It's always hated me and now it's not going to let me go.' Bill was, I think, pleased that the house was apparently regarding the Snowdens as interlopers and was possibly convinced that his presence persuaded the malignant forces to relent.

Somehow the Snowdens extracted themselves, and renovation began. Bill must have been given quarters in the school, picking up the threads of teaching again and returning to Shadwells for the holidays. Nothing further is heard of his applications for headmasterships, and the assumption must be that he was continually unsuccessful. I can just remember a later application that also failed to come off. In

140

discussing his chances with J.F. earlier, he cited lack of experience as a housemaster as a drawback, though feeling that the administrative experience he had gained in the army would counteract this. My instinct is however, that Bill's heart was so strongly set on teaching that he never really sold himself as a possible headmaster, only applying in the first place because he felt he ought. I can imagine too, that Patience would have had mixed feelings, enthusiasm for the position and extra money being counteracted by seeing her direct involvement with boys greatly curtailed by the more formal role of headmaster's wife.

Achievements continued, however, on the literary front. During 1946 Bill completed not only the Battalion History, but also what I think is a singularly depressing novel called *The Cure*. The plot was summarised neatly by the *Northern Whig*, which wrote that it was 'a rather drear story of a man's holiday at a small French watering place. There is an inconclusive love story which is improbable in its plot and unpleasant in its implications'. The hero lacks confidence in almost all areas of human contact, a man who regrets the loss of youth while being unable to value the benefits of maturity. A modestly successful businessman, he nonetheless fears the hotel staff and obsessively mulls over situations in which he feels he has cut a poor figure. It is difficult to know, now, how far this character reflected Bill's present state of mind. It is possible that the continuing difficulties in his marriage, combined with the failure to get the headmasterships and the transition back to a Stowe struggling to recover from its wartime battering, combined to undermine his confidence. The overall impression left by the book is of a deep mid-life crisis fuelled by regression to adolescent self-doubt. The ending is unhappy, with the gloom aroused by the sense of failure being difficult to shake off after finishing the book. Reviews were mostly muted and noted that it did not fulfil the promise Bill had shown in *The House*. However, one or two were enthusiastic, praising the delicacy of approach and the quality of his writing. The devoted *Buckingham Advertiser*, of course, writes that Bill had produced 'another novel of rare and charming qualities'.

Patience, meanwhile, had completed another lighthearted novel. Slighter than *Roman Holiday*, *Love, or Money* was the story of a brother and sister living, just postwar, in a vast and hideous inherited house, having lost all the money that formerly buttressed its upkeep. Much of the plot concerns their attempts to conceal the situation from their formidable mother, who is bent on pushing them into making 'good' marriages. Mysteriously, but possibly for reasons connected with wartime shortages, it was initially published in Egypt where, according to a local Sussex paper, it became an 'established "best-seller" among troops in the Middle East'.

When in the autumn of 1946 it came out in England, it was nothing like as widely reviewed as *Roman Holiday*, though local papers, including, of course, the *Buckingham Advertiser*, did it proud. Sussex newspapers made much of the family connections, with the *Sussex Daily News* headlining an article 'Prolific Output of Sussex Literary Family', adding a recently published novel by Patience's brother to *Love, or Money* and *The Cure*. She tells the paper that she wrote *Love, or Money* on the beach at Lancing while I played. It is an abiding memory of mine: Patience, with her back against a breakwater, an exercise book on her knees, absorbed in writing, always in pencil, I, in what must have been a revolting red seersucker bathing dress, distracting her at intervals with shells and shapeless sandcastles. Sometimes we took a picnic with jam sandwiches that crunched with sand. In another interview, Patience says that she has 'recently completed a much more serious work which is to be published under her maiden name'. Whether this signified a desire to end her marriage, or merely the fact that she felt the name of McElwee labelled her as a light romantic novelist, is now unknown. The book she talked of must have failed to find a publisher since her next novel, which was indeed much more serious, did not appear until 1950 and was based on events at Stowe which had not then occurred.

Another piece, from an unidentified paper, must have given the family much joy. It is headed 'Just Like Us' and goes on:

'When I met Lancing's popular novelist, Mrs McElwee, the other day, it was interesting to find that, woman-to-woman, her problems were identical with ours when she is not pounding away at her typewriter, turning out thousands of words in next to no time. Her concern is accommodation and home-help ... just as it is the problem of Mrs. Jones and Mrs. Smith – and at Mrs. McElwee's home at Stowe with oil to cope with, cooking and housework, plus a daughter now nearly four years old, was no joke, as she told me.'

The punctuation is reproduced verbatim.

Throughout 1946, Bill certainly returned to Shadwells during the holidays, though in August he spent time in Scotland researching the Battalion History. At Stowe he taught, but he was without Vancouver and no Shakespeare play was put on. Before Christmas he persuaded Patience to visit and to see Vancouver, which was being redecorated and having electricity installed. At this point he won his battle, and it was agreed that we should all move into the house for the start of the January term. The beginning of this new era was not auspicious. Our journey by train was hampered by the snow that was to make 1947 a legendary winter, and I remember the train had a tendency to go backwards, which worried me terribly, much to the amusement of the troops that crowded the train. We were also encumbered by my frightful black tomcat, Bouncer. One day, queuing for oranges, Patience and I had arrived at the stall, only to find that all the fruit had gone. Distressed by my obvious disappointment, the proprietor thrust the cat into my arms. He was somehow kept apart from Maudie's Pekes and lived to be a menace to other Dadford cat owners. On that memorable and endless journey, he naturally messed his travelling box while yowling loudly and continuously throughout his incarceration.

I remember nothing about our arrival, apart from the fact that I was afraid of going to sleep in the dark, something of which I would have been expected to be cured after living in the ill-lit and sinister Shadwells with its impenetrable corners. I had every chance to get entirely used to Vancouver, however, since we were promptly snowed in, being supplied by German prisoners of war who remained happily in the area, travelling about on a tractor. Later that spring they were repatriated, having presented me with some nice bedroom slippers they had made, but without having managed to sell a litter of fox cubs whom they had captured and, having docked them, tried to pass off as corgi puppies. Released back into the wild, the cubs enjoyed long and happy lives ravaging the local poultry. Foxes carry their scent in their brushes and are almost unhuntable if tailless.

The thaw came with a storm that ravaged the Stowe trees while causing widespread flooding, and Bill and Patience began, in spite of the losses and the austerity imposed by rationing, to recreate the spirit of Vancouver and the History Side. That spring, the rooks nested in the elms for, according to Patience, the first time in five years.

14

The History Side Renewed

The golden age of Roxburgh's Stowe was over. The charisma of J.F. had provided much of the glow, but he was now desperately tired after the struggle to maintain the place through the war, and deeply pained by the losses. Being such a young school, it was badly hit proportionately. Just under 2000 Stoics served in the war, with one in seven being killed. Of the 60 Historians Bill had so carefully listed in a maroon leather-bound book, 14 were killed in action. Possibly J.F.'s passionate commitment to the boys current and old, paradoxically weakened his legacy to Stowe as a whole. Noel Annan, in analysing J.F.'s methods and achievements, contrasts his failure to work closely with his staff compared with the direct, individual and strong relationships he had with the boys. Not only did he apparently deal himself with issues that should properly have been left to housemasters, but there was only so much of him to go round. No man could have had the time and energy to know and support his staff while maintaining the sort of involvement J.F. did with up to 500 boys in the school, as well as numerous Old Stoics. No wonder then that he was drained at the end of a war that had decimated the young men he loved so much. Had the balance of his concern been more equal, he might, in giving more to his staff, have in return found his own burdens lessened. Nor is it surprising that Bill found colleagues who had stayed at the school weary and complaining about the stress they had suffered. He was deeply intolerant of their grumbles, feeling that those who had gone off to fight had borne much more of the heat and burden of the war years, but in truth I think his five years away refreshed him. He returned to teaching full of energy and zest, more determined than ever to produce high-achieving scholars.

The school as a whole recovered its numbers quite quickly, but money was tight. Noel Annan notes that J.F. found it difficult to live with inflation, being used to unchanging fees and salaries. The group of Allied Schools, to which Stowe belonged, had helped out financially during the difficult war years, but with the numbers restored, the school was expected to stand on its own feet. Lord Annan also felt that had J.F been able to bring himself to take a sabbatical break in which to explore what was going on elsewhere in education, it would have refreshed him and been of benefit to Stowe. It is likely, however, that he did not have the necessary energy to undertake such a task. J.F. himself appears to have been clear that it was time for him to retire. He realised, however, that his name was an important element in persuading parents to send their sons to Stowe. The numbers, having settled at over 500 before the war, had dropped to about 400 by 1943.

J.F. waited until once again there were more than 500 boys in the school, before retiring in 1949 at the age of 61. Though there have been many successful Stoics and many men who enjoyed their time there, it does not seem that ultimately, J.F. succeeded in his ambition to create an exciting, innovative public school. My sense is that Stowe, like the curate's egg, was only ever good in parts, relying too heavily on J.F.'s personality and the magnificent setting. Stephen Whitwell feels that fundamentally J.F. ended up being ameliorative, putting tolerance and good manners above innovation, aiming for 'a kind Eton without the snobbery and traditional harsh punishment'. This lack of a particular, clear vision, together with J.F.'s inconsistency in picking of staff and failure to nurture properly those he had, made the baton difficult to pick up.

Nonetheless, Roxburgh remained a name to conjure within the public school world, and Eric Reynolds, who had been a housemaster at Rugby before he succeeded J.F, was always going to face an uphill task. Suffering a serious accident soon after he arrived, which left his face slightly distorted and his vision disturbed, did not help. Bill had hoped that the Governors would appoint Oliver Van Oss, a housemaster at Eton, and was furious when he heard that the Governors had apparently turned Van Oss down when he answered a question on how he managed administration, by saying that it was a thing he 'left to clerks'.

Reynolds had been a highly successful housemaster, which clearly impressed the Governors, but Bill and Patience labelled him as nothing more than an administrator, a dreary little man, not quite out of the top drawer in any respect. There was an occasion when Patience, watching a cricket match, became aware of Reynolds sitting nearby on a shooting stick and said to her companions in her carrying voice, '*Prenez garde. Maitre Corbeau sur un arbre perche.*' New masters though, regarded Reynolds with some affection. Joe Bain, a highly successful Reynolds appointee, gave a warm and wonderfully idiosyncratic address at Reynolds' Memorial Service in the Stowe Chapel, in which he notes the label 'dreary little man', as well as his awkwardness with parents and his shyness. However, he balances the derogatory labels by citing his warmth and tolerance and also the mutual trust and respect between him and those staff who did not hanker after the days of J.F. He also details the fact that Reynolds fought for halfway decent salaries for the masters, it being during his reign that the Burnham scale was introduced at Stowe. He introduced the limitation of tenure for housemasters to 15 years in post, something that J.F. had failed to tackle. There were considerable grumbles about this along the lines of it taking five years to get rid of the last boys who had known your predecessor and another five to get properly settled in. However, while there were some brilliant housemasters like Edward Capel Cure and Humphrey Playford, both of whom held their houses for almost 30 years, others were disastrous and, as a general principle, fresh directions seem better for both house and incumbent. My own memories of Reynolds are chiefly of his appearing self conscious and indeed awkward, but there is a letter from him written to Patience, thanking her for sending him a copy of her latest novel, which is warm, appreciative and funny.

Bill cannot have made his life easy. He was probably less disruptive than he sounded when talking about Reynolds, but the facts of his success in recruiting clever boys and then getting them scholarships, his war service, the local stature that he was to acquire, together with the subversion that flourished anew at Vancouver, must have made him difficult for the most confident man to handle. I suspect Reynolds did not even try. The one area in which he did try to impose restraint was singularly unsuccessful. The corgi I had been given for my fourth Christmas had not, as rumour still has it, been named Reynolds as a deliberate insult to the Headmaster. His arrival predated that of Eric Reynolds by two years, and I had actually called him after the man Patience and her brother Alan dealt with at Melrose, the publishers that had produced their most recent books. It was for my parents, however, a happy coincidence, seized upon by Bill, who would regularly take the dog up to the school. I suspect he never actually shouted, as he alleged, 'Reynolds, come away from that bitch' at the top of his voice on the populous North Front, but the Headmaster nonetheless asked him not to take the dog up to the school anymore, a request with which Bill entirely failed to comply.

The war years may have made the recruiting of boys difficult, but in 1946 there was no lack of talent for the re-invigorated Bill to work on. Alan Caiger-Smith had just joined the History Side when Bill returned and vividly remembers the contrast with Ben Fawcett, who had been in his place. Alan found Fawcett an uninspiring teacher and was immediately taken by Bill's style. J.F. had billed his return by saying that he was 'coming back, having covered himself in glory', and Alan felt that, indeed, Bill arrived 'wreathed in battle smoke.' In fact he first saw him taking a parade of the Corps and was struck instantly by his 'zing' and the fact that a 'real soldier' was commanding them. The older boys on the Side were apparently less enthusiastic, supporting the ousted Fawcett and resenting Bill's assumption that he was reclaiming his own. Alan recalls an enjoyable put-down to one of the 'Fawcett people' who had made a noise at the back of the classroom. Bill asked what he had done. 'I'm afraid I giggled, Sir,' replied the boy. 'Don't giggle,' said Bill, 'I find it's better to chuckle.' Alan did find, however, that the supposed glory days of before the war were a powerful pressure and felt he was expected to emulate the reputedly brilliant figures of the past, whom Bill saw as part of a golden age. Alongside this, though, he thought Bill had a strong belief in the abilities of his present pupils and felt very much encouraged to be himself, to explore all options and to pursue his artistic bent.

Toby Robertson, who has gone on to a distinguished career in theatre and film, provides another vivid description of Bill's return. He writes: 'I don't remember Life-much-before-Bill, but even at fifty years distance, Bill's return to Stowe remains vivid and exhilarating. He had always been a name to conjure with, but we were quite unprepared (perhaps rather dreading the threatened change) for the sheer ebullience he brought not only to the classroom, but life outside it. For him, there was no difference.' Toby felt that, with Roxburgh tired, the buildings and grounds of Stowe run down and academic standards faltering, Bill was determined to recreate the prewar History Side, once again establishing an elite. 'Above all style not sincerity was to be the vital thing. If style is defined as "a sense of superiority without much moral justification for it", then I think, that was us. Starved as we were,

147

Bill bombarded us with books – "a gentleman spends a third of his income on books" was one of his throwaway lines.' Toby goes on to list some of the books and authors they were expected to read: *The Strange Death of Liberal England*, Ronald Knox, Namier and Alan Taylor. He also recalls the revival of the Historians' photograph and the Shakespeare play. So satisfactory for Bill to be able to celebrate the renaissance of the Historians by reviving *Richard II*, the first play he had ever done there, since he had an excellent and moving Richard in Toby himself.

Similar themes come up for Toby as for others. Being treated as undergraduates rather than schoolboys, Vancouver, 'primitive by modern standards – the atmosphere, new to most of us, I now realise must have been a rather primitive Bohemianism', good food, astonishment at how Patience did it, past Stoics and others visiting, and the fact that while the talk was good, you were expected to 'sing for your supper'. He also notes that 'Bill's return put certain noses out of joint: Perrin and Traill animosities abounded. The Stowe climate had always been fairly laissez-faire, but with Bill all our energies were to be channelled and developed by him. He was demanding and would not let us be niggard of our qualities. When I failed to get a scholarship to The House and merely made it to Trinity, Cambridge ("The only Cambridge College where a House man could be happy" said Bill), I felt miserable because I had failed him, but my real sadness was not to have had him longer as the inspired teacher he was.' Bill's intensive reading lists and his expectation that his pupils use their 'qualities' to the full, suggests that 'sincerity' of some kind remained important.

Toby was not the only one to feel pressure to recapture the glorious past. Peter Leslie, who joined the Side in 1946, also felt he should achieve the fullest possible success for Bill and Patience, and still harbours some regrets for a particular ambition unattained, though he was subsequently enormously successful as a banker. I still remember Patience bursting into tears when he told her that he had passed a particularly important examination. Colin Anson, a contemporary of Peter's, cites Bill's conviction that with sufficient self-belief, he could succeed in going up to Oxford, though happily, Colin confounded him and went to the Slade, following which he had a fruitful career in the arts world.

David Part, Director of that beautiful Sloane Street shop, the General Trading Company, did not win his argument for going to Reading

Phoebe and Katherine Lloyd - Bill's grandmother and mother

Inspector General William Lloyd - Bill's grandfather

Bill McElwee and younger brother Patrick

Bill McElwee (in the right of the picture) aged eighteen, when a prefect at Sedbergh

The Historians' photograph, 1951 - the Temple of Friendship

Bill McElwee - 'The Author'

Portrait of Bill painted by Robin
Watt, Art Master at Stowe

Patience with foxhound
puppies

Bill and Patience by the Vancouver stables

Bill and Patience on the
north front of Stowe in 1938

Bill as a soldier and father

In the Rec Room 1 - a decorous occasion with Cyril Atkins and a member of the domestic staff

In the Rec Room 2 - 'Pity the poor drunkard's child' - with the School chef and his deputy

Buckingham Fair - Stephen Whitwell displays the winnings

Bill using the sewing machine
bought when he was born in 1907

to study art and design, but was pushed into going up to Christ Church, which he left after a year. He recalls a session Bill had with new recruits to the History Side, during which each was asked about their future ambitions. David blurted out that he wanted to be an interior decorator. 'Good God,' said Bill, 'all one's most bogus friends are interior decorators.' David nonetheless hugely valued the History Side and Vancouver. Brian Brindley, another of the 1946 intake, said revealingly, 'I got a History Scholarship which was what he (Bill) wanted,' though in no sense was he complaining about Bill's ambition for him, going on to say how happy he had been at Oxford. However, he also felt that Bill failed to take account of the changes wrought by the war in the educational establishment, continuing to see Oxford and Cambridge as the only possible destination for the Historians.

Alan Caiger-Smith left early to go to the Camberwell School of Art, but hated it and reverted to History, getting a scholarship to Kings, Cambridge. In his viva, Christopher Morris and two other Fellows hopelessly wrongfooted him, leaving him only able to acknowledge his muddle. Sometime later, having got to know Morris, he asked him why they had put him through this ordeal. 'Oh, because you were a pupil of McElwee's,' was the reply, 'we wanted to see if you would admit your difficulty.' Alan felt that this reflected his own experience of Bill's teaching as enormously stimulating, but lacking a system, and, like Toby Robertson, found that the content did not always match up to the style. He was not happy to be told by Bill that 'charm must be your long suit' when earlier trying for Oxford. However, Alan remembers his tutorials as being 'gold': Bill, rather slumped in his chair, rolling a cigarette, and discoursing fluently and with enormous enthusiasm about people and events. Alan saw less of Vancouver than the others, since he was of an earlier generation, but he enjoyed what he described as the 'elegant dilapidation'. He was aware of the alternative family element offered by Bill and Patience, but perhaps not quite so strongly as the other four men, who were passionate Vancouverites. All of them, however, relished the commitment to them all, the gossip and the appreciation of achievement. A number of birthday and Valentine offerings to Patience still exist where Colin Anson had produced a sketch or delicate watercolour, while Brian Brindley had written a verse. The *Vancouver Book of Nursery Rhymes* dates from this period, several items being highly scurrilous. The following rhyme summarises the general pattern:

There was a crooked Tutor who ran a crooked Side
And got a crooked scholarship for every crook who tried.
He had a crooked wife with a crooked kind of glamour
And earned a crooked living as a crooked kind of Crammer.

In addition there is a cookery book with recipes that makes puns of various masters' names, a delightful parody of the Historians' photograph, produced by Colin Anson, and a Masque apparently written by Colin Graham Bonnalie, who was later, as Colin Graham, to stage successful musical productions. Historians' paintings decorated the walls of Vancouver, including one of Alan Caiger-Smith's that Bill particularly treasured.

A thorough analysis of Bill as a tutor was given to me by Sam Adshead, now himself a Professor of History at the University of Canterbury in New Zealand and one of the 1947 vintage. He did not apparently experience the lack of system or the emphasis on style and writes: 'Simply, Bill taught me, as so many others, how to think.' Sam feels that he did this by a mixture of 'telling criticism and encouragement. He beguiled one into thinking.' Bill would apparently use the phrase, 'Well, that's nearly very good' after listening to an essay, and was 'like Capability Brown. He saw the possibilities of even the most unprepossessing landscape.' Sam goes on: 'I don't think he really wanted me on the History Side, and I don't blame him. After school certificate, I was a know-it-all Marxist, constantly talking with an appalling stammer.'

Destined for another Side, Sam went to J.F. and threatened to leave if he were not allowed onto the History Side. Having succeeded, he then suffered a check. He writes: 'For about a year, I learnt little from Bill and must have justified his worst fears. Only slowly did I begin to listen. Then, in the autumn of 1948, I think, he set everyone an essay on "Charm"! Marxism no help, so I tried to imitate a *Times* Fourth Leader, which Bill always made us read, and the key fitted and turned the lock. From that moment, I began to learn: Charles V and Luther completed the process by opening up new worlds. Bill taught by stories. All of us knew the one about someone who had failed a scholarship by writing "Scoundrels, like the Abbé Gregroire": choose words carefully, have evidence to back them up. He liked epigrams: "The Middle Ages died hard", but not at the price of meaning and evidence. What he sought for was profundity, and even a suspicion of it received praise: "It was not what Luther affirmed but what he denied that made him a heretic". The stories went beyond history. He had some quarrel with an odious housemaster. Namier came to stay, heard Bill out and then, pondering it, said "You are in the wrong, Bill, you must attack". Another maxim of Bill's I still cherish is "If you are losing an argument, widen it, if you are winning an argument, narrow it." Yet he never put dialectic before truth. He just didn't like to see truth defended by sloppy arguments or obscured by verbiage. Thus he gave us the golden gift of thinking.'

Sam Adshead feels that he was never one of Bill's favourites, which may be so, but I do know that he had a huge admiration for Sam's intellect. His scholarship to Christ Church and subsequent First were obvious reasons for his appreciation, but there was also an occasion when Sam deflated Dick Crossman which pleased Bill enormously. Crossman, whom Bill had known at Oxford and who had a stepson at Stowe, came down to talk to either the History Side or the Twelve Club. Sam describes it as follows: 'Dick had opened with a vivid account of standing on the Roman *limes* in Germany, and then expounded a view of the Germans as always half outside European civilization, barbarians to the West. I was very full, prompted by Bill of course, of A. J. P. Taylor's idea of the Germans as essentially the people of the middle, barbarians to the West but civilisers to the East.' With this in mind, Sam asked Dick about Poland, whereupon Dick said: 'Oh, if you mention Poland, my whole theory collapses.' A delighted Bill told the story whenever Crossman's name came up anywhere. Bill's stories of Christ Church determined Sam to go there, and he remembers Bill saying of Hugh Trevor-Roper, who was to teach him, 'He's just about the cleverest man in England, and you must learn from him, but I think you will end not entirely agreeing with him.' Sam was somewhat in awe of Patience, and remembers her making him read Isherwood's *Goodbye to Berlin*.

A year later, Simon Digby, a scholar who achieved a Starred First at Cambridge and later became a distinguished exponent of Indian history and culture, was another who was determined to join the History Side. Simon, having weighed up the rival merits of Classics and English, both of which had some appeal, settled on History not just for a love of the subject, but also because of the prestige of the History Side and 'the reputation of McElwee among the body of the schoolboys (as well as his colleagues) as a protector and patron of discontented and critical boys.' Simon was a determined nonconformist at Stowe, but found a happy niche on the History Side and greatly enjoyed

Bill's teaching, saying that at Cambridge, only Noel Annan showed Bill's skill as a lecturer.

In writing of his time at Stowe, Simon gives the first postwar description of Vancouver. It was, he said, 'by middle-class English standards of the late 1940s, dusty, not to say filthy. Patience, though admirably capable of providing tea for twenty hungry boys as well as some old and sometimes distinguished friends who had dropped in on their motorised passage through the English countryside, had no impulse to spend her days scrubbing and cleaning. Some distinguished figures of their generation ("gilded" Oxford 1920s or aggressively Marxist) or ex-pupils of the prewar generation, when they had come to stay for the night would be given instructions in our presence to share the bath water with their wives or companions.' Simon also gives a vivid description of his first visit to Vancouver with two other aspirant Historians. 'The two Patricks and I sat upon a large decrepit sofa, facing an equally decrepit chaise-longue placed in front of a French window leading out onto the lawn. On the chaise-longue Patience reclined. Bill was absent. Beyond her feet on the chaise longue stood a small jar of fish paste much of which had been spread on the brown bread that we hungry schoolboys had already devoured. A small, scrawny, grey cat leapt up onto the end of the chaise-longue and concentrated its attention on the jar of fish-paste. Patience was talking to us, but all three of us on the sofa watched the little grey cat with fascinated silent attention until it had devoured as much as its tongue could reach. By then Patience suddenly noticed the cat and slapped it down while continuing to talk.'

I well remember the shortage of hot water and Patience's fury when some guest had a lavish soak in the bath, making it impossible to wash up satisfactorily. I also remember some cleaning. Blitzes of dusting and sweeping did take place from time to time. Possibly it was fun to exaggerate rather the difference between Vancouver and the Historians' own middle-class homes.

Brian Brindley was another who had aimed for the History Side because he wanted to be a Historian rather than from a passion for history, and who also found Vancouver a refuge from much of school life. His father wanted him to study something more technical in order to join the family firm, and Brian clearly enlisted Bill's support in pursuing a quite different career. He found being taught by Bill an 'adventure' and recalls Bill, newly returned to Stowe, arriving to take one of the junior classes, looking 'immensely dashing', still trailing a military aura and much glamour. Brian was, he now feels, pushed rather too swiftly through the lower school, resulting in nearly four years on the History Side, during which he was allowed a comparatively free rein. He feels that a combination of his accelerated progress and Bill's particular methods and focus resulted in his general education being neglected. He regrets, for instance, that Geography never featured, something which echoes Noel Annan's comments on Bill's limitations. Bill would quote with relish: 'Geography isn't a thing gentlemen learn, it's a thing gentlemen know.' It was one of his dearest tenets and a regrettable blind spot.

Other areas of learning did get attention, however. Historians were taught English and languages by other members of staff, while the exploration of Plato's *Republic* was a regular part of Bill's teaching, something he added to his curriculum after the war. The highly regarded radio producer, Piers Plowright, who joined the Side much later in 1953, remembers the sessions on Plato more vividly than the history lectures. He described Bill entering the classroom, putting a copy of the *Republic* on the desk, and making the lesson a 'dialogue as Plato's own book was, between us, him, the text and ideas', a method he found very exciting.

Piers too, recalls Bill's physical presence, his first sighting of him being when Bill read the lesson in Chapel, something about which he took trouble, always ensuring that he had read the passage through, however well he knew it. Piers said: 'First of all his bow tie fascinated me and then the tone of his voice which was rather gravelly and attractive at the same time. There was power there and a physical handsomeness that impressed me very much.' He thought Bill's face attractive without being beautiful, 'rugged, ravaged, and of beautiful proportions, a handsome presence that also had a raffish quality'. This last Piers felt, had echoes of the thirties, conjuring up a period about which he wished to know more.

While history was one of his subjects, it was Bill's physical presence that drew Piers to the History Side. Once there, he found Bill rather formidable, quite tough in his teaching and so fluent a speaker that Piers felt at times intimidated and anxious about joining in discussions. Later Bill picked this up, encouraging him to be more confident. Piers felt there were several parts to Bill, the military one particularly being tempered by a wild streak, making him seem vividly unconventional compared with the people Piers had encountered in his 'middle-class Hampstead upbringing'. However, Bill's lasting legacy to him was, he thinks, being taught 'clarity in writing'. He quotes Bill as saying: 'Say what you mean, but don't be afraid of the fine phrase', describing Bill's own prose as: 'Latinate with no fat'. He also felt encouraged to read widely, in this comparing Bill favourably to F. R. Leavis at Cambridge, suggesting that he had fewer axes to grind than Leavis and therefore felt comfortable with a wider range of books.

Giles Rooke, now a Crown Court Judge, also remembers the stress Bill placed on good writing, describing his first tutorial as more concerned with composition than content, 'unfolding for the first time an essay from which pretension, repetitive adjectives, false sentiment or bad taste were progressively dissected.' Anthony Chamier, who came after Giles, vividly recalls climbing the dingy stairs to Bill's Stowe study, clutching four pages on ruled exercise paper which he would proceed to read aloud while Bill was apparently entirely absorbed in rolling his cigarette. 'The first paragraph having been delivered, he would reach out for the paper and say firmly that it was redundant.' Bill's theme was that there was no need to announce what you were going to say, you should get on and say it. The rest of the essay would be listened to in silence, unless Bill was 'goaded beyond endurance by sloppy use of language.' Anthony once referred to Cardinal Wolsey becoming Henry Vlll's 'bugbear'. Bill indignantly asked what he meant, and when Anthony was unable to produce a definition, pointed put that words of uncertain meaning should be avoided. At the end of the reading, there would be a short silence while Bill rolled another cigarette and Anthony felt inadequate. 'But then some balm as Bill kindly drew attention to some turns of phrase that he felt to be happy and to some thoughts he said were well founded. And so one went away with a spring in the step, determined to avoid first paragraphs and bugbears for ever after.' Giles Rooke returns to the prewar theme of Bill's teaching being more university than school, and also cites the value of the other activities, such as the Shakespeare plays and the Twelve Club. Bill picked up much the same extramural activities postwar, though he no longer managed the library and did not again supervise the fencing until well into the fifties. The Debating Society continued to flourish.

15

Domestic Affairs

Having agreed to go back to Stowe, Patience threw her heart into re-creating Vancouver for the Historians, with the birthday and Valentine tributes illustrating how brilliantly she succeeded. Probably the appalling winter helped her to overcome her anxieties since, as long as she had an audience, she always responded magnificently to external crises. Producing the teas when everything was rationed presented a major challenge, but somehow cakes continued to appear. She never categorically denied the rumour that she sometimes used liquid paraffin when unable to obtain butter or margarine, probably because it was too good a Historian story to spoil.

There was little change in her general housekeeping, and the state of Vancouver soon fulfilled all J.F.'s worst fears. Patience could not, however, be blamed for the sweating floors and peeling wallpaper. The 17 springs affected the house as much as the garden. Brian Brindley was one of the few who were censorious about the condition of the house. Knowing it from the immediately post-war redecorated state, he felt the subsequent neglect was sad, lamenting the fact that 'the pretty house with its pretty things' deteriorated so. He remembers the chaise-longue mentioned by Simon Digby arriving in a pristine state, and watched it become tatty and stained. His parents also found Patience's behaviour offensive on one occasion when they visited. She entertained them in the sitting room while peeling potatoes, saying that she had to get them done before the Bradleys arrived. Brian thinks that her intent was to imply that the Brindleys were greater kindred spirits than the smarter Bradleys, but Mrs Brindley took it the other way round. Peter Leslie was, however, another who treasured the state of Vancouver. He was delighted to come and stay and find a pair of hunting boots standing in the same spot in the passage as they had five years before.

Of course more effort could and probably should, have been made, but it was a sizeable house, and any form of electrical device Patience attempted to use would spit and throw out alarming sparks. Cleaning was thus a labourious process of sweeping up dust, much of which swirled about in the draughts before resettling. Animals and boys who had been working in the garden trooped in and out of the house, bringing in copious amounts of mud. Possibly money could have been found for a cleaner, but then there would have been less for the far more important entertaining, besides which Patience would have been awkward with help in the house. Her mother did have a cleaner for Shadwells before the war, but was so frightened of her that she was liable to clean the whole house before the cleaner arrived.

Patience's domestic standards were erratic, however. Meals were almost invariably eaten in the dining room, which was inevitably some distance from the kitchen. For breakfast they used a beautiful 'breakfast service' that had come down through Bill's family, and even when food was rationed, porridge, bacon and eggs would be served, kept hot in silver plated dishes. Cornflakes only appeared in the rare hot weather. There was always percolated coffee and toast accompanied by the jam Patience made in huge quantities, scraping the mould off the top as each batch aged. Preparing, clearing away and then washing up all this was a major operation. Bill generally returned for a cooked lunch, and there would be a further hot meal to prepare in the evening. Open house was kept on every day except Mondays, when the Combined Cadet Force paraded all afternoon, and even then the occasional boy would appear. Numbers were small during the week but could rise at the weekends, with Sundays being particularly popular. That was the day when outside visitors would appear and gatherings of more than 20 were frequent, packing the sitting room to capacity. For tea, the crockery was anything but formal, there being an incredible mixture of patterns among the cups and plates, with boys who were leaving being expected to donate any superfluous china.

Patience's favourite cup was one filched from British Rail, a thick, white upright affair with BR on it in black letters. She liked her tea immensely strong and in a cup that would keep it hot. She would then leave it to get practically cold before she drank it. Patience never poured out. Some boy would be designated to do so, though when I was old enough to be a permanent part of the gatherings and strong enough to wield the heavy teapots, one an elegant silver affair and one chipped blue-and-white china with 'For Auld Lang Syne' round the rim, I became the most regular pourer, developing an encyclopaedic memory for the tastes of regular attenders. Brian Brindley eventually found the household a copper urn, which improved production greatly.

Brian also shared Patience's love of Victoriana. This prompted him to present the household with an 'epergne' made of red glass, which he felt would be the perfect table centre. He celebrated this event and the advent of the first washing-up liquid, by writing a Betjemanesque poem:

The Pellucid Moment

Amid the humdrum cares of life just think what joy
you're giving
By spreading, as a Clever Wife, the cult of gracious living;
It's not alone the polished floors, the windows
gleaming brightly,
But other less familiar chores that must be done politely;
These small refinements should be shewn in cottage
or in chateau:
The doyley crisp beneath the scone, the frill around the gateau,
The sweet that's topped with whipped cremette, the salad
plates all hot,
The folding of a serviette to represent a yacht,
The dainty tea, the frozen pea, the glass of empire wine,
The gleam of spotless napery, the fragrant hint of pine;
The tin of beans the fingered fish achieve a real panache
If in a silver entree dish. Here's how to make a splash:
Place on your board some grand epergne with ivy
twining through it;
Rub up the ornamental urn and fill again the cruet.
Make sure your bathroom has appeal – neglect is sure to
spoil it,
For who can feel at all genteel who cannot flush the toilet?
China and silver must be clean: this task at least is easy
For anybody who has been presented with – a Squeezy.

The boys invariably rejected 'bought' cakes, so a continuous supply of sponge and chocolate cakes, flapjacks, rock buns and little cakes that were called ironically 'fancies', had to be maintained. Occasionally there were leftovers, and Paul Johnstone never lived down having once made the plaintive enquiry: 'Is stale cake good for training?'

Frequent guests at the weekends meant Saturday dinner and Sunday lunch, for which Patience managed to produce meals for six or more people that were always good and sometimes outstanding, while she miraculously appeared to be continuously present at pre-meal drinks. Much of her cooking was of the 'good plain English' kind, with recipes culled from her by now quite ancient *Mrs Beeton*, but nonetheless, even a straightforward roast meat and two veg requires considerable last-minute effort. Stephen Whitwell has a fond memory of curried prawns. She would sometimes pander to the particular tastes of guests, though not without grumbling. Norris Kennard was thus favoured, probably because she was so fond of Lee, his wife. Patience always gave him his favourite Sunday breakfast of a boiled egg, toast and Cooper's Oxford marmalade. She did not apparently grudge him the marmalade, which was not regularly eaten, since Bill, peculiarly, liked Golden Shred, but she did bitterly resent Norris' copious consumption of pepper with his egg. 'Does he realise it costs half-a-crown an ounce?' she would mutter furiously. Lee was less of a problem at breakfast, wanting only lots of black coffee, sometimes accompanied by aspirin, and, when it had been a really hard night, brandy. She was annoying over other meals, though. Since she had gourmet tastes, Patience would take immense trouble with the food, and while Lee was duly appreciative, she would leave half her plateful, light a cigarette and stub it out in the food, thus rendering it unfit for the cats.

The Kennards' alcohol consumption was another bone of contention. In spite of the limitations of Bill's salary, alcohol mostly flowed at Vancouver, though there would be much speculation about what kind of sherry they could get away with giving to parents on Sunday mornings, the decision generally being in favour of Spanish for those they liked and South African for the less popular. The Kennards, however, invariably drank very dry martinis, for which Bill and Patience flatly refused to supply the Noilly Prat. The Kennards therefore brought their own, but always took it away with them. Their really annoying meanness, though, was over the gin. If they brought any, it would be a half bottle that would barely last them an evening. Rich as they were, they could be heard through their bedroom wall arguing furiously far into the night, over which of them owed the other cigarettes. Old Historians were generally much more generous and would regularly bring bottles of gin or whisky. Norman Wates, grateful for Bill's teaching of his three sons, sent him a case of gin every Christmas until his death.

Probably the Kennards' bed, in which, reputedly, my great grand-father had been conceived, born and had died and which was probably the one the Longfords remembered as being infested with death watch beetle, was not of sufficient comfort to soothe their irritation with one another. Orthopaedic mattresses were not a feature of life at Vancouver. Some sagged so badly that you lay in a kind of trough, while sleeping in an elegant bed known as the French cot was like lying on the ground. One of the legs of this bed was broken for years, being propped up on several volumes of Gibbon's *Decline and Fall of the Roman Empire*. The rest of the set were substituting for a sofa-leg in the study. Stephen Whitwell, who stayed at Vancouver frequently while between Diplomatic postings abroad, reckoned, however, that the only really unbearable sleeping conditions he had encountered were on the occasion when the house was so full that he was allocated two car seats pushed together in the attics. The run on sheets at such periods posed difficulties in spite of the fact that Bill and Patience had been given Edwardian quantities of beautiful linen when they married.

Patience occasionally washed sheets using the traditional copper in the scullery, but mostly they were sent to the laundry. Of course, like the bathwater, there was considerable sharing, Patience making entirely arbitrary decisions about whose sheets could be slept in by someone else. Her judgements had almost nothing to do with cleanliness and everything to do with whether she liked someone and found them attractive. Sometimes, rather than get on with the washing-up, we would both linger among the ruins of breakfast after Bill had gone to work, classifying people by whether or not we could sleep in their sheets. Given the stream of visitors to Vancouver, Patience made it an absolute rule that she never sent on any belongings left behind by a guest. The only time she made an exception was after Peregrine Worsthorne had spent a weekend. His enthusiastic bread-and-butter letter ended with a plea that she might make an exception in the case of the razors he had left, 'since they belonged to Dame Nellie Melba.'

Another constant problem when living in Vancouver was keeping the place warm and dry. There was, of course, no kind of central heating, though at some point fires were installed in the sitting and dining rooms that would stay in all night if properly banked up. They also helped heat the water that was otherwise at the mercy of a 'Sadia'

159

which could manage no more than two modest baths or one bath and a large wash-up. While individual rooms could be made reasonably warm, the passages remained freezing, and the effort required to leave the fireside in the winter to go elsewhere was enormous. Large quantities of coal were needed as well as an endless supply of logs, and I soon became adept with a saw though never any good with an axe. Bedrooms had single-bar electric fires, though there were fireplaces that worked in all the bedrooms and I was sometimes allowed an open fire when I was ill. The glow in the dark was a particular comfort, but normally Patience would switch on a small fire when she woke me, and by the time I had to get up, it would have made no impression whatsoever on the frost patterns decorating the windows. Pipes regularly froze, though I do not remember any bursting. Bill became quite skilled at thawing them out gently with candles and oil fires.

The wet made the stone passages in the back part of the house sweat, and above the kitchen, the guttering had a nasty habit of getting blocked with leaves and then precipitating water through the ceiling by the back door. This would create a major flood that, if there were boys about, Patience would turn into an exciting drama, but which was a dreary nuisance if there was no audience. Brian Calvert, who piloted the first commercial Concorde flight to New York, was an expert at clearing the leaves, finding a bowler hat particularly suitable headgear for the task. The leaves were rarely cleared before disaster occurred, and the ceiling became became the home of a variety of fungi. Patience cherished these and would show them off to visitors.

Provision of all this food and drink taxed their slender means enormously, and one of Patience's recurring anxieties was over the butcher's bill. Supplies were eked out, therefore, by some living off the land. Rabbits were a major source of food, sometimes wild, but mainly tame, bred by Patience for the table. She was good at this, choosing a Dutch-Old English cross breed that she got from a breeder in a neighbouring village. The bucks and the breeding does were given rather grand names, generally of my choosing, while their offspring, which were to be eaten rapidly, remained anonymous. This was not an invariable practice, though I once announced cheerfully to an assembled company that 'we are eating Elaine today'. I was going through an Arthurian stage at the time, Elaine being one of the Knight's ladies.

Rabbits are notoriously difficult to sex, but Patience announced that bucks always had staring eyes, referring to a currently popular murder case, and was almost always right. Bill would dispatch and skin them while Patience had a variety of cooking methods, the best of which could produce a dish that resembled chicken, in those days an expensive treat. It was the American wife of Lord Quinton, who had been a war-time Historian, who once said that she believed 'in England, you actually eat rabbit?' while unaware that she was tucking into a delicious rabbit casserole. Feeding these creatures was of course another time-consuming activity, since they ate quantities of varied greenstuffs which had to be culled from the garden. When numbers were particularly high, Patience would resort to taking a sack down to the local allotments. The very first pair of rabbits Patience acquired provided me with an early lesson in the facts of life. Bill would recall with pleasure the occasion on which I came rushing into the house, demanding that he come and see 'Henry rumpling Primrose'.

Pigs were another source of home-grown food. After the war, there were subsidies for those who kept pigs, got their fattening just right, and sent them off to the bacon factory when they reached the required age and weight. Patience, who was much attached to Large Whites, probably began this activity when Bill successfully bowled for a pig at a local fête. She turned out to be skilled at feeding them to produce just the right balance of fat and lean, so a number of these creatures passed through her hands. When it was time for them to go, she would invariably weep copiously, but welcomed the side of bacon that was a perk of the operation. I joined in with the pig rearing, using the £5 sent to me unexpectedly by my godfather, Osy Darell, to buy a weaner. It sold for £10, with which it was decided that I should buy a New Forest pony from Buckingham Market. Consignments of these wretched foals would be hawked round the markets, with the best being bought for children and the rest ending up at the knackers for dog meat. William Rufus was only six months old, bright chestnut and terrified. It took a year of sitting in the field with him to get near enough to him to put on a head collar.

Besides the rabbits and bacon from the pigs, there were pigeons and, in the spring, rooks. Bill averred that the rooks would desert if their young were not culled, so each spring he and selected Historians would blast away at the tops of the elms in which they swayed, producing enough to make rook pie, made delicious mainly because of Patience's delectable, gooey pastry and the inclusion of hard-boiled eggs. The rook breasts, which were the only part eaten, were

161

probably fairly tasteless. Pigeons were tasty enough, though the ease with which they could be eaten depended on their age. When the deadline was approaching on a book, Bill would retire to work in the attic away from the telephone and other distractions, writing with a 2.2 rifle beside him. At intervals there would be a crack, and a pigeon happily feeding in the orchard would expire. One pigeon would feed the three of us bulked out with bread sauce and fried potatoes. Bill would also organise shoots in the grounds of Stowe, taking trusted boys. He must have had more than one gun of his own and would house weapons belonging to boys, regarding these expeditions as a further part of the general education they were getting. He was a stickler for care over where a gun was pointing and the need for cartridges to be removed when getting over fences. In those relaxed days, however, the weapons were kept propped in a corner of the study at Vancouver, the front door of which was never locked.

Tim Manville-Hales, a vulnerable boy with a difficult family background, was pointed towards the History Side by his housemaster, Edward Capel Cure, who was concerned for his well-being and thought that Vancouver might provide necessary support. Subsequently discovering a cache of guns in Tim's study, he suggested that Tim leave them in a drawer, from which Capel quietly abstracted them in Tim's absence. He later visited Tim's family and told Tim to go and look in the boot of his car. Following this episode and with what would now be seen as considerable foolhardiness, Reynolds agreed that Tim could keep a gun at Vancouver, which he was apparently allowed to take out on his own. No disaster resulted and Tim was no doubt much more prepared to conform in other areas, though betting got him into further trouble. Here again, Vancouver came to the rescue, with Patience agreeing to place his bets for him, the rationale presumably being that there was no way Tim would stop betting, and at least that way some check was kept on his expenditure while avoiding trouble with school rules. He was even encouraged to make positive use of his betting, being given £10 or £20 by Bill and Capel, and told to see if he could turn it into enough to go on a Culture Tour. Sadly he failed, but he still appreciates the gesture.

Tim was a participant in a major school scandal. At that time, Silverstone aerodrome had, with the war over, ceased to be needed and had not yet become a famous race track. It had been acquired by Rootes for the storage of new cars about to be put on the market. A group of boys, of whom Tim was one, spent one happy afternoon driving a number of cars round on the old runways, heedless of the fact that the vehicles lacked oil and had little water in the radiators. Some boys, realising that they would be late for prep, drove back to Stowe, taking not simply enough cars to accommodate them all, but one each. At this point, of course, they were caught, though not Tim, who had prudently noticed the time and returned on his bicycle. J.F., who was still in post, used all his charm on Rootes and persuaded them not to prosecute, thus avoiding the worst sort of publicity. As a coda to this story, Nicholas Beveridge, a Historian who was then a Communist, was apparently outraged by this example of privilege being used to avert what he saw as just deserts, composed a letter to the *Daily Worker*, which he asked Giles Rooke to type for him. Giles did so and then realised the potential disaster to Stowe and informed authority. Needless to say, the letter was stopped.

It was near Silverstone that Tim and others found an ammunition dump in some small Nissen huts with nothing more than sacking over the doors. Naturally they helped themselves to such things as .303 ammunition and grenades. Some of the grenades subsequently turned up, unexploded, in a sandpit that was part of the CCF assault course. 'Captain' Archer, who could look fiercely militaristic when helping to run the Corps, cheerfully told two boys to take these to the Armoury, having apparently no inkling of the appalling danger to which they were exposed. Freddy Archer ran the scouts before the war, owned an amiable spaniel called Boojum and had some difficulty with his Rs, with the result that he was inevitably known as 'Fweddie'.

Tim was not an academic, but says that he was taught to write essays and to read widely. He remembers Bill arranging for visiting lecturers to come and talk to them, in particular Alan Taylor and possibly Hugh Trevor-Roper, but also appreciated spending time at Vancouver, helping to keep the nettles down. Four-and-a-half acres, which as the extent of the Vancouver grounds, required considerable hard work, though whether more than the basics were done depended on the current History Side. Mowing the lawn required little skill, but tending the flower beds only happened erratically. The production of vegetables mostly ceased with the departure of 'Groundsel', but for a time Patience grew lettuces, and there was one bed in which first strawberries and then asparagus were grown. For several years we had a lavish and delicious crop of strawberries, in spite of having to share them with blackbirds. There was a net, but naturally it was full of holes. It is likely that the produce changed because they were given some asparagus corms and it was the only suitable space. The bed was not wildly prolific, but did turn out to be an excellent therapeutic tool. Patience would rope in a boy she felt was troubled by something and take him off to help her weed the asparagus bed. She was regularly correct in her diagnosis, and the bed would be tidied while whatever was wrong could be elicited informally.

Such selective cultivation was a drawback in a country district where everyone grew their own supplies of vegetables. We would sometimes be the beneficiaries of gluts on the allotments, but otherwise getting food generally was difficult. There was no shop in Dadford until the early fifties, so everything either had to be delivered or fetched from Buckingham, four miles away. The butcher, a Mr Gasson, who was highly successful and kept racing greyhounds, came twice a week, the next delivery being requested on each visit. Groceries came once a week, in response to a telephoned order, from a splendidly traditional shop in which goods were measured from jars and sacks, while Mr Archer regularly came round with beer and fizzy drinks. Any other alcohol had to be obtained in Buckingham. There was a bus into the town on Tuesdays, which was market day, and Saturdays, with one returning on Saturdays just late enough to allow a visit to the Chandos cinema. Since Patience never learnt to drive, it was either the bus or waiting until Bill was free to drive her – always assuming that his current car was working.

Visits to Buckingham were exciting outings, generally including for Bill and Patience a session in the bar of the White Hart Hotel while I was parked in the lounge with fizzy orange and a packet of crisps. Sadly, I left Buckingham at just about the time I was old enough to go into the bar, so I never experienced the rich gossip, the placing of illegal bets, or the anarchic management of local affairs that went on there. I would get tantalising glimpses of an exciting throng whenever the door opened. There were the Wheeler family who farmed what had once been Stowe land, and had deep, distinctive voices, other farmers in for the market, the local bookmaker, Patience's current favourite man, an austere and glamorous person called Guy who did something mysterious and rather grander than the other denizens, and Mr Reynolds the grocer, who was generally drunk by the middle of the morning. Bill once answered the telephone, correctly announcing that he was Buckingham 2212, only to have a slurred voice that he recognised immediately, say 'But that's my number, what am I doing ringing my own number?'

Bucks being a long, thin county meant that north and south were very different, something that is probably still just true. The south was populous and almost suburban, while the north was wild, wooded and a law unto itself. The county town of Aylesbury was 20 miles away and appeared to have little influence on Buckingham, which happily managed itself. Now it has expanded greatly, but in 1954, when it celebrated its Quatercentenary, having been granted a charter by Bloody Mary, the population was largely unchanged. It was also reputed to have the same number of pubs, 13 being thought slightly excessive for a small town. It was never a pretty town, but it has delightful corners and some elegant eighteenth-century houses. The earlier part is tucked away, and an effort is required to find the house with a twisted chimney which was the town's main architectural claim to fame.

Apart from the White Hart, Patience's favourite place was the dark and cluttered shop run by the splendid Kiddy Holton. 'Antique Shop' was almost too grand a title for it, but much of the stock was far from being junk, and wriggling round the packed furniture in the gloom, excellent pieces could be discerned. How Kiddy moved about his shop is a mystery, since he was so fat that on the occasion of the sixteenth-century fair arranged to celebrate the Quatercentenary, he was able to hire an outfit designed for Falstaff without the padding, the only man ever to have done so. He inherited his shop from his father, who had been a ruthless parent, refusing to support Kiddy once he had left school. Therefore Kiddy had, in his turn, to learn hard and not always honest dealing, at times managing successfully to diddle his parent. Bill would tell a story of the time Kiddy bought a table, only to be told by his furious father that it was worthless without its pair. Kiddy managed to slip the table into another sale without telling his father, who subsequently appeared triumphant, saying that he had, with great fortune, managed to save their bacon by finding the perfect pair.

Kiddy appeared to deal honestly with Patience who, when feeling particularly down, bought things – never clothes, like many women, but pieces of antique furniture, such as vast desks which she would swop one for another, as well as trays or even chairs made of papier-mâché and inlaid with mother-of-pearl. Because she had little money, the pieces were invariably damaged. On one occasion Colin Anson was deeply impressed by the enthusiasm Bill expressed on seeing a once beautiful, but now badly worm-eaten acquisition, feeling that this exemplified Bill's devotion to her. Sometimes she would set out to repair at least the surface of a table, but the task would never be completed and often a piece of furniture in comparatively good repair would be left under a sunny window. I got much pleasure from the small items that Kiddy Holton stocked, acquiring chipped pieces of china or damaged snuffboxes for a few shillings.

Sometimes, when spending a whole day in the town Patience would take me to have lunch at the Buckingham Bakery, which I regarded as a treat, happily tucking into the tomato soup, overcooked lamb and two veg, followed by ice cream or apple tart and custard. When I was small, she also accompanied me on my frequent, prolonged and painful visits to the dentist, castigating me for my sweet consumption although she equally worried that while rationing existed, I was not getting enough sugar. She also allowed me to accept portions of generous Stoics' sweet rations.

My happiest memory of the town, however, was Buckingham Fair. This was a less sophisticated version of the fairs that appear regularly in towns now, and arrived every October to take up the entire centre of the town for two consecutive Saturdays. It had what felt like a dramatically fast ride known as the 'Noah's Ark', dodgems, which I adored and drove with great efficiency, and stalls at which goldfish could be won by throwing ping pong balls in narrow necked jars. Our scores varied from year to year, the best one being the occasion when we won seven. Their survival was variable, ranging from a year or more to less than a week. One lived on happily alone, having chewed the tail fins of his companions, and several died within days after Colin James, later to be Bishop of Winchester, but then a Chaplain at Stowe, decided, during a post-fair drink in the White Hart, that tonic water would greatly improve conditions in their tiny bowl.

We generally went as a family, though Patience was there as a spectator rather than a participant. She accepted the goldfish as being decorative, but longed for someone to win her a budgerigar, prizes for balls thrown into high and awkwardly angled jars. A number of us uselessly expended much cash in attempting to secure this prize for her, but Susan Richards, author of a distinguished book on Russia, but then aged about seven, trounced us with her first go. Her father, Brooks Richards, who was a prewar Historian and was later to be Ambassador to Athens, had, that weekend, told an erudite and Vancouverish story about the pronunciation of the name Proust, so the budgerigar was christened Albertine. Her cage sat on a tall bookcase above Patience's chair in the sitting-room, and she twittered happily away for some time. Her nerves were eventually overcome by the cat, who developed the habit of sitting thoughtfully on the top of her cage.

Patience must have bought some clothes, but I mostly remember her in a longish, dreary, pleated skirt or corduroy trousers, worn with various layers topped by a cardigan, thick lisle stockings, a duffle coat for outdoors and what she always referred to as 'm'sneakers' on her feet. She did have an unbecomingly tight coat and skirt (she would never have called it a suit – that would have been non-U) for going to London, and a wonderful bright scarlet 'housecoat' which, as she triumphantly told Colin Anson, was made out of bunting which, she emphasised with delight, was coupon-free. It was full-length with a heavy zip up much of the front, and had improbable short, puffed sleeves. This garment eventually found its way into my dressing-up box.

When I was a child, Patience's main concern was that I should be warm. She fussed almost as badly as her mother and was convinced that if my legs got cold, I would get something wrong with my kidneys. To prevent this, she knitted me long woollen stockings which were kept up by suspenders sewn onto a liberty bodice. These stockings and an endless supply of socks were bits of knitting that she did finish, produced as they were on four needles with neatly turned heels. It was only on the hottest summer days that I was allowed to wear coveted white ankle socks. I spent most of my days in trousers or jodhpurs, all my smarter clothes being handed down from my Uncle Alan's stepdaughters, whom I always regarded as my cousins. My one party frock was faintly Victorian and pretty, but I hankered after the yards of net worn by my friends.

Concerning her appearance, Patience was, as over housework, arbitrary. Her hair, which was dark brown with a slight wave, was cut in a not-particularly-becoming long bob, with a side parting and a Kirbigrip holding it off her face. It became greasy quickly and was not washed often enough. On the other hand, she had an obsession about shiny noses, keeping hers carefully powdered and nagging me continuously about mine once I was adolescent. She also re-did her bright red lipstick regularly, and on occasions when we were settling down to something we wished to do undisturbed, would say 'Let's put our lipstick on and then no one will come'.

Her battle with her weight was continuous. She maintained that my birth had ruined her figure, and was always unsuccessfully trying new diets and getting depressed after using the sort of scales in public places into which you put a penny. Her other line of attack on her stomach was to confine it, and she was always searching for the perfect garment to flatten her. I remember a succession of elaborate boned and laced stays, the discomfort of which meant they never survived for long. She would sit, always in the same lopsided armchair by the sitting-room fire, wriggling and probing her waist until she extracted the fearful steel 'bone' that had started to stick into her. If someone then came, she would thrust this down the side of her chair, along with anything else that might be embarrassing if seen by one of their smarter visitors like a parent. Eventually she discovered the 'Playtex living girdle', which worked as well as anything without causing too much pain – besides having a name that enchanted her so much that she told almost everyone she was wearing it. It infuriated her that Bill could eat like a horse without putting on an ounce.

Getting to the stage of having to wear glasses was another source of pain to Patience, a derogatory remark of mine about how they looked making her cry. However, all her concerns about her appearance would vanish once she was in company, and she would charm her audience with her stories, her malicious enjoyment of gossip and, above all, with her interest in and concern with, those she liked. Both Bill and Patience felt strongly that the young, like dogs, always needed someone to whom they could 'bring their bones', and I remember feeling that no experience was complete until I had picked over every angle with her. Patience without an audience, however, could descend into deep gloom. She had a constant struggle with anxiety and frequently appeared irritated by my behaviour and that of my friends. Bill recalled coming home from Stowe one day to find me leaning against the front door jamb and looking apprehensive. When he asked me what was wrong, I jerked my head in the direction of the kitchen and said 'Mummy's savage'. While the rejection of a manuscript caused understandable despair, a burnt cake could also darken her mood, as could something lost or the failure of any boys to turn up for tea.

Patience struggled continuously with her mood swings, endlessly trying out remedies, ranging from vast bottles of Valerian to purple hearts and Librium, while for the regular migraines that attacked her, she went through a period of taking Hydrochloric Acid, a vicious remedy that appeared to do no good whatever. The migraines would often come on a day when she particularly wanted to do something, starting with violent sickness, going on to a blinding headache and gradually ameliorating to the point in late afternoon when she would demand a supply of water biscuits. There was also a lesser ailment that she dubbed a sick headache, but these did not last so long. For external injuries she would regularly raid remedies kept for the horses, lavishly applying something evil-smelling marked 'The Embrocation' to any strain. A severe backache was once cured by the administration of a remedy known to the horse world as 'The Drench' – in fact a massive dose of Epsom Salts. Anxiety about her health was fairly constant and probably resulted in her being labelled a malingerer by her doctor, but out of this too, Patience was able to make a good story. Having gone to the doctor with a major worry and been examined from head to toe, she recounted that he stood back from her and said: 'You know, I have never seen a body better fitted for hard work.' It is likely that current knowledge of allergies and pre-menstrual tension would have made a considerable difference to Patience's life.

16

Horses but no School for Harriet

Bill and Patience described prewar Dadford as having a shrinking and degenerating population with few children, and in some inhabitants, deformities that suggested serious inbreeding, 'Groundsel' and his two brothers being cases in point. All three were shrunken, two were profoundly deaf and one was brain-damaged. Probably echoing the attitudes of their class and generation, my parents regarded incest as a not too serious peccadillo of the lower orders. However, they welcomed the fact that when they returned after the war, the situation had greatly improved. With their usual eye for a good story, they put this down entirely to the activities of Seamus Stokes, who had had some ailment that prevented him from being called up, but who otherwise enjoyed splendid health. While the rest of the men were away, it was said, Seamus made hay, so that by the late forties, a blooming younger generation flourished. In 1948 my parents gave a Christmas party for most the children in the village, and certainly our dining room was full. The noise when they sang carols was such that the grandfather clock, that had been silent for years, started again and continued to work for years. Colin Graham was prominent in leading the singing.

I never asked why they gave that party. Possibly it was a bid to establish themselves squirearchically in the village. Because of the way the village had developed, this position was, in a sense, going begging. The official lady of the manor was Mrs Close-Smith, a daughter of Lady Kinloss, the last owner of Stowe. She lived in a hideous Victorian house some way from the village, and though she was a stalwart supporter of the church and sometimes walked to the village, the distance was too great for her to be of immediate practical help. Dadford, deprived of the church or manor house around which it might have clustered, was divided into chunks. The village was situated on

170

the road from Buckingham to Silverstone, and the first chunk encountered when driving into it was a lovely row of about six eighteenth-century cottages. They were opposite a Victorian village hall and close to a later house in which Annie M. Gregory sold cigarettes and peppermints. Annie had two club feet and made beautiful lace. Beyond these cottages were the allotments through the middle of which ran the brook, properly called the Dad. The Street, which was lined by about 14 dwellings, mostly Victorian or later, ran along the top of the allotments and ended in Vancouver Drive.

Further along the main road were the council houses, which outnumbered the earlier dwellings and felt like a separate community. In one of these was the only other commercial enterprise in Dadford, a Post Office that was no more than a counter fitted across Mrs Dormer's hallway. At the end of The Street there was a piece of grass, opposite which was a telephone box with some railings above the brook. This provided the only central gathering place in the village where teenagers hung around and gossiped. The biggest house was the Vicarage which, for this and other obvious reasons, would have been most likely to take on the Squire's role. However, Mr Fernihough, the gentle, asthmatic and bachelor vicar, was apt to be vague, unworldly, and not always the best source of advice. He kept bees that regularly swarmed, pursued by a breathless Fernihough in his protective clothing. Immediately after the war Stowe masters occupied the two other larger houses in the Street, but neither the Dams, who lived next door to us, nor the Zettls, in a pretty house further down The Street, had any children, and no doubt my village friendships were one reason why it was to Vancouver that people went for advice or with recalcitrant forms to be completed.

That I was permanently free to play in the village was probably due to the most eccentric decision Bill and Patience ever made. Apart from attending Stowe for lessons in French and music, they never sent me to school. The rationale for this was that girls did not need a formal education since marriage and children were their future, and that I would receive a better education in a cultural atmosphere that allowed me to read widely. They also thought that playing team games and holding positions of authority at school mitigated against women being attractive to men. Underlying these expressed reasons were, I suspect, Patience's dislike of school, where she had found it hard to make friends, the influence of Bill's governess, Miss Spraggs, who, while he had admired her teaching abilities enormously, had frightened him, and, finally, snobbery. They could not afford a private school, and while I could play happily throughout my childhood with the village children, they did not wish me to share their education. A close ear was kept on my accent and any tendency to adopt flat, Buckinghamshire vowels was jumped on heavily. Obviously, other parents have made a similar decision regarding their children's education, but have then created some structure within which they taught their children. Bill and Patience were a touch erratic in this, though they did begin well. They taught me to read very early, beginning with a Victorian 'Golden Primer' which traditionally involved cats, mats and hats along with elegant illustrations, before moving on to something more modern and extensive which I remember racing through while sitting on my father's bed at Shadwells. Now, I am unable to remember not being able to read. Writing copperplate in copy books was not such a success, and my handwriting has never been good. Patience must have read to me when I was very young, but my memories are of Bill's reading aloud to me. In particular I remember *The Wind in the Willows*, which I adored, and *Treasure Island*, which was exciting at the time, but to which I never returned.

Mathematics were a misery, though Bill thought I did well. When I gave them up at 12, having reluctantly reached algebra, he would say that I had learnt quite as much as 'it was decent for a woman to know'. Patience also had an inflated idea of my talents. In an undated letter to Bill, she writes 'Have got H v good arithmetic book for children just starting at a secondary school. She can sail through the first few pages, and I think she is really very forward.' It was probably from this book, which I remember as singularly unattractive, that Bill would set me a series of problems involving apples and buns, before he left for work in the mornings, expecting me to have completed them when he returned. In fact he would often have to spend much time working the damn things through with me. I recited tables in the bath and, at intervals during the day, Bill would suddenly say 'What's seven eights?' at which I would freeze and stutter. Part of my struggle was the need to please him, which made me overanxious and dogs me to this day if suddenly called upon for an answer in any kind of educational setting. For a brief period they arranged lessons once a week with a teacher from the village, and I actually enjoyed mental arithmetic. However, she must have moved away and was not replaced. I only remember Patience teaching me capital cities and their rivers, but she must have done a bit more than that.

I never learnt formal grammar, and Bill expected a daughter of his to be able to punctuate automatically by a process of osmosis. I did have a book called *Latin with Laughter*, but I think I was supposed to learn from it by myself as I can remember no formal work on it. They also gave me books about trees and plants, but I do not recall anyone working on these with me either. While I am an expert on what rabbits can eat, my ignorance about plant names is startling in a countrywoman. The only lessons I had outside the home were from Monsieur Chanson who, used to teaching adolescent boys, struggled with teaching French to a small girl, and I failed to progress. French versions of *The Tale of Peter Rabbit* and of *Mrs Tiggy-Winkle* were also unsuccessful. Having a good aural memory meant that I never learnt to read music properly, since I memorised each piece at speed. We did not possess a piano, and practising in other peoples' houses hampered my studies.

When I was young, the children of the village provided my peer group and some of the playground education that I would otherwise have missed. I would meet up with them during their holidays and when their school day was over, to be kept up-to-date with current games. Those were pre-television days, and we had a great deal of imaginative fun. Hopscotch, skipping games, tig, grandmothers' footsteps and Simon says all kept us going happily through the summer. When we were older, hide and seek in the winter dark was fun, and later still we went carol singing and collecting material for the enormous bonfire erected on a piece of waste ground near the brook. On Tuesday evenings, winter and summer, we would wait hopefully for the fish and chip van. This trundled round the villages driven by a man known as Fishy Hutt, and the timing of its arrival was erratic. Sometimes we would wait fruitlessly for what seemed like hours, only to have to trail home supperless. Patience particularly adored fish and chips, a pleasure heightened by the happy perusal of the *News of the World* in which they were wrapped. In the winter, we generally gathered in Vancouver, since there was more space, and went in for playing with dolls, dressing up and card games. Patience was disconcerted on coming into my room one day, to find a group of us in our underwear, playing what we called forfeits.

I attended an immensely staid Sunday School taken by Mr Fernihough. What we learnt there I do not remember, though I do recall being given two threepenny bits to put in the collection, but saving one of them to buy an ice cream from the van that always appeared

173

on Sunday afternoons. Inevitably Patience found out, since I was hopelessly unable to conceal any wrongdoing, and was furious. Her anxiety over any dishonesty of mine was chronic, and on the not particularly frequent occasions on which I lied, she would start worrying that I was going to turn into a juvenile delinquent. She would get angry too, over my carelessness with my possessions, many of which were Victorian toys bought in the Brighton Lanes during and immediately after the war, that would now be worth a fortune. However, given the state of Vancouver, Patience was not a good model in this respect. She enjoyed playing with dolls' houses of which I had several, one of which she had made for me out of an orange box, and would sometimes make clothes for my dolls, but otherwise I remember being left to get on with things by myself. Once I was in my teens our relationship became much more relaxed and companionable. We talked a great deal and listened to the radio together. *Take It from Here* delighted us all.

During term-time much of my day was solitary, but I found the Vancouver garden paradise. I would spend hours creating 'little houses' in various sheds and bushes, together with miniature gardens and graveyards. This last was a particular passion for a time, sparked off by the discovery of a dead heron floating in the brook. I constructed a fine grave in the shrubbery, using an elaborate edging tile for a headstone, but then being on his own did not seem right for him and I scoured the countryside for further corpses. A fresh impetus to this activity was provided by Stephen Whitwell, who declared that all mice were Muslims and had to have a separate burial ground. Since the cats left mice and shrews in varying stages of decomposition all over the place, I soon had a fine forest of lipstick tubes, which he said were just the right shape for appropriate monuments. (Barbara Cunliffe, mother of Adrian Evans who was at Stowe in the fifties, was staying at Vancouver when she found a dead mouse on the stairs. She mentioned this to Patience, who replied blithely that she rather thought it belonged to Magic, who would collect it later.)

The bottom area of the garden, with its decaying orchard, the pond and the brook, were a wonderful source of entertainment. I caught sticklebacks and minnows in jam jars, tried to keep the handsome newts in various receptacles, from which they invariably escaped, and would have large jars of frogspawn on the go in spring. I would spend hours just gazing at the things in the pond that wriggled and undulated over the delicious black mud, progressing later to lying motion-

174

less by the brook watching a kingfisher. The orchard was given to flooding regularly, and I much enjoyed wading about in the flood water, getting into serious trouble with Patience when the water went over the tops of my Wellingtons. An added bonus was sliding about on the ice when it subsequently froze.

The peonies and huge poppies, that somehow managed to flourish in spite of intermittent neglect, were another joy, the poppies being fun to peel back when still in bud, revealing the silky scarlet petals curled round the black stamens. It never occurred to me, though, that I could have made a proper study of these lovely things. The garden and surrounding countryside provided an idyllic part of my early child-hood, from the carpet of snowdrops that appeared in the spring, through the colour of summer and the spangled cobwebs of autumn to the frosted trees of winter. However, consideration of the sciences was not part of the Vancouver ethos, and while I would make collections of leaves and berries, it was of my own volition and without structure.

My sex education, on the other hand, having been started by the rabbits, was continued explicitly by the cats. Most of these were acquired by accident, like Bouncer, who had eventually perished, but whom the little grey cat mentioned by Simon Digby had succeeded. She had arrived at the house with a visiting pack of beagles, appearing when they returned for tea and settling immovably down by the fire. Patience christened her Tigri Moonette after the cat in the French version of *Mrs Tiggy-Winkle*. She produced kittens regularly for a time, before disappearing as mysteriously as she had come. She left behind Bodkin, a large mackerel-striped son named for a quotation in *Hamlet* that happened to be the play in hand when he was born. Her successor, who came from the Vicarage,was the only cat we ever set out to acquire. An immensely handsome long-haired tortoiseshell, we initially thought that she was male and called her Joseph on account of her many colours. Once her correct gender was established, this was changed to Josepha, which rapidly became Tufy for short. This was down to Patience, who always produced fresh versions of animals' names and who later, having seen the name in the schedule of a horse-show, announced that actually Tufy was called Mrs Roper-Caldbeck. 'She signs her letters Sincerely, Josepha Roper-Caldbeck,' she decided.

Tufy was as bad-tempered as she was beautiful, most of the time disliking any form of attention. The exception was when she was actually in labour. The conception of her numerous litters tended to

175

be a public affair, her partners in this being either a handsome black tom, in which case her kittens were beautiful, or a hideous striped brother of Bodkin's, which produced a singularly unattractive brood. When Patience reckoned parturition was due, she would prepare a comfortable lying-in box, despite the fact that Tufy invariably chose either the bottom of a cupboard littered with garments that Patience was uncertain about keeping, or the best spare bed, on which to give birth. If her family was moved following the birth, she would laboriously carry them back one by one. While giving birth, she liked company, purring ecstatically and expecting lavish praise as each repellent bundle arrived. She was a brilliant hunter and would appear dragging along moles and squirrels as well as the usual mice, bent on teaching the kittens to hunt rather than sustaining them, since all the cats were lavishly fed and were woefully inefficient at keeping down the stable rats.

The offspring of the black Tom were highly sought-after, but the tabbies had no market and frequently ended up being drowned or coming to some other sticky end. Even they could be enchanting as kittens and were an enormous source of pleasure to me. Once mobile, they were taken out on the lawn for highly entertaining kitten races, when they would charge along with their tails sticking up like little Christmas trees until some distraction caused them to veer off the course. They could be taught to crawl up Bill's trouser legs when he was asleep in his armchair by the fire and added to the general dereliction of the furniture. Five of Tufy's kittens remained at Vancouver, a beautiful and idiosyncratic collection, including Fergusson, a handsome ginger tom who had a passion for boiled egg. He would lie on Bill's lap at breakfast, impetuously raising his head over the edge of the table when he thought the time for his share of egg had arrived. He was allowed the last two spoonfuls, licking them ecstatically from the spoon. An almost total disregard for hygiene was a characteristic of life at Vancouver, the cats and their habits never being seen as a possible source of infection.

What eventually gave structure to my days, and provided some discipline, were first ponies and then horses. At the age of three, I had been treated to a ride on a pony plying for hire on Worthing beach. I can remember her now, she was piebald (black and white) and called Bluebell. I evinced such pleasure during the ride that Bill and Patience decided that I should have a pony once we were settled back at Vancouver. Brownie was a fifth birthday present, and obviously I was seen as an incredibly lucky child to be given such a treat. Brownie was a mixed blessing, however. At this stage Bill and Patience had no equine expertise and what was sold to them as an animal with a future was in fact nearly 20 years old, almost the end of the line for a horse. She had also been a riding school pony developing a mouth so hard that she was unstoppable, and an understandable determination to get back home as soon as she could. She regularly ran away with me in spite of the failing health which meant that she had to be put down after only two years.

I proved to have skill as a horsewoman, and other ponies were given to me to ride. In addition, there was my purchase of William Rufus from the market who, once Bill and I were able to handle him, was 'broken in', a large teddy bear being used to get him used to having a weight on his back. I was taken hunting from the start of my riding career, first with Patience leading the pony, then Bill. He decided, however, that it would be more satisfactory if he capitalised on the riding experience he gained as a boy in Devon and be mounted himself. At the time I was being taught at a local riding school, the proprietor of which had Irish connections, and he agreed to find Bill a horse. Wicklow, named after the county from which she came, was described by a later riding teacher of mine as having 'a head like a Duchess and a bottom like a Cook', but she suited Bill splendidly and he began hunting regularly with the Grafton Hounds, a pack that was not of the smartest, but which had a reputation for jumping formidably big fences. We lived in the 'Saturday Country' which was much the least grand, being heavily wooded and giving little chance for spectacular 'runs'. The 'Friday Country' was further north into Northamptonshire, bordering on the famed Leicestershire hunts, and was regarded as high-class hunting country, needing fast, expensive horses to keep up.

Hunting helped Bill to become a local figure and added to his Renaissance man persona. In the hunting field he was quickly accepted into a hierarchical world that tended to be divided between landowners together with army officers on the one hand, and farmers on the other, with the man who helped run the Buckingham off-licence hovering somewhere between. Dress and behaviour were carefully coded, farmers always wearing black coats or occasionally tweed jackets, known as 'ratcatcher'. They also wore caps. Top hats were for the gentry. Tweed was de rigueur for everyone going cubbing, the culling of young foxes before the season proper started.

Bill began his hunting career wearing a black coat and top hat, thus firmly labelling himself gentry, but was soon 'given the Hunt Button', which meant that he was entitled to wear a scarlet coat, correctly known as 'pink', with Grafton buttons on it. This acceptance pleased him enormously and was a measure of his ability to charm as well as his courage in the hunting field, since schoolmasters theoretically ranked somewhere along with the off-licence owners.

We were only marginally part of the social world of the landowners, and found the farming fraternity infinitely more welcoming and congenial. Bill was delighted when, needing a cup of tea after a long day's hunting, he and another farming friend called in on a delightful man called Gerald Dancer, who had gone home earlier. They found him shaving, and asked why. He replied that he felt he must improve his appearance before doing the milking. That Gerald's cows were of more account than the snooty members of the hunt gave Bill much pleasure. At the other end of the social spectrum, Lady Hesketh was a particular hunting companion since she and Bill were both seventeenth-century historians. They would discuss their trade loudly and happily during the frequent hiatuses with which hunting is punctuated. She was the chatelaine of Easton Neston, a lovely house in which Elizabeth of Austria had stayed when she was undertaking her enjoyable hunting in England. Bill was a somewhat ruthless parent in the hunting field, expecting me, on a small pony that was sometimes difficult to manage, to keep up and look after myself. There was no question of my finding a way round the formidable fences, despite the fact that I regularly fell off when jumping them, and I generally had to find my way home by myself.

Patience never fulfilled her youthful ambition to learn to ride for Bill's sake, freely admitting her fear of horses and determination not to ride them. However, her knowledge of racing, culled from her father and brother, meant that she took a passionate interest in their breeding and achievements. She was a brilliant 'horse bore', able to sustain endless conversations with hunting and racing friends about the provenance and behaviour of their animals. She would occasionally help in the stables if I were ill, but really disliked even this contact. This attitude was instantly spotted by my much-loved William Rufus, who was normally affectionate and biddable, but who teased Patience by making vicious faces at her the moment she appeared.

The contact with the Hunt did offer her something that she particularly enjoyed. Those concerned with the rearing of foxhounds, reckoned that puppies, once weaned, benefited from the individual attention

178

of being 'walked' in private homes that could offer space and some knowledge of how they should be fed. Patience agreed to add two puppies to the Vancouver manège for the summer months. She became so skilled in feeding them up that the kennels would ask her to take on those that were failing to thrive. The process of preparing their food was not for the squeamish. Greenish horsemeat, supplied by the kennels, needed no cooking, but when that was not available, Patience would boil sheeps' heads, the evil smell of which would pervade the whole house. She would then pick off the meat, mixing it with dog biscuits and various nutritious additions designed to build the necessary stamina for the formidable Grafton country. The puppies were never taken for formal walks, being expected to show initiative in using the garden to occupy themselves much as I did, though they did enjoy accompanying us on expeditions to collect wood or rabbit food. Coming into the house was strictly forbidden, there being one awful occasion when some visitor, calling on a wet day and finding us out, saw the two pathetic-looking puppies lying in the porch. Knowing that the door would be unlocked, they let them in, and when we returned half an hour later, they had perpetrated £60 worth of damage – no mean sum in the fifties.

Once they found their way to the village, it was generally time for the puppies to be returned to the kennels. One lot discovered someone's chickens and lovingly brought Patience still-warm pullets, while another pair started lifting milk bottles from doorsteps, dropping them in their delight at seeing a friend. The following summer there would be a puppy show, with the walkers of the winners being given quite lavish prizes. Patience almost invariably won something, but the gloom when she did not was awful. Later, just before they left Stowe, she walked several beagle puppies and acquired a whole fresh lot of trophies.

Patience's attitude to my riding was ambivalent. On the one hand she worried desperately about my safety, and I would regularly meet her in the village when I rode back from hunting, ostensibly collecting rabbit food, but in fact having been too anxious to stay in the house. This was compounded after someone she met at a Hunt sherry party told her how much Bill neglected me when out hunting. In her usual fashion, she made this into a funny story, but it did increase her worry nonetheless. Conversely, she was ambitious for me and once I began to ride in gymkhanas, was keen that I should do well. My early experience of horse shows was acquired in Lancing, based round the riding school from which Brownie had come. The school owned a pair of Shetland ponies that a child called Lindsey and I sometimes rode in very local competitions for pony pairs. It was decided that we should be entered in the grander Worthing Horse Show, and Patience described the result in a letter to Peter Leslie: 'Harriet covered herself with glory the other day, riding herself into the money on a pony taken from the beach against some of the best ponies in England. It was like the best kind of dream.' Most of this is fantasy. I do not recall that the pony had been taken off the beach, there were no handsome ponies in the line-up below us, and while they gave us rosettes saying Highly Commended, partly because we had ridden nicely and kept together, it was also because the Shetlands were much smaller than the other ponies and we looked sweet. 'Give the Shelties a clap' said the announcer as we cantered round the ring with the long ribbons on the rosettes flying. Seeing this letter recently for the first time was startling.

It was in the same riding school that Patience discovered Beaufort, one of the most beautiful horses that I have ever seen. She bought him for £60 because she thought it was unbearably degrading that an ex-race horse of impeccable breeding who, until something went wrong with his legs, had belonged to the wealthy owner and breeder of race-horses, Dorothy Paget, should be ridden in fancy-dress competitions by the incompetent, badly taught pupils of the school. Bill was initially furious, but presented with the fait accompli of the near-starving animal who only just survived the train journey from Sussex to Bucks, entirely changed his tune and announced that he had always wanted to ride in point-to-points and if he did not do it before he was 45, he never would. An elderly and bad-tempered groom was engaged to live in, and Bill began to train himself and the horse, who was now being properly fed. This training took place under the auspices of a remarkable ex-sergeant of the Royal Scots Greys, who had learnt to ride and train horses, principally to jump, under the aegis of Colonel Rodzianko, who had been a Central European landowner. Alex Tait had come from Glasgow originally and had just set up in the business of teaching riding and training horses in a nearby village. Some acquaintance had recommended him as possibly being able to teach me to stay on over jumps, something that he certainly achieved though my current pony came to dislike his rather cruel methods intensely. Beaufort, who, once properly fed, became nearly unmanageable, was a stronger candidate for Alex's methods and became somewhat better behaved. He learnt to jump rather too successfully, though, since in racing, horses are required to jump fast and off the shoulder, while show-jumpers, which Alex normally trained, need to take it more slowly and jump off their hocks.

In the spring of 1952 Bill entered Beaufort for three point-to-points, the whole enterprise being entirely amateur. Bill's colours were combined in a sweater specially knitted for him by a devoted female friend. They were white with cherry-red sleeves and collar, accompanied by a black cap. Reluctant to carry too many lead weights, Bill had to stuff himself to reach the stipulated weight, and I well remember him before one race, irritable with nerves, trying to force down quantities of bacon and eggs. It was all singularly unsuccessful, and in only one race did they finish the course. In another, Beaufort was pulled up, and in the third they had a spectacular fall. He was an idle horse who reckoned that four miles was his limit, whereas most point-to-point courses were four and a half. Feeling him flag coming up to the seventeenth fence in his final race, Bill pushed him on, but perhaps Beaufort was genuinely tired since he failed to rise to the fence at all, took it with his chest and exactly illustrated what is meant when a fall is described as going 'arse over tip'.

Patience had resisted her instinct, which was to hide in the car with a flask of brandy, and was bravely watching the race, though at too great a distance from the fall to see in any detail. Shortly after it happened, the Clerk of the Course rode up to her and enquired genially: 'Is that your outfit down there?' Patience wanly said that it was. 'Well, we thought he had broken his back at first, but he's eating grass now so we think he's probably all right.' Confusedly wondering whether apparent madness was better than being crippled, Patience had forgotten that the state of the horse is of paramount importance on a race course. In fact Bill had been well-instructed that the most important thing was to avoid the horse falling on you, so had hit the ground instructing himself to 'roll, you silly bugger', ending up yards from Beaufort and unhurt. The horse had winded himself and, when he got his breath back, had helped himself to delicious grass without bothering to get up. Bill, when he noticed this, hauled the animal to his feet, and he came back to his box wildly pleased with himself as if he had done something enormously clever.

Bill had at least achieved his ambition, but it was at enormous financial cost, it taking years before the debts were finally cleared. Beaufort was unsaleable and had to be given away, ending up with Group-

Captain Townsend, who took him out to Belgium. Here, he developed the habit of firmly lying down whenever anyone went into his stable carrying a saddle. Since he was very big, people gave up challenging this behaviour, and I believe he ended his days in peace. Bill now contented himself with Wicklow, while I had a succession of animals of varying charm and ability.

The Local Education Authority never questioned my upbringing. Bill would have been considered qualified to teach me, and presumably his standing in the local community would have prevented questions about the standards I was achieving. There was a sticky moment when the Chief Education Officer came to lunch in the middle of a term-time week. Patience chose to have a migraine that day and I, aged 12, acted as hostess. It was characteristic of the way that Buckingham operated that no action was taken then or later.

Once we became adolescent, I drifted apart from most of my village friends though a small group of us came together when I was about 17, to start a rather limited youth club in Dadford. June Turney, now Hall, who was one of the group, became close to Bill and Patience during their final years at Stowe, and remembers with pleasure the encouragement she got from them and the seriousness with which they listened to her ideas. They felt strongly that girls should be thoughtful, well-read and able to express their ideas fluently, but were ultimately inconsistent about women's education and careers. The bright female contemporaries of Historians at university were admired, and one was castigated for 'wasting' her Double First when she married and became absorbed in her children. However, that may have been due to the fact her first baby was, at the time, unprepossessing and because she changed his nappy in the sitting-room at Vancouver. Motherhood might be considered the ultimate destiny of women, but the detail of child care must be kept from public view.

17

Plays and Travel Postwar

One part of my parents' educational method was to take me with them almost wherever they went. I would be part of gatherings in the Art School, still, immediately after the war, run by Robin and Dodie Watt. They would also take me to lunch and cocktail parties given by old Historians who had moved on to Oxford and Cambridge. Patience castigated me on one of these occasions for crying when the Taj Mahal in Oxford was unable to supply me with ice cream, Peter Leslie having generously taken us to dine there. I must have been about seven and can just remember feeling exhausted after an entirely adult day. The lack of ice cream was the final straw. I was subsequently made to write Peter an appallingly ill-typed letter apologising. Once I was adolescent, accompanying them was much more enjoyable. Generous parents would take us all out to the few good local restaurants. Outstanding among these was Wicken Rectory, a beautiful eighteenth-century house. This was run by an eccentric Parson who hunted regularly and was known in Grafton circles as 'the mad Parson of Wicken'. He was in constant trouble with his Bishop for his provision of delicious and quite expensive meals, but since he invariably had a full church, his position was difficult to assail. Patience was not always an ideal person to take out to meals. If food was delayed she was apt to faint and she was a bad chooser of food. She would examine other people's plates and say: 'I like what you've got better than mine. Swop?'

From the age of five, I would sometimes accompany Bill on Combined Cadet Force afternoons, when I would be allowed to sit astride one of the elegant lions gracing the south front of Stowe, watching the parade. I was a witness to his running battle with the Bandmaster who was also one of the music masters and who was convinced that the boys in the band were unable to march and play at the same time. Bill was equally convinced otherwise and eventually won. At one parade, however, the Bandmaster entirely failed to pick up his cue and continued playing endlessly. Bill's clear, carrying voice rang out: 'Put a sock in it, Mr Webb.'

When small I would dip in and out of the tea parties and similarly with the Shakespeare productions, though, when very young, I was sent away for the actual weekend of the play. I would go and stay with the Connors who ran the local riding school, something I enjoyed enormously. For a time, this gave me a second family where I was allowed to behave childishly and to be happily employed, not only with the ponies, but also with feeding the hens and haymaking. The Connors' daughter Mary, who must have been about 17 when I first knew her, was an encouraging teacher who not only taught me to ride, but also to swim in the icy Stowe lakes. Patience had never learnt, and if Bill spent as little as ten minutes in cold water, he promptly developed bronchitis. When I was about 12 however, these idyllic episodes ended and I took a full and mostly enjoyable part in the tea parties and was encouraged by Bill to become a fixture at play rehearsals, a position I loved. I thus received a thorough grounding in whichever Shakespeare play was being produced.

These began postwar in the summer of 1947 with his successful *Richard II*, a joint production by Bill and the Congreve Club, a body that existed solely to put on plays and regularly did so with great success. For some reason the Queen's Temple was unusable, so the play took place in the Gym. Beverly Baxter, who was then the drama critic for the *Evening Standard*, who had a son at Stowe, reviewed the production for *The Stoic*. He began by describing the lack of enthusiasm with which he faced this busman's holiday, going on to say that, to his surprise, he 'thoroughly enjoyed the play at Stowe. When the three hours had ended, I would gladly have sat through another hour if the cast had cared to give encores after the new fashion set by the companies playing *Oklahoma* and *Annie Get Your Gun*.' He was deeply impressed by Toby Robertson, whom he felt resembled the young Gielgud, and particularly noted Giles Rooke playing the Bishop of Carlisle and displaying the 'granite courage of the character' in spite of the smallness of the part. He also noted the 'admirable diction' of Michael Morland, later the judge in the case of Jamie Bulger's murder, commenting that: 'it was not his fault that he did not look as near death as is customary when making the great speech on England.'

Stephen Whitwell remembers John Stoye, Gaunt in the 1935 production, looking like death. Beverley Baxter's final paragraph states: 'It was not, and could not be, a professional performance, but to a remarkable degree the spirit and cruel beauty of this exquisite play were maintained. Stowe has every reason to be proud of this production.'

The Gym was again the setting for a lively production of *Twelfth Night*, the reviewer in *The Stoic* being John Saunders, who then ran the Congreve Club and might have regarded himself as a rival to Bill. He was generous in his praise, however, and argued the virtues of the Gym as a setting, writing that 'the uniquely exasperating quality of the Gym stage induces ingenuity'. John Saunders felt that they would do better not returning to the Queen's Temple, but in 1949 *Richard III* was produced there, with a real horse appearing at the end. I, aged seven, was allowed to stay for the first half in order to see the little princes, whom I viewed as a romantic pair. This production was reviewed for *The Stoic* by Peregrine Worsthorne, who opened by writing: 'To sit in the elegant grounds of Stowe on a fine summer's evening is to taste life at a ducal level and if, in addition, some obliging company, preferably of course, The Historians, produce on the steps of the Queen's Temple an excellent Shakespearean performance the evening becomes even richer and more memorable. It does not really matter to any great degree what play is chosen, for the play is essentially not the thing. Stowe is the thing, and in such a triumphantly artificial setting any performance, unless it is of Olympian grandeur, becomes a play within a play.' Having praised individual performances, the final line of the review says: 'A summer term without a Historians' play, a Historians' play not at the Queen's Temple, – those austere days are gone. Thanks be to McElwee.'

A *Julius Caesar* which *The Stoic* commended for its determination to let the audience decide on the hero was put on in 1950, followed by the much more ambitious venture of *Othello*. This was possibly inspired by the performance of Simon Chalton as Casca the previous year, suggesting to Bill that he might make a good Iago, which indeed he did. *The Stoic* was unenthusiastic, but *The Times* liked it. Both praised the clothes which were a particular tribute to Bill. Hiring by this time had become too expensive, and the woman in Buckingham who usually made the costumes fell ill at the last minute, so Bill made them all himself, using the 1907 sewing machine. It was a tour de force, with rich-looking garments created out of cheap taffeta. There exists a splendid photograph of Desdemona wearing pants with a

185

suspender belt over them holding up his stockings and, on top, Mrs Purefoy's bust bodice being adjusted by Patience.

Brian Calvert's performance as Cassius inspired the next year's highly successful *Hamlet* and, with few 'stars' around, *Henry VIII* seemed suitable for Coronation Year. In 1954 Bill had to go into hospital to have his sinuses drained – he kept falling inconveniently asleep – and John Saunders put on *The Merchant of Venice*. This production marked the emergence of Piers Plowright as a formidable force on various Stowe stages. Reviews of the play were few, but the *Buckingham Advertiser* commended his Portia as 'nobly-drawn', and the following year he made a magnificent Coriolanus. This play, the first of which I was able to form a moderately independent opinion, seemed a touch under-rehearsed, but Piers had enormous authority and was matched by Brook Williams, son of Emlyn, as Tullus Aufidius. Of his performance *The Times* said that: 'the part of Aufidius was played with a polish one does not expect of a schoolboy actor.' At the end of the play, the dead Coriolanus, wrapped in a scarlet cloak, rolled all the way down the Temple steps. It was splendidly effective, and Bill always said that he had to do it first to demonstrate to Piers that it could be done without pain.

Piers gave a hilarious performance as Mrs Peachum in a delightful *Beggars' Opera* put on by his house, and Brook made a compelling Henry IV in a Congreve Club production of the Pirandello play, again a startling performance from a boy. Finally, they came together again when Bill did another *Twelfth Night* with Piers as Malvolio and Brook as Aguecheek. It was probably one of the best productions the Historians ever did, having an excellent Belch, a moving Feste and convincing boys in the womens' parts, as well as the two stars. John Saunders in *The Stoic* said: 'It would not be right to end this review without saying a grateful farewell to those distinguished actors Plowright and Williams.' After noting their starring roles, he finishes: 'here was God's plenty. The stage at Stowe will be fortunate indeed when it can show such a pair again.' After this, a rather patchy *Midsummer Night's Dream* seemed anticlimatic. The apparent lack of future talent made another *Julius Caesar* inevitable, but this was good, with Cassius and Mark Anthony suggesting themselves respectively as Richard II and Bolingbroke for 1959.

By this time Patience had, unofficially, conceded her role as wardrobe mistress. She remained thus designated on the programmes, since my name there would have generated horror among the housemasters. She also continued to dispense some sewing up, aspirin and much general support. I was no better needlewoman than she was, but I learnt how to order wigs from 'Bert', to track down Roman armour among the theatrical costumiers of the West End, and how to complete complex measurement forms. For *Richard II* we were able to hire gorgeous costumes from Nathans thanks to Geoffrey Russell, now Lord Ampthill, who said that the firm owed him and would be happy to supply us free. Nathan's 'expert' was a genius at coming up with appropriate costumes, and Christopher Gauvain, who was playing Richard, and I, had a wonderful time selecting hampers full of velvet and brocade. I particularly cherished the velvet tabard with the arms of England in gold wire that we chose for Richard's return from Ireland. The following year Bill chose to do *The Winter's Tale* in seventeenth-century dress, and Nathans again helped. When discussing the costume for Mamillius with the expert, I simply said 'When did you last see your father?' Without a word he fetched the perfect blue satin suit.

Richard II and *The Winter's Tale* were both put on at Wardour Castle, a gaunt, but romantic ruin in Wiltshire. This came about through the influence of Edmund Rolfe, a thirties Historian who continues to live in the house next door to the castle. The Rolfes' barn housed many of the cast, and the fact that some of the proceeds of the ticket sales went to the Catholic Church was carefully concealed from the Headmaster of Stowe. Edmund had played a second Lady in the 1935 production of *Richard*, but rose to play Gloucester in the *Lear* of 1939. Term being over and school discipline distant, made for a certain amount of relaxed behaviour, but both productions were successful. During *The Winter's Tale* Patience became aware that Mopsa's bosom had become somewhat misshapen. When she asked Prince Nicholas of Prussia what had gone wrong, he replied that it must be his cigarettes and whipped out a box of 50. He played Lady Macbeth in Bill's swansong production, his 'What, in our house?' being a masterpiece of upper-class outrage. Eric Reynolds had always forbidden Bill to put on *Macbeth*. Apparently Reynolds had produced it himself when at Rugby, and just before one performance overheard two women from the local Woman's Royal Army Corps Camp, who had been allocated free tickets, saying 'Oh Christ, it's *Macbeth* again.' Normally Bill carefully documented each play, sticking a copy of the programme and all the reviews together in his press-cutting album. For *Macbeth,* the last play he did, there is nothing.

187

Brian Brindley felt that Bill was not a particularly successful director of the plays, saying in particular that his crowd scenes, on which he prided himself, were not as effective as they might have been. Glowing reviews in the *Buckingham Advertiser* are no real guide, *The Times* write-ups may not have been unbiased, and the whole process so enthralled me that I am unable to be objective. I do remember that Neville Coghill was as enthusiastic about one of the postwar productions as he had been about the earlier *Henry IV*, but in fact the quality of the productions was not in the end the most important factor. Boys were challenged to think way beyond their own experience, much was learnt by those doing scenery, lighting and music, and any involvement in the play, however minor, was much sought after throughout the school. When doing *The Winter's Tale*, Bill was delighted when the Captain of Rugger came up to him and said that he had always wanted to be part of the Historians' play, but being no actor, had felt he had little chance. This year, however, he had heard there was a bear. The costume Nathans supplied was realistic, and Christopher Clucas was a great success. At Wardour he was seen rolling down a bank while getting himself into the part.

The work involved every year was enormous, the worry about the weather continuous, but the adrenaline ran high and the enjoyment was huge. No production was rained off, though the third production of *Twelfth Night* had to break for a thunderstorm on the first night, giving particular pertinence to 'The rain it raineth every day'.

During the immediate postwar period, the Shakespeare plays were not the only theatricals in which Bill and Patience became involved. Along with his tutorship, Bill was under-housemaster to Edward Capel Cure, who ran Temple House which, for several years, put on a pantomime. The first, *Red Riding Hood*, put on in 1948, was co-authored by Tony, now Lord Quinton, but sadly the script has vanished. Capel, as he was invariably known, always wrote the music, and Colin Graham was much involved in all four productions. Alan Caiger-Smith wrote the 1949 *Puss In Bags*, which has also disappeared, but the last two, *Jack and the Beanstalk* and *Cinderella*, were written by Patience and Christopher Cash, and the words still exist. The description of the first scene in *Jack and the Beanstalk* is redolent of the postwar period, the entire pantomime being a satire on postwar life under the Labour Government, with some swipes at the upper classes in the guise of a pantomime dame called Lady Florence. The Giant is the Civil Service, and there are topical references to shortages, queuing and Snoek. The villain turns out to be Lady Florence's long-lost son, and Tory virtues win out in the end.

The last pantomime for which there is any documentation is *Cinderella*, which was put on in 1950 and which had a hunting theme and rather more of what was known as 'basic'. This referred to local topics, and much laughter could follow the mere mention of certain names. The Ball in *Cinderella* provided the opportunity to include members of the Stowe staff in unlikely pairings and guises, and the first entry of the Fairy Godmother (played by Colin Graham) 'dressed as Lady Keyes', got in a reference to a slightly eccentric member of the Grafton hunt. Tragically, Capel died of leukaemia at about this time and the pantomimes ceased. His successor as Housemaster of Temple, though a regular enemy of Bill's, went on to stage some delightful productions of Gilbert and Sullivan.

In 1948, the Historians seem to have taken over the Puppet Club to produce *The Barber of Seville*, the beautifully dressed puppets continuing to be found in corners of the Vancouver attics for some time. Colin Graham must have been a moving spirit in many of these enterprises, appearing in all four pantomimes and being part of the puppet show. He was Feste in *Twelfth Night* as well as Buckingham in *Richard III*. However, the History Side of this period seem in general to have been inspired to become widely involved in numerous projects. Clearly they were determined to rise above the gloom of postwar England.

The resumption of the Culture Tours must have provided a further boost to the Historians' morale. These began again in 1948 and continued annually until 1959. Bill, however, only once deviated from alternating France and Italy, this being in 1957, when he went to Spain. In place of train travel or two Lancias, eight boys were packed into a minibus, the driving of which was shared between Bill and Peter Leslie. From the descriptions in the diary, it was a successful venture, though for the co-drivers, the distances were punishing. During this tour Bill celebrated his fiftieth birthday with a grand dinner in Bordeaux funded by George Kenyon, the generous parent of Christopher, who was one of the party and who wrote the diary. This is a succinct and vivid document, marred only slightly by the self-consciousness that featured in all the Culture Tour diaries that have survived. Bill's panama hat, which featured in the 1937 diary, appears again in Spain. Two French tourists were overheard to remark that the hat reminded them strongly of Monsieur Hulot.

The following year Bill and Humphrey Playford took only three boys to France in Humphrey's car. This appears to have been an enjoyable and peaceful party and, indeed, it was only the last tour of all that Bill felt was a failure. By the end of the fifties, people were travelling more and the party he took had not only experienced staying in Europe, but many of them had done so in greater comfort than could be afforded either by Bill or by the poorest member of the party. It was on this tour that his 1932 Delage broke down irreparably. The travellers had to return by train while the Italians made an enormous fuss about the car being officially broken up. They seemed convinced that Bill wished to import this impossible vehicle into the country by a back door. It was possibly this disaster which most affected Bill and, understandably, clouded his final assessment of the Tour. Stephen Whitwell, who joined them for part of the time, remembers the party gaining much enjoyment and value from their travels. The photographs he has confirm this. There was never any question of my joining a Culture Tour. Cost and propriety would have been implacably against it.

Something that is frequently mentioned in any Culture Tour diary recording a drive through France is Bill's habit of saluting magpies. Since these arrogant birds are particularly prevalent in northern France, his hand can never have been still. In theory his gesture was to ward off the bad luck brought by the appearance of single birds, but just to be on the safe side, he would salute magpies in whatever numbers they were seen. It was one manifestation of the superstition that dogged both his and Patience's lives, though she worried more about omens and portents than he did. Bill was probably influenced partly by a Celtic culture of propitiating the spirits, and Patience by Maudie, who was always anxious to propitiate everything in all dimensions. Both were also likely to have had old-fashioned nannies when they were at their most impressionable. Neither would ever walk under a ladder, and Bill would never cut his nails on a Friday or a Sunday or fail to make a cross in the bottom of a boiled egg so that the witches could not go to sea in it. Patience was terrified of seeing the new moon through glass, of breaking a mirror, and would never allow May blossom or an opened umbrella into the house. Eating 'bread and cheese', the hawthorn leaves when just in bud, was considered lucky, as was going under a railway bridge when a train was going over, and seeing a shooting star.

As a child, all this strongly influenced me, and I would hang around under bridges and at night would walk along with my eyes dangerously glued to the sky. Tufy's black daughter crossing our paths was also greeted as a good omen. I was in my thirties when I virtually freed myself of their rituals, but my hand still twitches when I see a single magpie, I have to make a conscious effort not to make a cross in my eggshells and I always stop a glass ringing. At the time it all added to the excitement of life at Vancouver, but also increased the anxiety. Patience would make a good story out of the speed with which she could visualise disaster whenever the telephone rang, but her fears were real and were greatly increased when either of us was away. Accompanying Bill on the Culture Tours would however, have been infinitely worse for her than sitting at home waiting to hear that death and destruction had occurred. She remained adamant in her determination never to leave England's shores, and as long as the telephone was quiet, spent the time writing and undertaking her hugely enjoyed annual reading of Dickens. Someone had given her a complete set of his books, and I can vividly remember her, curled up in the corner of her tatty chaise longue with a bag of sweets, tears pouring down her face as she read yet again about the death of Dora, the child bride in *David Copperfield.*

18

The Popular Historian and the Lady Novelist at Home

In spite of the physical distance, Patience continued to be strongly influenced by her mother Maudie. They wrote to each other regularly and, for some years after we returned to Stowe, we continued to spend the holidays at Shadwells. I can remember the enormous excitement of arriving at the house and seeing Maudie, whom I adored. It is likely that Maudie had mixed feelings about these invasions. She was already becoming reclusive, having few friends and allowing her life to revolve round her son Alan and her Pekes. Alan was, by this time, producing a stream of novels and radio plays, most of which Bill was apt to dismiss as 'potboilers', commending only *Fritzi*, his first book, as being really good. They got published, though, and, like Patience's books, were always immensely readable. *The Night Has Eyes* was made into a film which still occasionally surfaces on television, and his plays were regularly broadcast. His writing did not provide enough to live on, however, and all his working life was spent teaching at St Aubyns', a prep school in Rottingdean.

Alan was an enormously successful teacher, beloved by his pupils and expert at getting them through Common Entrance to their public schools. During the war, the school was evacuated to Wales and there Alan met Tonti, a married woman with two daughters who had also been evacuated. They fell in love, she was divorced, and, to Maudie's distress, they married. After the war they settled in Lancing in a flat rented from Maudie's lesbian sister Theo, who lived above them, and during the holidays Alan would arrive at Shadwells every morning to write, carrying his work in a small, battered blue suitcase.

He worked in a room that was theoretically my 'nursery', but in which my toys vied with his beautiful butterfly collection for space. The walls were entirely papered with pin-up pictures of thirties musical comedy stars which, if removed, took the plaster away with them. Alan would always start his working day with a session on the lavatory, studying the racing pages of the *Daily Express*, a process that inevitably gave him piles. His betting was continuous, causing endless financial problems. Maudie bailed him out as much as she could, and I recall one awful lunch when Patience suddenly burst into tears and accused her mother of having favoured Alan all their lives, allowing him to have her share of what money there was. Maudie said nothing, simply bowing her head to the storm. The family, led by Maudie, disapproved of Tonti. A polite relationship was maintained, however, and I regularly rode with her daughters, who were the only cousins I had.

Around 1953 our visits to North Lancing ceased, largely because Shadwells was becoming uninhabitable. The roof had resembled a sieve throughout my childhood and, as the years passed, the various chamber pots, basins and buckets set out to catch the drips when it rained, would set up an ever louder, ill-tuned cacophony. That Maudie managed to produce perfectly roasted meat, lovely, soapy steamed potatoes and delicious gravy from her incredibly primitive kitchen for as long as she did, was a miracle. Even when ivy was actually growing in her bedroom, she flatly refused to ask for something to be done. The peppercorn rent she paid left her feeling insecure, and she was convinced that if she made a fuss they would have turned her out. The state of repair was such that her landlords would almost certainly have insisted on rehousing her, which she would have hated. Bill and Patience regularly asked her to live with us in Vancouver, but she remained adamant that she wished to stay in Shadwells. She managed to create oases of comfort without, I think, any of the usual support available to the elderly, while the pieces of lovely Victorian furniture that had not been sold to pay Alan's racing debts crumbled away. She had a wholly Dickensian drawing room into which no one ever went. It was a complete period piece, with needlework chairs, beaded fire-screens and wax fruits under glass domes, but everything was covered in mould and cobwebs. If the door were opened, the room emitted a chill miasma.

In 1960, when Maudie was 80, she fell while trying to board a bus, broke her arm and was taken into hospital. While there, she caught an infection and died within a week. Since she had not spent a night outside Shadwells for 30 years, she must have been like a snail deprived of its shell. I was away from home when she died and Patience, matter-of-fact when telephoning me with the news, insisted that I did not come home for the funeral. I much regret that I lost contact with, and failed to say goodbye to, someone who was enormously important to me as a child. With Maudie gone, however, it was possible for some myths to be dispelled, for Tonti to become a close friend and support in times of trouble, and for all of us to value fully Alan's charm, humour and wide knowledge. Shadwells, in spite of its Queen Anne beauty, was pulled down. No doubt repairing it had proved too daunting and expensive.

Bill was not good at cherishing family ties. Before the war they stayed with his mother in Devon occasionally, but I only remember one visit when I developed a pain in my stomach which Patience thought must be acute appendicitis, but probably stemmed from my habit of illicitly eating under-ripe fruit. Kitty had given up Tapscott, the family home, and lived in London during the war, braving the blitz and, in spite of being 70, spending a year working an eight-hour day packing parcels for the Red Cross. When her younger son Patrick came back from the war to teach Modern Languages at Blundells, she moved into a school house with him. She died in 1948 aged 76, having been a widow for more than 30 years. She occupied herself with her exquisite embroidery, the Woman's Institute, the Nursing Association and gardening, a brave and deeply inhibited woman. Bill regretted his somewhat distant relationship with her, but made little attempt to see more of his brother.

Patrick came to stay at Vancouver occasionally and, rather surprisingly, gave me a copy of *Bonjour Tristesse*. He was a delightful, diffident man with a great sense of humour. He never married, lived in a muddle and spent much of his spare time researching the family history. Unlike Bill, he wrote a great many letters, keeping a carbon copy of everything. There was a suggestion of some scandal, possibily involving a homosexual connection, but details were never made public. Bill was probably right in saying that Patrick should have gone to a different school and university. He might not then have been so overshadowed.

Bill, unlike Patience, who used aspects of Maudie in at least two books, did not appear to put any of his family into his novels, though he did use many aspects of himself. *Final Objective*, his war novel and last work of fiction, was, like *The House*, nearly a great success. The book was published in the autumn of 1950, and the *New Statesman* wrote: 'Had this novel appeared two or three years ago, it would probably have become a best-seller and later become "The Book of the Film".' The review goes on: 'Mr McElwee may be excused his conventional happy ending for his description of an infantry attack. This is one of the best accounts of actual fighting that I have read for a long time.' Other reviews mostly agreed, though the *Buckingham Advertiser* went further, ending their review by saying: 'The closing chapters rise to heights of sublimity that could never have been suspected in the earlier passages of the book. It is a novel of a man of action and a poet.' As with The House, Roxburgh wrote to Bill, this time revealing more of his romantic streak. Writing that he had finished the book 'in the early hours of the morning', he went on:

'Everyone will be telling you that the battle is marvellously described – surely the tale of McCann the soldier (not the lover!) is autobiography: if it isn't, it is magic – but frankly what has won my heart is the Gerda story. I feel inclined to say of the early part "how did you know it felt like that?" and of the last part "Thank God you realized how she would react". If the end had not been what you make it the whole book would have been spoiled, but I suppose when you had once created Gerda she more or less took charge. Anyway Gerda has another lover since last night – a rival to John McCann – and that is Yours ever gratefully, JFR.'

Had the book achieved best-seller status Bill might have continued writing novels, but commissioned history books provided advance royalties and a steady, if limited, income. *The Murder of Sir Thomas Overbury*, which appeared in 1952, could be seen as a transition between the two genres. In his introduction, Bill wrote: 'A piece of history, if properly written, is a better story than any novel which can be written about it'. His account of the machinations of Frances Howard, Countess of Essex and Somerset, and her accomplices, in their struggles for power and happiness is balanced, thoughtful and vivid. It was widely and well reviewed, being given a whole page in the glossy *Illustrated London News*, then an upmarket magazine. The photograph of Bill that accompanied the article shows him as dark, serious and good-looking. A bow tie adds a faintly raffish touch.

Faber and Faber, for whom he had written the book on Overbury, now commissioned a History of England to be no more than 200,000 words long and to be aimed at 'the average intelligent general reader'.

With such limited space, *The Story of England* is inevitably a gallop through history, but it reads well and provides a satisfying outline of the major events. As always with Bill's view of history, much of the book concerned people and politics, but a review in *The Times Literary Supplement*, noting the difficulty of compression he faced, adds that 'Major McElwee has not dealt with this problem by writing an exclusively political history. Literature, religion, industry and the social life of England are all discussed, and so successfully are they included in the narrative that one is reminded more of a miniature than a mosaic.' Bill passes confident judgement on the main players, as his description of the shift from Plantagenet to Tudor illustrates. He would have no truck with attempts to rehabilitate Richard III and to clear him of the murder of the little princes in the Tower. He wrote: 'None of the many attempts that have been made to clear Richard of the crime has yet succeeded; and indeed historians are still bewildered, as his contemporaries were, by the character of the last Plantagenet. Many of the contradictions can be traced easily to the formative influences of his youth: the high renaissance culture which produced not only the Italian masterpieces, but also the civilization of the Borgias; and the wolfishly brutal background of a world in which Queen Margaret would delightedly encourage her eight-year-old son to condemn Yorkist prisoners to death, and Tiptoft, the scholarly Earl of Worcester, amused himself by watching Lancastrians being impaled on spears. Certainly Richard might, in other circumstances, have made a very good king. All that he did in his short two years suggested a thoroughly businesslike reorganisation of the government. But there was too much blood...'

Henry VII, however, who succeeded Richard, was one of Bill's heroes. While Patience condemned Henry's meanness, Bill lauded him for the careful economic management which actually put the exchequer in the black. Other reviews of *The Story of England* broadly concurred with the *TLS*, and the book provided a regular supplement to the McElwee income for many years. Later he was to compress the story even more tightly for the *Teach Yourself* series. When negotiating this deal, he was offered some samples of previous works in the same series. He always expressed regret that he did not have the face to ask for a copy of *Teach Yourself Sex*, which he could just see tucked away in a bottom shelf.

The seventeenth century was Bill's favourite period of history, and he got enormous enjoyment from writing *England's Precedence*, a general history of the principal Stuarts published in 1956. The title was a wonderfully arrogant quotation from Milton: 'Let not England forget her precedence of teaching the nations how to live'. Writing histories in which he distilled the research of more serious historians into manageable and readable chunks, was clearly a sensible move, given his particular talents and other commitments. He justifies the practice in an author's note at the start of the book, outlining the tendency of historians to compartmentalise history into such areas as constitutional or social, adding that a gulf existed between serious historical works, textbooks and historical romances. *England's Precedence* successfully filled this gap, though one reviewer did take Bill to task for overemphasising the political at the expense of the cultural.

The period covered was from the accession of James I to that of William and Mary, with some description of the situations preceding and following these events. By this time I had developed a romantic passion for the same period, Prince Rupert being a particular hero. It was a delight, therefore, to be allowed to go with Patience to the National Portrait Gallery to choose the illustrations for the book. It was a measure of their mutual understanding that Bill should assign her this task. Assisted by the then curator, David Piper, who tempered Patience's romantic tendencies with his passion for authenticity, we had an entrancing day and one that I must admit would not have been included in any school curriculum. We emerged much better educated in the provenance and background of a number of portraits. The book was again well received, with the highly thought-of historian, C. V. Wedgwood, giving him a lengthy and enthusiastic write-up, followed by a personal letter. She particularly liked his description of Prince Henry, eldest son of James l, an idealised youth who died young and could therefore be lamented as a great king we never had. Bill wrote of him: 'He was good at games, passionately interested in ships and shipbuilding, hero-worshipped Raleigh and had all the sound insular prejudices about foreigners.'

Bill expanded on some of the material acquired in researching *England's Precedence* to write a life of James VI and I, using that well-known quotation *The Wisest Fool in Christendom* as a title. Halfway through writing the book, Bill learnt that a similar biography was being written by an American and thus found himself under even more pressure than usual to meet his contracted deadline. The books did coincide and his sales were affected, though the reviews were as

197

widespread and as enthusiastic as ever. He again had a full-page spread in the *Illustrated London News* written by Sir Charles Petrie. Christopher Hill, writing in the *Spectator*, preferred a life of Gustavus Adolphus, saying that: 'Mr McElwee's book is slighter and less original. His main contributions are a vivid sketching of James's experiences as King of Scotland, and some subtle analyses of his relations with his wife and favourites, and of his early degeneration.' I think Bill is good too on the difficult legacy James inherited from Elizabeth, the different talents needed for ruling the two countries, and the effect on James of an appalling upbringing. The book was published in America and was again well reviewed, the *Herald Tribune* saying: 'Mr McElwee's success in writing a fascinating biography about such a sorry effigy of a king is a triumph of art and scholarship.'

Even if Bill's books were not works of extensive historical research, it was still an achievement that he was able to produce them at two-yearly intervals. Meeting the deadlines was always a struggle, given that it was difficult for him to write much during the term, and while he could work at great speed when he got down to it, he was easily beguiled by a detective story or the latest Georgette Heyer, a visit to the pub or gossiping with a guest. Also, he talked endlessly to Patience and quite a bit to me. All these factors are likely to have contributed to the fact that his next book did not appear until 1962. In addition he chose, or Fabers' persuaded him, to change periods dramatically and write about England between the last two wars. He had done some work on this for the *Story of England*, which extended to the coronation of the present Queen, but it was not in his bones as the seventeenth century was, and the reading he undertook was extensive. *Britain's Locust Years* followed his usual fashion, being some 300 pages as opposed to the 600 of what was then seen as the definitive work on the period, written by C. L. Mowat. Bill cheerfully acknowledged his debt to Mowat, and reviewers mostly commended the sharpened focus of a shorter work.

Alan Taylor reviewed the book entertainingly in the *New Statesman*. He began his piece by exploring the idea that the period had not been as bleak as it had been painted. Having praised the readability of Bill's book, he goes on: 'As his title suggests, he started out with the conventional picture of the wasted years. Much of this picture has crumbled under the impact of his sharp and questing mind. He has discovered two heroes, no doubt to his own annoyance. They are Ramsay MacDonald and Stanley Baldwin. I fear he is right. They were, of all the statesmen during my lifetime, the two I most disliked. Yet I must confess that they did more than anyone else to turn England into the happy, civilised country it is now.' Later in the review Alan says: 'Towards the end, Mr McElwee slips back into "contemporary" attitudes, and cheers for Churchill. The historian ought rather to explain why so few cheered at the time. Mr McElwee quotes contemptuously Chamberlain's claim that he had saved the Czechs for a happier future. It was no doubt a foolish and offensive thing to say. Yet I wonder, looking at what happened between 1939 and 1945, whether there was not something to be said for being a "betrayed" Czech rather than a "guaranteed" Pole. The British people saved their honour in 1939. They did not save Poland. Indeed it was the Poles who paid the price for British heroics.' Alan ends his review by saying: 'Mr McElwee says, in his preface, that I may be exasperated by some of his conclusions. I wish I could be exasperated by more of them.'

J. R. Campbell reviewed the book for the *Daily Worker* and takes Bill to task for his description of events connected with the General Strike, of which he, Campbell, was part. He shows greater enthusiasm for Bill's treatment of the thirties and ends by writing: 'The upshot is that Mr McElwee has written a very exciting political book but his judgements are very mixed indeed.' Almost certainly the book sold less well than it deserved, given the reviews. It was not easy to write, Bill saying that judging a period through which you have lived yourself requires disciplined analysis. I think he succeeded, but I am frustrated that I cannot remember what he himself did during the General Strike.

The serious novel that Patience had promised in her immediately post-war interview with a Sussex paper took some years to appear. Probably the book she had trailed to local journalists while she was still living at Shadwells, had been rejected since *Pride of Place*, published in 1950, was inspired by events that occurred at Stowe following their return. The hero is a young man returning to teach at a public school at which he had been both pupil and teacher before the war. He is put in charge of a house containing his younger brother, a boy who has suffered from a self-centred mother and a rackety London life. Simon is almost seduced by his tutor, a brilliant, but destructive man.

This character was based on a master called Peter Wiener, who arrived at Stowe in 1946 after an immensely exciting war, probably

199

as part of the Special Operations Executive. He spoke completely fluent French and German and apparently undertook a series of hair-raising exploits with the French Resistance. Schoolmastering must have seemed tame after this, but he was, apparently, an exciting if irresponsible teacher. Alan Caiger-Smith was taken up by him and describes how he and another Stoic visited Paris, where he found himself abandoned in the city's most notorious homosexual nightclub. Peter and the other boy had disappeared and Alan, a beautiful 17-year-old, was left to extract himself as best he could. Peter Wiener and Edward Capel Cure were friends, and Alan also recalls being part of their late-night drinking sessions when they would gossip uninhibitedly about staff and pupils. Alan was never caught. However, another boy, emerging drunk from Peter Wiener's rooms, was apprehended and expelled. Peter Wiener was sacked immediately.

Alan Caiger-Smith remembers Wiener's charm, intellectual stimulation and the fun to be had with him in a Paris café, when he would use his linguistic skills to adopt different characters, drawing in other diners. Patience, however, judging by her book, was implacable in her dislike. There are no redeeming features in her characterisation, which is a weakness of the book since it becomes difficult to understand why the man is so seductive. The picture she paints of him is also deeply anti-Semitic, though she does attempt to leaven and explain when the younger brother, excusing the Wiener character's behaviour to his brother, says: 'He's so possessive you see. I suppose it comes from his race having been homeless and possessionless for thousands of years. He wants his friends completely. Whether he has got a further kink that makes him discard them once he's got them, I don't know.' Another character in the book that appears to be a target for bitter anger is the Headmaster's daughter, who becomes engaged to the hero. She appears sympathetic early in the book, but as the story progresses, becomes thoroughly unpleasant, the repository for Patience's dislike of other master's wives. She was generally vituperative about these, apparently despising them for being middle-class and uninterested in the boys. I think she feared their disapproval and aimed at getting her blow in first.

In spite of the prejudices, however, *Pride of Place* was one of her best books. It was, as always, beautifully written, other characters were vivid and rounded, while the pictures she created, both of the country school and postwar London, were real and lively. She got mostly good reviews, including one in the *Yorkshire Post* that perceptively notes that the female characters are less convincing than the male, and, in the *Oxford Mail*, an incredible eulogy from S. P. B. Mais. He writes: 'I am going to find it difficult to speak with moderation about this novel. I have never before heard of Patience McElwee. It is to my mind almost impossible to believe that any woman could know so much of what goes on behind the scenes in a boys' public school as is betrayed in *Pride of Place*. Presumably her father or husband is a public-school master. Even so... The next thing I find difficult not to overpraise is her architecture. This is one of the neatest examples of novel planning that I have ever come across. It is about as perfectly constructed as Salisbury Cathedral.'

There was probably at least one rejection before the publication of *Wintersweet* in 1954, but thereafter she established something of a formula and brought out a book at least annually for the next seven years. Only one of the adult novels lived up to *Pride of Place*, though they were all well-written and highly readable. Her heroes were invariably bad-tempered and good at concealing the affection they felt for the heroine. Possibly there were aspects of her father in them, but Mr Rochester and Heathcliff were her fundamental models, with her life-enhancing humour tempering both the romance and irritability, thus avoiding any saccharine quality. The sexual tension is generated verbally, with very little description of physical contact. Patience's belief in marriage as the only real future for a woman underpins all the books and is illustrated in a snatch of dialogue in *Gainfully Employed*, written in 1955. The hero says: 'If I told you all the qualities I wanted in a wife you might ask me what I had to offer in exchange.' 'I shouldn't,' says the heroine, 'I'm old-fashioned enough to believe men confer a favour on women by asking them in marriage.' 'Do you really think that?' he asks, 'Most people nowadays believe or claim to, in the equality of the sexes, and poor old marriage seems the Cinderella of the professions.' To which she replies: 'Perhaps I shall believe in the equality of the sexes when I am too old to fall in love.' Later in the book, she says to the hero: 'I expect my desires are the same as anyone else's who hasn't seriously started to look for a husband instead of waiting for one to come along. A combination of Sir Galahad and Mr Rochester; a mixture of integrity and brutality, and by the time marriage has become an economic or emotional necessity one is able to make do quite happily with someone like George.' (A minor, unattractive character in the book.) The heroines are generally well-bred but down on their luck, while the heroes are upper-class and mostly well-off. Though the love affair in *Gainfully Employed* is tiresome, the book contains a vivid and moving description of the end of the summer season in a seaside town, describing the ponies giving occasional rides to chilled children and landladies anxious to accommodate what few visitors remain. Situations involving genteel poverty inspired some of her best writing.

Wintersweet, which S. P. B. Mais thought should have been nominated as a Book of the Month, is different in that the heroine is a widow with a 16-year-old son. It is written in the first person, and in one revealing passage the narrator contemplates another character, a woman with an only daughter. 'She was so determined, and she seemed to have all the attributes of success that I knew were lacking in myself. She knew what she wanted and how to get it, and, most enviable trait of all, remained satisfied when she had it. She never looked over her shoulder, I was sure; never feared remorse, shame, a mortal illness, or even ridicule. The possession of an only child did not tear at her bowels. I could not imagine her suffering searing anxiety at children's parties. She would bear unmoved the failure in competitive games. She would have seen Shirley off to school with a calm that was not assumed, because Shirley would be making such nice friends there and learning to correct the slight flatness of her accent. Not for her the misery of the last night of the holidays, with the gala supper and the treat that turned to sawdust.'

Time's Fool, published in 1957, also featured a widow with an only child, a daughter this time. The heroine Kate, a romantic novelist, in love with the local landowner, wants her daughter to marry his son, a consummation that just fails to happen. The daughter has been given a formal boarding school and Oxford education, but had failed to get as good a degree as she hoped, found a dull job, and, having jilted the suitable son, ends up living with an undesirable man. Perhaps Patience was convincing herself of the rightness of their decision over my education. The book also contains another regular character of Patience's, the hard-boiled, still beautiful, middle-aged woman who behaves badly, generally by leaving home and husband. Divorce packed a powerful stigma in the fifties, and I can remember feeling that people whom I otherwise loved and admired were seriously flawed by having been divorced. While it made no difference to their friendships, Bill and Patience were deeply disapproving in principle, and this came through strongly in her novels. In *Time's Fool*, this woman denies Kate her happy ending by returning to her ex-husband, but the final gloom is leavened on the last page when Kate takes a sheet of paper and, with a deep sense of satisfaction, begins a new book.

The year before *Time's Fool* appeared, however, Patience had produced a pony book. It was my experiences at Pony Club camp, the nearest I ever came to boarding-school life, that prompted *Match Pair*. It is the story of identical twins sent to stay with their youthful Uncle William while their father, a diplomat, is sent somewhere insalubrious. They are expected to ride unruly twin horses and to help William run his ramshackle farm. The essence of the book would have gone straight over the heads of most pony-minded 11- to 14-year-olds since it was fundamentally a splendid caricature of the people running the Grafton Hunt Pony Club. Christopher Kenyon, reviewing the book for *The Stoic*, wrote: 'This is not just another "book about ponies" such as proudly fill the shelves and stagnate the minds of the future county marriage-market, but is in fact a shrewd study of this very class. There is perhaps too much of Mrs McElwee herself in the youthful heroine to whose eyes she has entrusted her own view of that class which still exists in the heart of old England amidst Coca-Cola and chewing-gum, whose sole preoccupation is the keeping and riding of horses, whose only means of educating its young is through the Pony Club.' Patience hugely enjoyed writing the book and it was a joy for those close to her, but it had little chance of commercial success. She wrote two further children's books of considerable charm, but neither sold particularly well. Her humour remained too sophisticated and was not balanced by sufficiently gripping plots.

Judging by a letter from John Attenborough with whom she dealt at her publishers, Hodder and Stoughton, she wanted to continue writing children's books. This was apparently fuelled by her disappointment over the reviews and sales of her 1958 novel, *Malice Domestic*. Attenborough pointed out the range of reviews that she had received, said that though it was a bad year, her sales compared favourably with others, and, with careful wording, that her children's books were unlikely to be successful – sentiments that must regularly trip off publishers' tongues.

I think *Malice Domestic* ranks along with *Pride of Place* as one of her best books, a view shared by the publisher's reader who reported on it. 'I thought this a most successful novel, easily the best Mrs McElwee has written for you. She seems to me at last to have hit the right level. Her book is readable and unpretentious, yet it deals with real people, genuine problems and convincing situations. It has a firm shape, yet one does not feel that plot has been contrived. As always she writes amusingly and the dialogues in particular are very wittily observed, but in this novel she is also writing with sympathy and understanding, and not trying to write down to a public she does not really respect. On its own level this book seems to me an entire success which should be enjoyed by many people.' It was sad that after such a glowing write-up, the book did not do better.

Malice Domestic described a large landowning family struggling with a variety of emotional problems brought to a head by the strains of a wet weekend and organising the annual fête. A central figure is the charming, anxious and selfishly autocratic widowed matriarch. This character, while having rather more iron in her than the prototype who appeared in *Roman Holiday*, is nonetheless a character who has strong echoes of Maudie.

Patience's last published novel, *A House for Olivia*, was initially inspired by an early romantic experience of mine. The heroine, emotionally damaged by a youthful love affair, comtemplates marriage with a man she does not love rather than continue her career as a successful secretary. Patience paints a chilling picture of the likely decline in Olivia's career prospects as her looks and energy fade. However, the portrayal of her intended is so vicious that it is hard to believe she could ever have contemplated the alternative of marrying him. The happy ending is surprising, but improbable.

19

Televison and Politics

In the early fifties, the immediate post-war pressures had eased, the History Side was flourishing, Patience was contributing strongly to the Historians' well-being and had established herself as a novelist, while both she and Bill had become a part of the wider community. At 46 and with the point-to-pointing episode behind him, Bill was ready to explore avenues other than teaching and writing. One of these was his venture into television. Paul Johnstone, who continued to remain closely in touch with Vancouver, had become a successful producer for the BBC. When in 1953 he was charged with producing *The Balloon Game*, in which six panellists had to argue in front of a jury over whom among three famous historical figures should be thrown out of a sinking balloon, he decided that Bill would make a good chairman. Though deeply disapproving of television (he refused all his life to own a set), Bill was unable to resist such a challenge. Twenty-five guineas an appearance would have been an added encouragement.

Patience and I watched the game on the only television in the Street. I retain an impression of a ponderous affair with an over-pedantic Bill, and a pernicious voting system for the jury involving black balls that kept getting stuck in the chutes while Bill encouraged the jury to 'bang it'. Such programmes then went out at erratic intervals, with there being four or five *Balloon Games* between October and March. Before the first programme, Bill was facetiously written up in the *Sunday Chronicle* by Robert Robinson in an article that started: 'A great big watery eye will be on William McElwee next Friday. It is a corporate eye and belongs to a nation gone mad playing parlour games.' Robinson goes on to surmise that Bill will either find himself the 'apple of that big watery eye' or 'the surprised target of abuse.' 'McElwee is confident' he writes.

Of course reaction to the game was much more mixed than Robinson predicted. Jill Craigie, writing in the *Evening Standard*, was rescued by the programme from a dreadful week of viewing and thought that it was 'television at its best', while C.A. Lejeune in the *Observer* reserved judgment. The *Manchester Guardian* was magisterial and patronising, saying: 'To have G. M. Young, Noel Annan, Asa Briggs and several other interesting and knowledgeable people discussing the merits of Bernard Shaw, Mrs Beeton, and King Alfred was quite an achievement for the television service and one that suggests the rest of the series will be well worth seeing.' King Alfred was saved on that occasion.

The next programme pitted Beethoven against Isaac Newton and Florence Nightingale. Some viewers were outraged that Beethoven stayed in, with one person writing in saying that a 'dreadful mistake' had been made, adding that 'if music is divine then Christ would have been a musician.' Queen Elizabeth I beat Captain Scott and Nelson in spite of the fact that A. L. Rowse was deemed to have gone on far too long about her. The only other trio recorded were Lucrezia Borgia, the last Kaiser Wilhelm, and King John, who survived. By the end however, the reviews were dire, and an episode planned for May 1954 was dropped. Noel Annan thinks it was a 'footling game' and that he as a panellist 'was perfectly hopeless'. Since he was one of the few who were asked to take part more than once, this modesty is certainly misplaced. The reviews say little about Bill's skill as a chairman, though one mentions his improved grasp of the system which suggests that, not surprisingly, it took him time to get used to the medium that must then have been developing along with those taking part. What comes across strongly now is how amateurish it all was. I still have some of the scripts with pencilled comments from Paul, and these, together with his letters setting the whole thing up, suggest a wonderfully casual, cosy approach. The contrast with the current slick technology is so great that it is impossible to make comparative judgments. Overall, some of the programmes were clearly successful and Bill got much enjoyment from taking part. He met historians whom he admired, liked Nancy Spain who defended Mrs Beeton, and was taken up for a time by Gilbert Harding.

If he was disappointed that *The Balloon Game* folded, Bill soon had local fish to fry. It must have been at about this time that he became Chairman of the Governors of the Royal Latin School, a most successful grammar school in Buckingham. Bill was effective in this role,

206

which lasted some years, and found it another source of enjoyment. It naturally pleased him that Eric Reynolds, his own Headmaster at Stowe, was a Governor under his chairmanship. He was full of enthusiasm for the annual productions of Gilbert and Sullivan operas that they staged and, to my later chagrin, was just as encouraging to the girls in the school as the boys.

George Embleton, the Headmaster of the Latin School, was valued not only for the success of his school, but also for being able to tell the story of how, as a gunnery officer in the Navy, he had managed on D-Day, to 'miss France'. He was clearly concerned about my education and would lend me esoteric critiques of English language and literature. Not having done the preparatory work in these areas, I found these books baffling and would desperately hope that he would not question me about my reading. It was probably because of this local connection that Bill became a member of the managing committee that organised a sixteenth-century fair in Buckingham to celebrate the Quatercentenary of the granting of a Charter to the town by Mary Tudor. The headmasters of the secondary modern school and the Catholic boys' college were also part of this committee, and Bill would recall how gloomy he felt at their first meeting which seemed destined to be woefully formal. His gloom deepened when the Catholic Father arrived carrying a large briefcase, but was wholly lifted when the case proved to contain nothing but a bottle of whisky. The whole atmosphere changed and they got down to planning a procession and tableau of Mary Tudor's visit, some appropriate dancing, a few sideshows and the roasting of a whole ox by the official hangman. He was possibly better at his day job, since the ox took much longer than expected to cook and, even when it was declared done, remained very rare indeed. The evening ended with the burning of a witch – in effigy, something that was probably Bill's idea. Many more people turned up than expected, there was not really enough for them to do and the Council wrangled for months afterwards about the bills, but on the whole, the evening was declared a success.

My increasing involvement in show-jumping provided Bill with another much relished role, as a collecting-ring father. With his cap at an even more rakish angle than usual, he would gather with the farming and horse-coping parents of children who were infinitely more professional than I was. Among the fathers there was tremendous camaraderie and at least an appearance of philosophy when their offspring failed, but the mothers, apart from Patience, were much more ruthless. Patience agonised over my efforts and would probably have much preferred not to come. Heroically, she would watch rather than hide in the car, and never actually reveal how much she minded for me. To them both it was almost more important that I should be a good loser than that I should win, though Bill did get exasperated when I twice took the wrong course. He made me play 'Kim's game' endlessly which successfully cured me. Alex Tait, my riding teacher, said that I had a 'ring complex', which meant that I became paralysed by nerves and failed to do my mounts justice.

I did win the occasional rosette against some good ponies and riders, but I was better at schooling horses when there was no element of performance. For a brief period I became friends with Jan White, one of the most successful among the young people riding then. I went to stay with her and witnessed her mother's fury when Jan had one fence down at the Horse of the Year Show. The storm raged all the way home: Jan was to give up riding, Full Cry, her brilliant pony, was to be sold and regular school was to be Jan's fate. Passionately partisan on Jan's behalf, I suggested that we teach her mother a lesson by dismantling the massive display of prizes and rosettes. 'That'll teach her,' I remarked when we had finished. Within 24 hours the whole thing had blown over and my remark was treated as a huge family joke.

Given this experience and his local connections, Bill got roped in by the local show in Buckingham to provide commentary on the showjumping competitions. Buckingham Show epitomised local agricultural shows and provided a much-enjoyed day out for the farming fraternity. Not only horses were on show, but also cattle, sheep, flowers, produce and dogs. Before the jumping began there would be a parade of prize winners, where the beautifully plaited and oiled show horses would vie for attention with magnificent and unwieldy bulls, who were led on inadequate-looking rope halters and were eyed with much apprehension. The flowers and produce would include the inevitably vast marrows, limp-looking gardens in plates constructed by local children, and vases of blowzy roses. Prizes in these competitions and the dog show were rosettes worn on the lapels by the winners.

Alcohol flowed, and Bill was kept well supplied with whisky to prevent his voice from drying up. His immaculate diction never sounded blurred as he announced each competitor, but by the time his stint was over and he was able to head for serious drinking in the National

Farmers' Union tent, he was generally in excellent form. This tent was the hub of the show. In the late afternoon of one show we met Lil Wheeler, matriarch of the remarkable farming family. Placidly she told us that she had received word that her husband Chubb had started to sing in the NFU tent, and that she rather thought it was time to take him home. George Morgan, descendant of one of the several local Welsh farmers who had dropped off the old sheep trail from Wales to London, was, on one occasion, shovelled into the back of his own cattle truck by his disrespectful sons following a session in the tent.

It was in the NFU tent at the end of one show that Bill came face to face with Robert Maxwell. This was the first year that Maxwell stood as Labour candidate for Buckingham, and he clearly viewed the Show as a good place to canvas. He had pinned a large red rosette to his lapel, and Bill, instantly and loudly, wanted to know what he had won it for. The NFU tent must have been something of a lions' den for Maxwell, since those drinking there were likely to be Tory to a man and woman. Chubb Wheeler was also present and suggested that Maxwell might buy him a drink. Maxwell refused on the grounds that such a gesture might be seen as an inducement. Chubb told him that was no problem: 'You can buy me a drink and I still won't vote for you,' he said cheerfully.

Bill, having always been a committed Tory, was most disapproving when the father of two of my particular friends put a 'Vote Labour' sign in his front window. Thus he supported Frank Markham, the worthy if rather dull Tory candidate for Buckingham, and was delighted to be asked to speak at an eve of poll meeting in Buckingham Town Hall. His task, upon which he entered with zest, was to keep the assembled voters happy until the candidate arrived to speak. He did this largely by abusing Maxwell, who had made the mistake of saying that he felt he had been sent by God to represent the interests of the people of Buckingham. Bill's line was to ask his audience to consider other phenomena supposedly sent by the Almighty, and to speculate on which of the plagues of Egypt Maxwell resembled. He relished hecklers, responding to a continuous, eldritch shriek of 'What about the Rent Act?' with 'What about the Rent Act, indeed?' and evading an actual answer. On that occasion Maxwell lost and at a post-poll party, someone came up to Patience and said: 'Do go and be nice to Walter (Frank Markham's agent), he is the only member of the team whom Maxwell has not served with a writ and he is feeling so out of it.' Though, with hindsight, traces of what was to come can then be

209

seen in Maxwell's behaviour, there was also a nasty undercurrent of chauvinism and anti-Semitism in the campaign against him. Bill and Patience certainly joined in condemning the possible representation of Buckingham by a Czech Jew.

Elections were taken very seriously in Buckingham, and during each campaign I would not be on speaking terms with the daughters of the declared Labour voter. The first declaration of poll that I remember must have been 1950, when Frank Markham lost to Aidan Crawley. Counting was not the speedy affair of these days, and the result was not announced until nearly noon, when the returning officer would come out onto the balcony of the Town Hall to address a large crowd assembled in the market square. Feelings ran high and I, who was clutching the lead of a bulldog we owned at the time, his collar decorated with a large blue bow, was hissed by the large number of Labour supporters. I burst into tears and announced that I did not like elections. This incident turned into one of Patience's much relished stories.

Another of her favourite election tales was of the time that she managed to arrange for the Conservative candidate to address the Stowe domestic staff gathered in a depressing area generally hidden from parents and known as the Power House Yard. She somehow failed to make the same arrangement for Aidan Crawley, who was known to Bill and Patience, and on that occasion, the Conservative won by 54 votes – the exact number of staff eligible to vote. Bill maliciously described Aidan Crawley as being exactly half-witted'. Patience also enjoyed the occasion when one candidate turned up in Dadford in a loudspeaker van, parked by the telephone box in the centre of the village, and made a long speech promising endless economic goodies to an audience consisting entirely of the herd of bullocks grazing in an adjacent field. They were apparently rivetted, breathing ever deeper as each commitment was made.

Bill belonged very much to the one-nation Tory tradition, though his connections with Alan Taylor and Dick Crossman were far stronger than with Quintin Hailsham, to whom he had been close at Oxford. His loyalty to the Tories, though, clearly wavered in 1956. A letter to him from Dick Crossman suggests that they should meet: 'Then I should be able to satisfy my curiosity over what it is precisely about the present administration which drives you to the desperate remedy of wishing prosperity to my kind of politics!' The obvious cause of Bill's disaffection would have been Suez, and perhaps it was what he saw as the Government's failure to follow through that got to him. He was alarmingly militant when it all blew up, being rude about the Egyptians and giving up the *Observer* because of their stand against the British actions. The political balance in *Britain's Locust Years* was exemplary, however, and it was only late in life that he lost some of the historian's perspective on politics, becoming deeply gloomy about the state of the world. He would have been appalled by Thatcherism, by sleaze and by the determination of politicians to hang on to office at all costs. William Whitelaw was probably the last politician he admired, his view being enhanced by the fact that they had met while both were fighting successfully across Normandy. He was opposed to Britain joining the European Union, largely on the grounds that in ceasing to offer favourable trading concessions to the Commonwealth countries like Australia and New Zealand, Britain was letting down those who had supported her so strongly during the war, something about which he felt quite passionately. Heath was therefore unpopular with him, but as much for his accent as his politics.

Labour politicians with regional accents were fine, Conservatives should not flatten their vowels. Bill and Patience waged an endless, Nancy Mitford-like war on middle-class words and expressions, in particular bitterly condemning the use of 'pardon' and 'toilet'. 'Settee', 'lounge', 'mirror' and 'notepaper' were out, and any kind of decor or object not considered quite right was labelled 'Pont Street'. Their attitude was slightly mitigated by their delighted collection of snobbish absurdities. The family favourite was the edict of one smart Ascot mother of a debutante, who told her daughter that she would be socially ruined if she had a bath at night or drank her coffee white. This story originated with Christopher Cash, a happy chronicler of the smart world who was probably also responsible for 'Pont Street'.

Both Bill and Patience had a strong sense of the gradations of class. They valued titles, and enjoyed the period when the Count Zamoyski and the Knight of Glin were both on the History Side. Patience in particular relished the romantic history of aristocratic families and would know their origins, seeing a recently created duke as being of lesser status than an ancient barony. In this they were aided and abetted by Iain Moncreiffe, the prewar historian who labelled himself 'the Arch-Snob' and once explained to me how much longer his family had occupied their Scottish lands than had the ancestors of his then wife, for all that she was the Countess of Errol and Hereditary High Constable of Scotland. Patience also had a passion for the history of the Raj, being a great fan of Kipling and loving the idea of British India combined with the Indian princes. Black people were then pretty well unknown in Buckingham and its environs, so the issue of racism rarely arose. Their attitude to black Africans and Afro-Caribbeans was, therefore, until they went to the Royal Military Academy in the early sixties, in the abstract. They would certainly deplore explicit racism, but would casually remark of someone with a dark skin, 'a touch of the tar-brush there, I should think,' – just as they would deplore overt anti-Semitism, but would say things like 'they may call themselves Colquhoun now, but I bet they started life as Cohen.' Africa was not a place that caught Patience's imagination as India did, but later in his life Bill said that were he younger and fitter, he would love to become involved in African affairs. Quite what he envisaged doing, I never discovered. At the same time he apparently agreed with the proposition that Africa should be left entirely alone for a hundred years so that it might sort itself out.

Their attitudes were very much of their generation, and remained paternalistic partly through the ignorance that continues to pervade some country areas. No black people were living locally, and I do not, at that time, remember any at Stowe. I was brought up to have a rather patronising attitude, but was entirely without the sort of fear that caused a young woman whom I knew briefly, to say that she would be unable to approach a black person in the street. Bill certainly showed the conventional appreciation of the sporting achievements of black people, which were then only just coming to prominence, but their interest in national sport was limited. Patience remained passionate about racing and Bill had some interest in international rugger, but otherwise for both of them their sporting involvement was purely local. Living in a school meant that rugby and cricket were regularly watched, particularly when there were one or more Historians in either team. Having members of either first team on the History Side was regarded as adding greatly to its status. Rugby meant cold feet on wet duckboards while observing the mixed success of the First Fifteen in their garish royal blue and gold-banded shirts, while cricket was often almost equally chilly and of similarly mixed fortune, while being infinitely more boring. Despite cold or boredom, however, distant away matches would be attended if either Patience or I minded about a particular boy. Patience spent rugby matches disapproving of other master's wives who shouted their support to the Stowe team,

212

and, when watching cricket, expected unoccupied Historians to come and entertain her.

Every summer the Historians were expected to play a cricket match against a Dadford team. This idea and its execution showed Bill at his most squirearchical. A cherry-and-white cap was specially designed for the Historians and sold through the school shop, while I still possess the battered and symbolic Historians' cricket bat. The Stowe kitchens would provide tea, and Bill would buy a barrel of beer to be consumed after the match. This event never took place on any of the manicured Stowe pitches, but always in one of two local fields, which sometimes still contained the resident cattle. Hitting a cow was six and out. One of these fields had a hazardous bog and the other sloped sharply away from one boundary edge, so at least one extra ball was essential. It was not quite the kind of idyllic village green envisaged by John Major. Both teams showed wildly fluctuating ability, with members of the First Eleven generally doing very badly. Scoring tended to be low, though on one occasion a Dadford player achieved 38. Total scores only once topped a hundred, and Bill liked the margin either way to be as close as possible. The most exciting occasion was when the Historians won by one run after their final bowler, a Belgian called Eric Le Jeune, who normally never played cricket, took out the last three Dadford batsmen with a hat-trick. David Mann, a fifties Historian, presented the cricket team with a proper scoring book which I learnt to fill in, though without emulating Patience's prewar feat of giving her side victory by inadvertently adding the date to the final score.

One of Bill's other regular summer activities was the Staff College Battlefield Tour. Officers deemed sufficiently talented to be considered for staff jobs are, when aged about 30, sent off to the College to learn about tactics, strategy and generally how to manage armies. Part of their studies includes examining particular campaigns in detail, and for some years one of these was Normandy in 1944. The campaign was then sufficiently recent for the participants to be available to describe the events, and together with the students, they were taken off for the inside of a week on what, to outside observers, appeared a massive 'jolly'. The battles would be described on the ground by a mixture of still-serving soldiers and 'guest-artists', of whom Bill was one. The bridges over the River Odon would be visited and, after one of the senior Commanders had described the battle plans, Bill would prop himself on a shooting stick and give his view of what had happened on the ground when all their beautiful plans went wrong. That was during the day. In the evening the local inhabitants would vie with one another in expressing their continuing appreciation of their liberation while old comrades reminisced. Bill would return to Stowe with a hangover of monumental proportions.

Taking time off from the school for the tours seems to have caused no problems until the late fifties when, possibly, Donald Crichton-Miller, the then Headmaster, was difficult about it. The upshot was that, in order to minimise Bill's time away, he would be collected in a helicopter which landed on the South Front. This added enormously to Bill's kudos and entranced the boys. On Bill's Stowe file are two letters from General Hewetson, then Commandant of the Staff College, thanking the Headmaster for allowing Bill the time away. In the first written in 1959, he was lyrical:

'He made all the difference to this particular presentation and our students were fascinated and inspired by what he had to say, and they learnt a great deal from him. He is as you know a marvellous raconteur, and this combined with the fact that he has a very proud and noble story to tell makes his description of the battle really memorable. By listening to him the students were able to get the atmosphere and feel of the battle most vividly.'

The second, written the following year was briefer, but equally enthusiastic. After the formal typed paragraphs, General Hewetson had scrawled: 'Does he talk "in school" as much as he does "out" of it?!' To that letter Crichton-Miller replied: 'Thank you for your letter. I am so pleased that you were able to make use of Bill McElwee. It does him a lot of good. Yes, he talks without ceasing, both in school and out!'

20

Friends

Buckingham Show was also a treat for PC Petty, the man responsible for law and order in Dadford and the surrounding villages. His patch was a huge rural one, and he covered it by attending every race-meeting, meet of hounds and horse show, as well as a huge variety of social events. His transport was a small motorcycle, though he had a van for occasions when he was really off-duty. This, though, was never an easy distinction to make. He invariably turned up to the after-play party in the Queens Temple and somehow sniffed out my tenth birth-day party, which was a rather adult evening meal. I do not recall that his being in uniform was ever a bar to his accepting a pint of beer. Official visits to Vancouver were always to remind Bill to renew his gun licence, but concern was never expressed about where and how the guns were kept – propped in a corner of the study, as it happened, with the front door permanently unlocked. Once a police officer other than Petty came to see him about the licence and expressed concern about these casual arrangements. Bill was intensely irritated and did nothing to improve the security.

Petty had a boon companion in the force who ran his patch in much the same way, resulting in both men being hauled in front of their superiors because of their failure to make any arrests. Nettled, they went out and pulled in two Americans from the local airbase who had parked illegally in Buckingham. The truth was that Petty knew his patch so well that potential trouble was often headed off, and he had been known to sit up all night with people in distress. Of course it cannot have been as idyllic as it seems in retrospect, but there was very little overtly serious crime. There was one adult in Dadford who used intermittently to disappear briefly from circulation, and a youth who was occasionally part of my gang and who stole my mother's diamond engagement ring during a period when it was not in the hands of Coutts as security against her overdraft. He subsequently swopped it for 50 cigarette cards. Violence between adult males caused less concern then and poaching, if limited, was to some extent tolerated. No doubt domestic violence and the abuse of children took place largely unchecked. Some years after leaving Stowe, I returned with my husband for a dance. We stayed with the farming Wheelers, and much of the early evening was spent regaling David with stories about Petty and his party-going. To my enormous delight, the first person we saw when we arrived at the dance was PC Petty, who had some-how managed to be part of the official security, but was really there to see everyone.

One of Petty's fans was another constant figure at Vancouver, Christabel, Lady Ampthill. Christabel had remained a family friend long after her son Geoffrey left Stowe in the thirties, and was a com-pletely original personality. A biography of her written by Eileen Hunter details her fearlessness, her lack of convention and her ability to live totally in the present without ever expressing a shred of regret over the events of her life. Almost any other woman in the world would have been marked for life by the trauma of her divorce case. Christabel apparently went through the initial court case, a lost appeal and a final triumph in the House of Lords with remarkable strength, shrugging off any suggestion that it might have been a strain by saying that her knowledge that she was in the right sustained her throughout.

Her husband, John Russell, stated that their son Geoffrey could not possibly be his because they had never achieved full intercourse. She was adamant in saying that she had slept with no one else, and it was contended on her behalf that Geoffrey had been conceived during what were described as 'incomplete relations'. Christabel herself described them as 'hunnish scenes'. A number of co-respondents were cited and eliminated, with the eventual verdict being that she had committed adultery with an unknown man. Since she led a very separate life from her husband, went dancing almost every night and was happy enough to spend the night at a man's lodgings when she had lost her key, it is hardly surprising that, in 1922, this was the jury's conclusion. Possibly they were sceptical of medical evidence stating that, in spite of her pregnancy, an examination showed her to be still a virgin. A formidable legal team battled it out, with Marshall Hall appearing for John Russell while Patrick Hastings represented Christabel. Her case was eventually won in the Lords on a legal technicality regarding the admissibility of John Russell's evidence. Bill and Patience always said that she waited until he inherited the title before divorcing John Russell, but in fact proceedings had already been instigated before his father died.

Clearly she was remarkably unconventional, but also, in Eileen Hunter's view, innocent. In an article about her which must have been written in 1975, Catherine Stott quotes Christabel as saying, 'I always adored the *company* of men, but it was so pure. You see nothing is more sacred than somebody who knows nothing of life. The only proposals I have ever had have been courteous proposals of marriage. And if anyone *had* said anything to me I wouldn't have known what they were talking about, because I hadn't the faintest idea of what any of it was. I never thought about it and that's why I had such a perfect youth. There was nothing wicked or unkind. So go on keeping your children knowing nothing. Not going to school saved us – we never met any of those horrid little gels who delight in telling each other frightful stories.'

The intrusion of at least a partial reality in the shape of a husband must have been a shock, and when I was about 12 she said to me with strong feeling, 'men are such brutes', which confirmed how deeply distasteful the 'hunnish scenes' had been to her. She told Eileen Hunter that she had married to stop men 'pestering her'. Her ruse did not succeed. Men continued to adore her and remained devoted for years fulfilling her outrageous demands, but only permitted to worship from afar. She was devoted to Geoffrey, and Eileen Hunter describes wonderful hair-raising holidays that he had with her. In reality, she was in the position of many single parents now, in having to provide for him and herself as there was little Russell money – even if she had been offered or accepted any – and she did not come from a wealthy background.

She supported herself by running a highly successful dress shop in Mayfair simply called Christabel Russell, where the designs were made up to fit each purchaser and were expensive. She was able to indulge her passion for hunting, often through riding other people's horses offered to her to either train or sell. Riding sidesaddle, she would take on the most difficult creatures and produce them behaving themselves immaculately and looking wonderful. Given the force of her personality, I cannot imagine how I withstood her determination that I too should ride sidesaddle. Christabel also enjoyed buying houses, doing them up and selling them at a profit. Eileen Hunter quotes Geoffrey as saying that he never knew where he would be living during the school holidays. In spite of all this physical activity and her refusal to learn to read before she was 12, she was erudite and educated in the widest sense. Bill sent her a copy of *The House*, and she responded by writing:

Bill dear your book has filled me with delight. I spent a quite entrancing day reading it – a terrible cold in the head became a pleasure. Your poetry is like Meltis walking.

I wish it were really less good as it is only the Ethel M. Dells of this world who seem to make big money and I do so want Patience to dress exclusively at C.R. Ltd!

Love to you both,

Chris.

It is a letter that is hard to beat for concise charm.

When I first met her, she had a pretty house in Kent which was a touch olde-worlde, but with a lovely garden complete with a stream and, very grandly for those days, a swimming pool. We went to stay with her in the summer holidays on several occasions, probably staying for a week at a time. Life there was a constant obstacle race, with Christabel going off to work each morning, leaving written instructions as to what we were to do in her absence. Bill and I would be detailed to exercise at least one horse and pony, while Patience would be told to graze another horse in the orchard without allowing him to eat the fallen plums. This was impossible, as the fruit was all over the grass and the horse had a passion for them. Only Christabel's formidable will could have forced Patience to overcome her terror of horses sufficiently to undertake this task, but even she could not prevent the consumption of plums. Other fruit had to be picked and a number of tasks completed before her return, at which point a different round of activity would begin. Meals were mostly eaten out of doors, which meant a literally running battle with wasps.

Christabel's passion for the open air did mean that I was once allowed to sleep outside, which was a huge delight, in spite of much concern from Patience about whether I would be warm enough. The sound of the running brook with a range of nocturnal animal noises is an enduring memory. I was still unable to swim at this time, but baulked of being able to persuade either of my parents to swim, Christabel would insist that I went into the pool whatever the weather.

I also suffered from an invariable supper of cornflakes and stewed fruit, until one evening Patience managed to sneak into the kitchen and fry me some delicious potato cakes. Christabel neither drank nor smoked, but presumably endured my parent's cigarettes. Possibly they provided their own drink as I cannot imagine that, even for Christabel, they would have suffered an alcohol-free week. Once when staying at Vancouver, shivering in our draughty dining-room, she remarked, 'Darlings, if you only gave up gin, you could afford central heating,' a plea that fell on deaf ears. Feeling the cold and an inability to deal with animal (and probably human) vomit were her only weaknesses.

Of course, Christabel's charm, sense of humour and huge zest for life outweighed the exhausting struggle to keep up with her and her dictatorial behaviour. Bill and Patience in fact managed to stand up to her successfully, which made it possible for her to stay at Vancouver for much of one winter when she was hunting regularly with the Bicester Hounds. In the visitors' book she has signed once for the period October 1954 to April 1955. She must have been a paying guest in order to cover the constant electric fire and her appetite, which was enormous and legendary. Catherine Stott describes her as 'eating like a horse' and asking Ms Stott when she refused a third helping, if she 'was off her feed?' She never put on an ounce, no doubt burning up an enormous amount of calories by her constant activity. She would dash in and out, exciting a mixture of apprehension and delight in me, enchanting the boys and bemusing any other adult visitors.

I was at times her slave and also her companion on a number of cross-country expeditions concerned mainly with horses. Her car was an elegant, silvery, open Lea Francis, a make that has long since vanished from the market. She kept the hood down in almost all weathers, which helped keep my inherited motion sickness at bay, and would allow me to sit on her lap and steer the car, an indication of her enormous encouragement of children, whom she treated as equal companions in whatever adventure she was planning. She never patronised or talked down to them, though she would cheerfully put them at risk. A friend of mine has never forgotten an occasion when, bicycling to see us, she was overtaken by Christabel in the Lea Francis. Seizing Diana's hand, Christabel towed her along the road for some miles. She would also play up to silly jokes. When living in Kent she had a lovely solid, friendly white cat called Syringa. One summer I decided he was rather grand and christened him Sir Ringa. The next Christmas we got a card from her on which she had had printed: 'From Christabel Lady Ampthill and Sir Ringa'.

Christabel was enormously elegant, always appearing beautifully dressed and made up, with her long, immaculate honey-coloured hair done in a perfect bun. The cut of a riding habit mattered enormously to her, and she once whipped a riding skirt off some wretched woman at the end of a day's hunting and took it off to London, announcing that it did not fit at all and that she knew just the person to make the necessary adjustment. However, her natural figure did not conform to her standard of elegance, and she once delighted us when she came down to breakfast on a hunting day, looked at herself in the mirror, and announced crossly, 'Damn. I shall have to alter either my bosom or my stock.' She was not amused, however, when an inquisitive cat extracted her false bosom from her suitcase and dragged it round the house. Deportment mattered too, and she came into my bedroom once when we were staying with her in Kent, to give me a lecture and demonstration on how to sit properly with knees or ankles crossed, but never with knees apart.

She would have been coming up to 60 when she spent the winter with us though until she was nearly 80, she refused to admit to more than 58, her fitness and energy making this an entirely plausible claim. She had broken every bone in her body, some of them more than once, including having cracked her skull three times. When she was well over 70, a frustrated letter from her complained that she had 'fallen into a pit', and the resultant skull fracture had caused her to miss *three weeks* hunting. Her age and earlier youthful behaviour not withstanding, she had become ruthless about propriety, once descending on us late at night because one of her admirers, with whom she had been to a dance, was expecting her to spend the night in his house unchaperoned. He had an unfortunate name, which inspired Bill to remark 'That's not a person, Chris, that's something you get a plumber in to see to.' Bill and Patience bravely took her to a Grafton Hunt Ball, and she disconcerted Eric Reynolds, the then Headmaster of Stowe, and a fellow guest, by replying to an offer of more coffee by saying, 'Oh, but it might keep me awake at the Ball.' I suspect she got more enjoyment from the time she accompanied us to the domestic staff's annual Christmas Dance. She took this occasion entirely seriously, dressed up to the nines, and was delighted to be asked to judge the competitions for the 'prettiest lady' and 'most handsome man'. With unerring skill, she chose PC Petty as the winner of this last.

It was on a day when Christabel was hunting with the Bicester that the event occurred upon which Bill dined out most happily. I, then aged eleven, was also hunting with the Grafton, and while riding along the road to the meet, on a pony in fact bestowed on me by Christabel, my liking for running water led me to look down into a stream. To my amazement there was the body of a man lying face down and fully clothed in water that was just deep enough to run over him. No person or building being anywhere near, I flagged down the first car that came along, which luckily turned out to contain a phlegmatic, but helpful man who decided that the body was very dead and said that he would drive to Westbury, which was where dear PC Petty lived, and report the matter. Feeling that I had acted responsibly and realising that I had a good story to tell, I continued on my way. My parents, driving to the meet behind me, came upon a farmer friend looking bright green and trying to control his wildly upset horse. He pointed wordlessly into the water, and they too set out to report the matter, only to find that I had already instigated action. PC Petty would no doubt have been irritated that he was thus unable to join the hunt.

At the meet people kept telling my parents how upset I would be when what I had seen sank in, and by the end of the day their anxiety began to rise. In fact the concern only made me more nauseatingly pleased with myself, and when Christabel returned I rushed out as soon as I heard her car, crying, 'Chris, Chris I found a body today!' 'Darling, how splendid,' said Christabel in her beautifully modulated tones, 'did they give you the mask?' The whole episode was thus both appreciated and deflated most satisfactorily if cruelly. A lengthy report subsequently appeared in the *Buckingham Advertiser*, at which point some awareness of human misery did hit. The man had bicycled all the way from St Albans, pushed his bicycle under the bridge, attempted to slash his wrists and then drowned himself in 12 inches of water. He was described as having been attending a 'Nerve Clinic'.

The pony I was riding on that occasion was the cause of the only occasion when we fell seriously foul of Christabel. How she acquired Twopence I can no longer remember, but when she gave him to me it was seen as an incredibly generous present – and she entirely failed to mention the fact that before I got him, eleven children had fallen off him and had all firmly refused to get on him again. In appearance he was extraordinary, looking rather as if he had been put together from three entirely different animals. His quarters were wide, with sharply defined 'hip' bones, his middle in contrast was rather weedy, but it was his front end that looked particularly strange. He had a massively thick neck with lumpy bits under an inadequate mane, a wide brow and melting brown eyes. His legs were short and stocky, being mostly black in colour while the rest of him was a bright coppery bay with pale beige areas round his muzzle. Sadly no photograph exists of him, but any illustration of Eohippus, the earliest type of horse, gives some idea of his contours. His expression gave an impression of innocence and a desire to please that wholly belied his true nature, and his method of unseating his rider was highly skilled. He would hump his back slightly to unbalance you, then his head would go down and his shoulder drop to the point where there was nothing between you and the ground. Occasionally he added to this heinous behaviour by lashing out at his prone victim. My friend Diana Green has problems with her back to this day thanks to a well-placed kick from Twopence. His only virtue was his phlegm, which meant that virtually nothing frightened him. He was therefore entirely safe to ride out in traffic and wholly unfazed by any whiff of death from the wretched body in the stream, it being a usual equine failing to become upset in the presence of death.

He also had one habit that appealed to me. The parents of Stoics would regularly come to pre-lunch drinks on Sundays to discuss their offspring with my father, and often brought younger daughters. I would be detailed to take these young things all dressed up for Sunday Chapel out to see my ponies, a task I did not much relish. Twopence, liquid-eyed, would nuzzle their smart, velvet-collared tweed coats with apparent affection, and it was only after they moved away that the surgical removal of a button was revealed. Twopence would have swallowed it.

Luckily for me, after being thrown only once, I learnt to read Twopence's mind and realised that he could only buck me off if he got his head down. By ruthlessly preventing this, I managed to control him, at which point Alex Tait decided that, in spite of his ungainly shape, he had the makings of a show-jumper. He could indeed jump considerable heights, but hated doing so and would canter up to a fence, stop and then heave himself over while I got castigated for not kicking him on hard enough. More regularly, he would refuse to jump altogether, which meant that in the show-jumping arena, without Alex threatening him from behind, we got nowhere.

After an exhausting season, during which I never once managed to complete a course, even Alex's optimism failed and it was decided that Twopence was more bother than he was worth. He had not helped his own cause by killing and eating three chickens belonging to the landlord of the Royal Oak in Tingewick, in whose field he was being grazed. He also removed the family washing from the line and ate it. Selling him in the usual way could not be done, since we could not bring ourselves to lie about his antisocial behaviour, so we sent him to the horse and pony sales at Leicester. To horse lovers, selling animals through such sales was seen as terribly cruel, since there could be no guarantee of a good home and proper treatment. Twopence seemed so tough and unpleasant that we felt he could hold his own in any circumstances, and he was duly sold for £40. A friend driving through Leicester some time later, swore that they saw him in a field, as fat as butter and looking as if he were leading a life of complete idleness.

Christabel was livid and wrote my father one of her most stinking letters. I do not think she actually said that she had always known he was not quite a gentleman, which phrase she was wont to use to men who had let her down, but it was nonetheless vituperative. Looking back, I cannot imagine why we did not simply ask her to take Twopence back. Perhaps we did and she refused. Nor can I remember if she was paid the £40 or whether her reaction much upset my parents. Possibly the absence of her name from the visitors' book for the years 1956 and 57 is connected to this incident – the dates would fit. After that she is down as having visited every year in the spring until we left Vancouver, so the rift was healed.

The lessening of contact was anyway explained by the fact that following her season with the Bicester, Christabel had, for fiscal reasons, transferred her hunting and house-restoring activities to Ireland, where she became master of the Ballymacad hounds, point-to-pointed riding sidesaddle and bought a derelict castle in Galway Bay. She remained based in Ireland for the rest of her life, and by the time Catherine Stott interviewed her at the age of 80, had sold the castle and was living in a caravan while a cottage was done up. She travelled widely, riding across chunks of largely empty Australia and going to the Himalayas on a bus – not a comfortable coach tour, but more probably a series of local buses. We saw little of her towards the end of her life, but she did come and stay with me after I was married and living in a Wiltshire village.

She had lost none of her energy, charm or dictatorialness. She arrived accompanied by a retired foxhound called Potent, who enchanted our very small daughter, but outraged the cats. Christabel insisted on making a pudding involving orange jelly and cornflakes. She also set saucers of milk all round the Aga in the hope that the milk would curdle nicely, becoming furious when she discovered it was pasteurised and would not. Finally, she insisted that David persuade the village Post Office to sell her stamps in spite of the fact that it was early closing. Her splendid body did finally let her down with her muscles, long overstrained, giving up. She died in 1977, the only person I have ever known to be without regrets or self-doubt. It was a delightful and terrifying combination.

Gavin Maxwell was another colourful figure who stayed regularly at Vancouver after the war. Like the Kennards, he had a passion for racing vintage cars and frequently stayed on the same occasions. Both Norris Kennard and Bill found his egotism tiresome, but Lee and Patience loved and cherished him, his self-dramatisation touching chords in both of them. There was an episode involving Lee and Gavin that was enough to satisfy anyone's sense of drama. The pair of them set out one Saturday to come to Vancouver for lunch, driving Lee's vintage white Mercedes. At some point on the journey, the car caught fire, burning out the back of Gavin's coat and reducing Lee to near hysteria. Remarkably, the fire was extinguished and they were able to continue on their way, arriving in a highly emotional state and telling the story with maximum drama. Having been soothed with food and, above all, gin, they set out to drive back to London. They got no further than the village of Chackmore when the car again burst into flames. This time there was no question of going further, and they returned to Vancouver crackling with adrenalin. Following their original departure, Vancouver had assumed a very different aspect, since it was the annual School Dance and among others, Antonia Pakenham, later Fraser, was staying, in order to attend the dance with Peter Powers, an American and much-cherished Historian. Lee and Gavin entirely disrupted this most decorous party. After the further administration of gin and possibly some food, Gavin was found some corner in which to sleep, but there was nowhere suitable for Lee, whom a kind neighbour took in. After Lee had finally departed, her hostess, when stripping the bed, was electrified to discover that she had left a pistol under her pillow.

During the period he stayed most regularly at Vancouver, Gavin was in the process of writing his early books. *Harpoon at a Venture* had just been published, Patience helped him with the tangled galley proofs of his book about Sicily, and we were all rivetted by his photographs and descriptions of the Marsh Arabs. To maintain his adventurous image, he must have glossed over the appalling discomfort he had suffered during this expedition. According to Douglas Botting, Gavin's biographer, the austere Wilfred Thesiger made no concessions to Gavin at all, his methods of travel being spartan in the extreme and wildly uncomfortable to anyone unused to squatting like an Arab. He talked vividly about his travels, and when in good form, was an exciting guest. He once took me out in his beautiful Maserati and drove at 100 miles an hour so that I could see what it felt like. Gavin then did the same to Patience when in a different mood, shouting to her above the noise of their progress, 'Of course, I don't care if I live or die.' On one occasion, following a bout of illness and depression, he arrived laden with champagne, announcing that it was the only thing he was allowed to drink. It was possibly during that visit that he remarked bitterly that 'Of course, I have to buy my friends.'

At one point Gavin decided that I had the makings of a child film star, making me act out a scene in which I had to come into the room and find my mother dead. He thought my performance was highly promising and said he would arrange a screen test, but nothing further was heard of this. When I was about 15 and suffering all the usual insecurities of that age, he took me out to dinner in London and flirted charmingly, boosting my morale enormously. After he moved to Scotland, we saw almost nothing of him. Bill and Patience despised *Ring of Bright Water* for being lightweight and unworthy of Gavin's literary skill, but possibly they were a touch jealous of the money he made. After 1956 Gavin never returned to Vancouver, though we were asked to the grand reception he gave following his marriage. I met him at the Kennards shortly before he died, and was deeply disappointed to find that the warmth I had always experienced when with him had quite vanished. He was uncomfortably cold and withdrawn. Probably this stemmed from the illness and unhappiness that dogged the last part of his life, but at the time it was distressing.

The Kennards remained close to us all their lives. After the war, they settled in Chelsea and led extravagant lives. Besides the white car, Lee also had an enormous black Mercedes that was beautiful but not entirely suitable for being driven about London. Bill alleged that once, when he was a passenger, Lee had managed to stall the car when coming out of St James' into Piccadilly and thus block both lines of traffic – Piccadilly being two-way in those days. Bill's favourite Kennard story, however, was of the Sunday drinks party that reached the point where people felt that they should eat something. This time it was Norris' green vintage Bentley that they took, but before piling in, each guest thoughtfully provided themselves with a sword and mediaeval tilting helmet from Norris' excellent collection of armour. They set off down the King's Road waving their swords and shouting, 'For God and St Denis', until a very young policeman stopped them, which, even though this was pre-breathalyser days, still caused them some sobering anxiety. All he wished to know, however, was whether the driver could see properly through the slits in his visor.

Lee was a splendid godmother, providing lavish presents, including a pretty, candy-striped outfit for my confirmation, which was regrettably preferable to the nicely bound book of devotions bestowed on me by Mary McClelland. She also helped me to choose a bright red suit in which to get married. Their life became less like something out of an Evelyn Waugh novel when they moved to Little Venice, and positively staid when they finally bought a house in Bath. When they were in London, they would ask us to dinner at the Cavalry Club. It was on one of these occasions in the early eighties, when we had just moved ourselves into south London, that Lee asked earnestly, 'Do tell me, where exactly *is* Wandsworth?'

The other couple who visited regularly and were particularly loved by us all, were Colin and Sybil Welch. Like Perry Worsthorne, Colin had experienced Bill's teaching, but had not gone into the Upper School at Stowe until after Bill had left to fight. Colin's idiosyncratic and compassionate brand of right-wing politics was much appreciated by Bill, who also loved his *Peter Simple* column. We all loved Colin's impersonations of important figures in the world of journalism, particularly that of his then editor at the *Daily Telegraph*, Colin Coote. Sybil was equally if not even more amusing than Colin, having a talent for mimicry that greatly exceeded his. She was an excellent linguist and therefore could do accents. She put together a cabaret act which she performed in a London club for a time, consisting of a series of vignettes of au pair girls. She had employed several of different nationalities, and was unerring in catching not only their accents, but a flavour of their national characteristics. Sybil could also do effortless Glasgow, producing entrancing monologues, and would embark on wonderful dialogues with Patience. They inspired each other, christening themselves Ma Welch and Mum McElwee. Sybil had the gift of making other people funnier that they might normally be, and both she and Colin were enormously kind to me. Following one of their weekend visits in the summer of 1959, Colin wrote what was, for once, a serious paragraph in his column, which he headed 'Dissonance':

'At Stowe on Sunday I went to see the final run-through of the Historians' play, to be given this Friday and Saturday. The setting was the exquisite classical Queen's Temple, the play, Shakespeare's gothic *King Richard II*; the one standing for elegance, order and symmetry, for leisure, conversation and repose; the other standing for darkness, treason, bloodshed and disorder; the one lit by the serene sun of the afternoon, the other lit fitfully by the flickering torches of murderers; the one blessed by the grace of this world, the other, if at all, by the grace of the next; the one recalling the majesty of Rome, the other the rude chaos that succeeded it; masterpieces both, together powerfully symbolising our divided nature, our rich and dissonant inheritance.'

Colin and Bill argued, generally about politics, with enormous zest and enjoyment. Bill, when feeling strongly about something, pulled no punches which, when the subject of the argument was abstract, created no difficulties. However, if matters became personal, he could be offensive. In standing up to Christabel on an unreasonable high horse, this worked well, since ultimately, she depised someone she could bully. However, his determination to avoid hypocrisy could be upsetting. His contempt for the grief of one Historian's mother at the death of her much-complained-about husband angered other members of the family, and Carroll Macnamara, who left Stowe in 1941, had an unpleasant experience of what seems to have been indiscretion and downright rudeness. He had enjoyed his time on the History Side, but this subsequent incident coloured his memory of Bill. He writes: 'It was unfortunate that when my my brother-in-law was at Stowe, Bill met his parents, though Darrell was not a Historian, and somehow dined out with them in a grand hotel in Rome. Bill, never a dull guest anywhere, clearly did not help family relationships by being unkind about my father. My late mother-in-law was not one to miss an opportunity for a bit of acidity.' Carroll Macnamara acknowledges that there might anyway have been a family row, but Bill seems to have provided the tinder. On that occasion, it is likely that he had too much to drink and got carried away, but had he been confronted with his thoughtlessness, he would probably have stoutly defended his right to express his opinion.

21

More Historians, Colleagues and Culture

To some extent, Bill had always judged his performance as a teacher and the success of the History Side by the number of scholarships and exhibitions obtained at Oxford and Cambridge. Prewar, his percentages were generally high, with at least one award from every intake onto the Side. The numbers joining the side each year varied between five and thirteen with the best year being the class of 1938, when out of ten coming on to the Side, six got some sort of University award. Postwar, five out of thirteen, from the 1946 intake was the record. Throughout the fifties, the number of awards declined, with several blank years. Possibly Bill became less in touch with university requirements or, in an increasingly technological age, brighter scholars eschewed studying history. Not that academic success at this early stage in life, was necessarily any guide to Historians' later achievement, and in the worldly terms that had always seemed to matter so much to Bill, his own career had not fulfilled the promise of his scholarship and First Class degree. My sense is that he had widened his ambitions for his tutees, now inclining to the view that performing well in whatever field was chosen should be as highly valued as achievement in academic or public office. When asked by parents 'But, Mr McElwee, what does history lead to?', he would contrast Noel Annan, who was then Provost of Kings, Cambridge, with a successful Cardiff bookmaker. He was certainly enormously proud of having taught such people as Brian Calvert, who flew Concorde's first commercial Transatlantic flight, Richard Temple, who is an expert on Icons, and Paul Whitfield, who became Managing Director of Christies, none of whom chose to go to university.

Bill was also proud of Anthony Philippi, who was, he thinks, 'the only so-called Historian that your wonderful father ever "crammed" to get into the army'. Anthony was subsequently commissioned in the Coldstream Guards, later becoming part of the 'Certificate A Examining Board', regularly visiting Stowe to put members of the school Cadet Force through some sort of test. He fondly remembers an occasion when he failed some 80 per cent of the candidates – mostly for being unshaven. Bill would have been delighted.

In fact the History Side had earlier been chosen as preparation for an army career by Angus Fairrie. He felt that 'Having no marked aptitude for any subject, it took only brief reflection to conclude that Major W. L. McElwee MC was the right tutor for me.' Angus goes on: 'I had anticipated a sticky meeting between my new mentor and my father, a sociable but short-fused retired Colonel of the Cameron Highlanders, with rather a blind spot for academics. But when we all met for lunch in the Crown Hotel in Brackley, Bill the history tutor became Bill the Highland officer, and the two established instant rapport. School was hardly mentioned, and Highland Brigade affairs reigned supreme. Meanwhile Patience entertained my mother with a hilarious tale of the upper-crust mother of a Historian who came to call at Vancouver on washing day. The lady, consumed with curiosity, peered ever closer into the suds, while Patience poured in ever more soap flakes to conceal the ragged state of the McElwee underclothes.' Angus was one of those who shot with Bill and appreciated being given a small part in the Shakespeare plays, which meant that even if much of the performance was spent waiting in the wings, he got to know the plots of *Othello* and *Hamlet*. He was also charmed by a Culture Tour to northern Italy, saying, 'Although I suspect that I set out with an overriding interest in becoming better acquainted with Chianti and Cinzano, it was a measure of Bill's talent that the Philistine minority to which I belonged was wholly absorbed by the culture to which he introduced us. I remain a convert to this day.'

In the latter part of the fifties, Bill's urge to recreate the prewar age appeared to have eased. On the other hand, his concern to 'rescue' those who had fallen foul of the school system or of family pressures, had increased. Bright boys who had dropped behind, their abilities untapped, or who were without academic ambition, were welcomed onto the History Side and encouraged to acquire a general education. Dick Temple remembers being told at his first tutorial that Bill expected all his tutees to write good English. Bill quoted Tim White's guide to writing essays, in particular saying, 'Don't mix your metaphors or you will find yourself barking up the wrong kettle of fish.' For the first time, the world of books and ideas was opened up for him, as was travel when he joined a Culture Tour.

Dick also felt that they were expected to perform for visitors to Vancouver, such as Oscar Hahn, a clever, stimulating and charming man who refused to be hampered by disablement; or Christabel Ampthill, who was deeply appreciative of charm and wit. Dick saw Bill and Patience as indivisible in their support and encouragement, but Paul Whitfield felt that Patience acted as a foil and that while Bill could give boys 'a grilling', Patience would bring in 'the shyer numbers lurking behind the curtains'. Paul has found Bill hugely influential all his life, though he felt enthusiasm for the visual arts and for music was lacking in the general Vancouver education. He also recalled that 'Bill disliked the eighteenth century so none of us ever learnt anything about it.' Like prewar Historians, he found Vancouver different from school and home, a place where boys were encouraged to be adult and were taken seriously. Paul also described an occasion when another boy became 'prissy' about one of the cats, who had peed on him. Bill passed the boy a gun and told him to go and shoot it, only issuing a reprieve at the last minute.

As far as their interest in and knowledge of art was concerned, Paul's judgement may be slightly harsh. While Bill and Patience certainly had little interest in modern art, their awareness of pictures and painting, from the Renaissance to the nineteenth century, was considerable. I was much encouraged to go and look at pictures, being taken by Patience to the Wallace Collection during one visit to London. Bill regularly visited the big, well-known galleries in the course of the Culture Tours and, while Robin and Dodie Watt ran the Art School, Bill and Patience were deeply interested in what was being produced there. In spite of their conservative tastes, however, they much appreciated the contemporary print of his own work, presented to Bill by Bill (Stanley) Hayter when his son William left Stowe.

Their taste in music, though, was, for serious musicians, questionable. In spite of their Viennese operatic education and an ancient collection of what would now be greatly treasured 78 records, ranging from a Galli-Curci recital to a splendid rendering of *Home James and Don't Spare the Horses*, their enthusiasms had become pure Light Programme. Patience, and I, when I was resisting getting down to work in the stables, would listen to *Housewives Choice*, the electric organ recital that followed, and finish with *Music While You Work*. We never became addicted to *Mrs Dale's Diary*, which followed. Bill was

231

furious if he missed *Grand Hotel* or *Friday Night is Music Night*, and later in life became much attached to a programme called *Sing Something Simple*. Whatever their tastes, however, Bill and Patience loyally attended school concerts, though they might then be rude about the performances. They had both loved and admired Leslie Huggins, Director of Music until his death from cancer in the early fifties, and therefore tended to be dismissive of the achievements of his successors. They rarely attended concerts outside the school, but were occasionally given theatre tickets by kind parents. They disliked *Beyond the Fringe*, loved *At the Drop of a Hat* and, to their surprise, enjoyed *My Fair Lady*, having initially been outraged over what they saw as the vandalising of *Pygmalion*. It was Christopher Wates, now knighted and running the Wates building firm, who widened my musical education, making me sit and listen to Beethoven symphonies.

Books, therefore, were the chief weapon in the Vancouver educational armoury, as Jeremy Jessel, who was rescued by Bill when he was at the point of being expelled, remembers. A risk-taking rebel, Jeremy described exploits, such as dangerous excursions on to the roof of the main Stowe building and riding a bicycle the length of the frozen, and very deep, Eleven-Acre lake with the ice cracking behind him. Charged with keeping Jeremy in the school for a year, Bill gave him a reading list that included Vicki Baum's *Grand Hotel* and most of Hardy. He was made to research the life of Christopher Wren and then present a paper on him to the History Side, as well as being given the task of designing scenery and costumes for *A Midsummer Night's Dream*. He was allowed to experiment with phosphorescent lighting, which, he says, did not work, but he was still allowed a free hand.

Jeremy liked being made to defend an intellectual position once taken. He says there was teasing, but it was tempered to the weaker members of the Side. He found Stowe as a whole anti-Semitic, but did not experience it personally from Bill and Patience. They were open about their prejudices and snobberies, he felt, so that you knew where you were with them. Anti-Semitism was only one of the discomforts Jeremy experienced at Stowe. He found it cold, with bad food and a strong pressure to conform. Corporal punishment flourished, something about which Bill took a traditional view, though he did feel that it should be used sparingly. He thought that it worked for some boys and was better than a massive accumulation of lines, but acknowledged that for some it was deeply upsetting and therefore inappropriate.

232

In spite of his dislike of the school generally and his wild escapades, Jeremy survived his year and went out to Canada. There he applied for work in a bank, but was scuppered by a reference from Bill that said, 'This man is not to be trusted with money.' Jeremy thinks this was in fact accurate at the time, but when he subsequently tackled Bill about his reasons for making such a statement, Bill said he wrote it because he felt the job was wrong for him. Jeremy was subsequently grateful for this high-handed behaviour, which eventually led to his doing what he really wanted, which was to go to Art School and become a painter. Bill pulled the same trick of writing a bad reference for Charles Cox, who was applying to Shell as his time at Cambridge came to an end. Charles also acknowledges that Bill was probably correct in his judgement, but was rightly furious at the time.

William, now Augy, Hayter, son of the artist Stanley Hayter and the sculptress Helen Phillips, was another boy who was hauled out of the doldrums. When Bill died, he felt the need to record his feeling that Bill had transformed his life and changed his Stowe career out of all recognition. He wrote to another master: 'My scholastic career started at the bottom of the lowest form in school, and although I was top of my class three years later, it was still such a slow stream that it would have taken me five years to get to "O" level. I met Bill at one of the Historians' plays and he decided to adopt me and take me in hand: he went to the Headmaster and persuaded him to let me jump a full year in one term and do "O" and "A" levels at the same time, with an attempt at a scholarship to Oxford thrown in for good measure. Well of course Bill's Pygmalion was never rewarded as it deserved; I passed most of my exams but never became the Galatea he hoped for. But the quality of the attention that he gave me entirely changed my attitude towards myself. The fact that he believed in my potential caused me to believe in it too and it broke a certain kind of self-disparagement that my difficulties at the beginning of my school career had led me into. And then you can't imagine the joy of those teas at Vancouver. We were drunk with the power of our newly found intellects, sounding off with pimply vehemence about life, art and literature and God knows what...'

William adds that Bill 'was not without vanity and had his faults, but I'm still willing to wager that the good he has done has earned him his place in Paradise.' Bill's attitude to 'A' Levels was cavalier. He said that the syllabus encouraged learning by rote rather than analytical thought, and was therefore unconcerned by the grades his pupils

233

achieved. In those days, while 'A' Levels were necessary for university entrance, there was still a separate examination, so the grades were of less importance.

Christopher Kenyon, on the History Side between 1954 and 1958, was less sanguine about the teasing than Jeremy Jessel. He felt that the gibes aimed at the North Country son of the owner of a textile firm were unkind and too much concerned with his accent. Patience would recount a story of this boy's mother 'dripping with diamonds' and saying wistfully: 'I suppose you are the sort of people who have a late dinner *every* night?' Coals of fire were heaped on Bill and Patience when a generous amount of material was provided to make good the damage wreaked on the already tatty Vancouver upholstery by the foxhound puppies. For himself, though, Christopher Kenyon found strong and sensitive support from Bill. He echoes many comments made by others on the subversive elements of Vancouver, the uniqueness of the History Side and the sense of superiority this engendered, together with the passionate concern Bill and Patience had for the boys.

Academically, Christopher particularly valued Bill's almost noteless lectures on the nineteenth century and the personal attention that saw him through a difficult patch in his adolescence. He has kept his school reports, and Bill's comments chart the highly promising start, the difficult and uncertain period, through to greater confidence and maturity. Given little space, Bill describes vividly the early intolerance, a growing understanding and a period when 'a mistrust of all forms of embellishment sometimes make his history essays extremely dull to read, but most of them are very good indeed'. Particular difficulties and a loss of confidence are noted, and there is a suggestion that pressure will be lifted while these doubts are sorted. Finally, he celebrates the resolution of the problems and Christopher's readiness for university. Christopher himself feels that his difficulties arose from the need to find a sense of direction and to make a decision about entering the family firm. He went on to manage it most successfully, as well as taking a major role in the management of Manchester University and becoming Chair of the Quality Assurance Agency.

Simon Brown, not a scholar, but now a Lord Justice and as successful as ever Bill could have wished, is another man who felt transformed by Bill's teaching. First encountering this in the Lower School, he found it a 'revelation'. He writes: 'Although no doubt I was reasonably bright, I was in those days a complete Philistine. Bill immediately saw through all that and did what school masters are always supposed to do but in reality almost never do: he fired my enthusiasm – not so much for history qua history, but rather for wider intellectual interests, pursuits and attainments generally. Like, no doubt, many others recruited to the History Side I was enslaved. He was seductively intimate – who else called one by one's first name at that stage? – no one as I recall. He was hugely flattering, knowing that to praise is to encourage, to make one crave more. And he was wonderfully irreverent, gossiping indiscreetly (on occasions disgracefully!) about other staff, ever careless of the boundaries of school life, drawing one irresistibly into the ethos of Vancouver life, making one feel deliciously mature, select, la creme de la creme.'

During the fifties some of the younger masters appointed by Reynolds also became regular attenders at Vancouver teas. They were a group who brightened life at Stowe academically, theatrically and spiritually. Joe Bain, who taught English and Modern Languages as well as producing some outstanding plays with the Congreve Club, became a particular Vancouverite. He had first to overcome Patience's initial impression that he was affected and her cracks about 'Precious Bane', made in reference to a novel by Mary Webb. However, Joe's wit and erudition quickly won her over, and not only did he come to tea regularly, but also, having no family of his own, spent Christmas with us several years running. Joe felt that boys and masters went to Vancouver to see Patience rather than Bill, describing her as the 'Witch of Endor', always sitting in her battered arm chair by the fire in the winter and on the grotty chaise-longue in the summer, weaving her spells of gossip and sympathy. He remembered her as unable to resist the witty, generally biting one-liner, citing her ruthless send-up of a hapless master's wife who had talked about Tolstoy's *Peace and War*. Both Bill and Patience, he felt, responded to challenge and were kind, but astringent. Bill, he thought, would never have made a Headmaster, his skills lying in teaching rather than the necessary administration.

Joe introduced Vancouver to Tom Lehrer and Anna Russell, allowing their records to remain in the house over long periods, during which they were played to teatime gatherings. Bill and Patience reacted to the Lehrer songs with a mixture of disapproval and delight. Anna Russell, however, was an unqualified success, her sending up of Wagner's Ring Cycle and all Gilbert and Sullivan operas being particularly beloved. Joe also felt that the difficulties other masters had with Bill sprang from their inability to stand up to him. He cited an

235

occasion when, needing to spend a day in London, he asked Bill to mind his form, a bright lot of pre-'O' Level boys with whom he was working on Wordsworth. When he returned, he found Remove C, with much giggling, talking about 'Gaffer Wordsworth', ridicule of Wordsworth being a regular theme of Bill's discourse. Furious, Joe attacked Bill, emphasising the trouble he had taken to instil appreciation of the poet into the boys, all of which work he said, was now undone. Bill was genuinely apologetic, acknowledging that he had allowed himself to get carried away and that it had been inappropriate.

Brian Stephan echoed Joe's judgement that Bill would respond if his colleagues stood up to him, but was sympathetic to the difficulties some of them had in doing so. He recalled the Senior Tutor, Patrick Hunter, being worried and angry about something he thought Bill was doing. Brian asked him why he did not do something about it, but Hunter replied that it was very difficult to do anything about a man who was so successful. Brian felt that the other tutors were deeply jealous of Bill and furious that he creamed off the brightest boys. There was a cabal, he said, between Bill, Edward Capel Cure, Humphrey Playford, and Brian Gibson, all three of them Housemasters and therefore not competitors for tutees. They were also sufficiently confident men not to feel threatened by the influence of Vancouver. Between Bill and Brian Stephan there existed a mutually wary respect. Brian was prepared to stand up to him, which might irritate Bill at the time, but they each admired the other's teaching skills. Had Patrick Hunter summoned up his courage and challenged him, Bill might have despised him less and valued the qualities which were appreciated by many who equally admired Bill. Instead, Bill perfected his cruel imitation of Hunter's unfortunate facial tick. Robin Watt had apparently thought that Bill's war service would give him a greater sense of loyalty to his colleagues. In fact, while he became intensely loyal to the Argylls and his military comrades, he became, if anything, more intolerant of the masters who were unable to stand up to him.

Brian Stephan did have concerns about Vancouver being an 'alternative house', and must have been worried about the rumours that boys were encouraged to drink and smoke, indeed being seen as cissy if they did not. The reality was that boys were in fact allowed a glass of sherry or the maximum of a pint of beer, generally following physical activity in the garden. Sixth Formers asked to dinner would be given wine and allowed a cigarette after the meal. Bill had a theory that if adolescents were allowed to drink sensibly, they would

236

be less likely to drink illicitly in school or to consume inappropriate quantities of alcohol when they were free of the place. He also felt entirely confident of being able to control the boys' behaviour while they were with him either at Vancouver or during Culture Tours. Young women, Bill felt, were in danger of being seduced if they did not learn to hold their drink so, his mission was to educate us to consume modestly. I was therefore encouraged to drink a little sherry from the age of 14. It did not, of course, prevent boys consuming alcohol in school, but may well have fostered a sensible attitude to drink generally.

However, with one boy Bill's methods failed entirely and alcohol caused his spectacular downfall. Asked to undertake a major rescue job on a young man with an unsupportive family background, who was floundering in every direction, Bill thought, at the end of Richard's first term on the Side that he was getting somewhere. The boy's work had improved and he was becoming infinitely more sociable. Alas, such virtue could not withstand the excitement of the end of the Christmas term. With three others, a party was planned, the ingredients of which consisted of five bottles of cheap South African hock, a Christmas pudding and a pint of cream. This orgy took place in a ground-floor study in the early evening. Two, more senior, Historians in the same House discovered Richard, comatose among the empty bottles and vomit, and, aware of Bill's investment in saving the boy's career, attempted a rescue. They cleaned up the study and, having been reading a book on eighteenth-century boxing, set about reviving Richard, slapping him, biting his ears and dosing him with strong coffee. Sadly, their efforts were in vain, since higher authority had earlier witnessed the debauchery and Richard's Housemaster was already planning expulsion. Richard's final fling was to stand on the House central staircase, hurling at his Housemaster, the Reverend Windsor Richards, known inevitably as Windy Dick, every obscenity of which he could think.

Colin James, appointed as a Chaplain, was another master who became a regular visitor to Vancouver. In spite of slightly High Church leanings which Bill, remembering his Irish Protestant ancestry, regarded with suspicion, Colin became a close friend of both Bill and Patience. He, too, was frequently part of Vancouver tea-parties, forums in which he was able to indulge an occasional taste for amusing malice. Along with this, he offered much spiritual support to those in need of it. Colin was greatly missed when he left Stowe for the BBC, en route to the Bishoprics of Wakefield and Winchester, but he

237

remained in touch with Bill and officiated at his memorial service. Colin, like Joe Bain, was not intimidated by Bill. They were both able to stand up to him, to laugh at him and challenge him when he was at his most outrageous. Both could also see how difficult he could be for other colleagues. John Hunt, who was to go on to become Headmaster of Roedean, and who taught geography at Stowe, became equally unfazed by Bill, though he says he was 'conscious of being given the once-over' when he first met them, 'and, fortunately for me, passed. Just at first Bill and Patience could be rather alarming to a young and very green member of staff.' John adds that he 'enjoyed much hospitality and talk at Vancouver Lodge, which was not a household where the fruits of domestic order were startlingly apparent.'

Away from Vancouver, one of the Stowe circles in which Bill and Patience moved most happily was that of the domestic staff. The living conditions provided for them were not good, but there was, among the hideous conglomeration of well-concealed buildings that made up the Power House Yard, a bar known as the 'Rec Room', where those who cooked, cleaned and maintained the place could meet and relax. It was a dreary-looking room, redeemed by the charm and humour of those who frequented it. Cyril Atkins, the Domestic Bursar, was a moving light behind the Rec Room entertainment. He shared Patience's passion for antiques and welcomed the few masters who, at times, chose to go and drink there rather than in the Master's Mess. A bonus was that Patience and I could join Bill there when we were forbidden the Master's Mess. It remained, however, a largely male gathering, with few of the female domestic staff spending time there. Apart from her own sitting-room, the Rec Room was one of the places where Patience flourished most confidently. There she felt no need to perform, revealing a spontaneous warmth and revelling in the gossip that flowed as happily there as ever at Vancouver. Party nights were presumably linked to Christmas or the ending of term, but whatever the reason, they provided what seemed at the time to be riotous entertainment. There was one where Patience became distinctly drunk, something that happened rarely since she was a modest drinker, certainly in comparison to Bill. On this occasion she was hilarious, being seized with infectious giggles.

There was another evening when she and Freddie Gunthorpe, who, when on duty, would be found swabbing down the endless subterranean stone passages of the main building, were seen to be propping each other up while taking part in the final dance of the Staff

Christmas party. When sober they would exchange racing tips. Up to the age of about 14, I would be 'minded' in the Rec Room while my parents attended Masters' cocktail parties. I would sit happily in a corner imbibing an endless supply of a lurid fizzy orange drink and Smith's crisps, which were delicious as long the salt wrapped in its twist of blue paper had not got damp. Dougie Richardson, the chef, and Eric, his deputy, would vie with each other about which of them was actually the official baby-sitter.

The school provided a considerable amount of entertainment. There were the concerts, with visiting orchestras sometimes supplementing those given by the school orchestra. These were generally a mixed experience. The brass section was often very good, but there were rarely enough good string players to make some pieces anything but uncomfortable for sensitive ears. Congreve Club and House plays could also resemble the curate's egg, but despite being bad in parts, were sometimes outstanding. A House production of Charles Morgan's *The River Line* was particularly memorable. Films, which I enjoyed, were regularly screened, but I learnt early that if I wished to be taken to them, I had to do my homework. In my early teens, enamoured of the 'Drinking Song', I insisted that Bill take me to see the film *The Student Prince*. He rightly thought the film dreadful, and made such a fuss that for the rest of his life I took enormous care over his screen entertainment. Patience was less selective, happily enjoying quite lurid films put on at the Chandos cinema in Buckingham, an outing which she regarded as a high treat. I was never allowed the Saturday morning cinematic entertainment though, and the early Disney cartoons remained unknown to me until I had children of my own. My first experience of the screen was when Patience took me to see Ingrid Bergman playing St Joan, who was a heroine of mine at the time. I must have been about seven, and Patience insisted that we left before Joan was burnt.

Away from Stowe, Bill and Patience's social life fell somewhat between stools. There were not many local friends with whom they were on entertaining terms, and though they were asked to the occasional drinks and dinner parties, I do not remember reciprocal invitations. They had more than enough to do with the endless stream of current and old Historians, and would have regarded money spent on their neighbours as wasted. Some of their acquaintances in the Grafton Hunt would ask them out, but they were more likely to become involved in fund-raising events for the hunt. Patience, in particular, organised several dances at Stowe for that curious entity, the 'Wire Fund'. Horses are unable to see wire and therefore cannot jump over the strands of barbed wire used as fencing. The fund existed to assist farmers in equipping their fields with the much more expensive cut and laid hedges or nice solid posts and rails so that the hunt could proceed unhindered. Bob Wheeler, a member of the farming clan and a close friend of Bill and Patience, remembers Patience arriving at one of these dances and finding, as she ascended the steps of the North Front, that her dress was much too long. Bill dealt with this smartly by borrowing a pair of scissors and slicing a chunk off the bottom, Patience apparently happily accepting this solution. Money to buy tickets for these occasions remained tight, but they nonetheless managed the Hunt Ball proper several times. For this Bill acquired the correct scarlet tail coat, which cannot have been cheap.

One dreadful 1 January in the days before it was a Bank Holiday, Coutts, no doubt cross about an unarranged overdraft, failed to send the £50 that normally arrived in a registered envelope and sustained them financially for the month. Panic was succeeded by euphoria when, towards the end of a desperate hunt through pockets and down the sides of chairs, 10/- was discovered in Bill's hunt dress coat. All three of us promptly repaired to the Queen's Head at Chackmore, another favoured source of entertainment, where the 10/- vanished as rounds of drinks were stood to those celebrating the New Year. The Queen's Head, provider of excellent company who could entertain with songs and recitals, was one pub where the landlady disapproved of my presence. She was, of course, quite right, but at the time I bitterly resented being made to retire to a kind of cubbyhole beside the bar.

Throughout the fifties, in spite of the books, money continued to be a major source of worry for Patience. Bill worried less, relying on charm to buy time in which to pay bills which, in any case, he never paid until they came in covered in pleas written in scarlet ink. He had a theory that as long as he continued to appear in the hunting field, his creditors would hold off. Patience would buy an expensive piece of antique furniture and then panic about the weekly bills, thus becoming easy prey for plausible men coming to the door in search of objets d'art. Bill never really forgave her for selling a pair of Georgian silver sauce boats at infinitely less than their real value. Once she asked Adrian Evans, who was then Head of School and somehow able to get permission to make regular visits to London, if he would sell some jewellery for her. He took them to Tessier, jewellers used by his stepfather and, as he says, 'immediately realised that they were not saleable, at least not at Tessier's. When I explained to Patience that Tessier admired them but felt that these particular settings were, for the moment, no longer fashionable, and therefore not likely to attract a sensible price, she smiled and took them back. Somehow she did it very sweetly.'

22

Harriet

Though lacking the youthful fireworks of the prewar period, the fifties was nonetheless a period of solid achievement for Bill and Patience. Books were written and received good reviews, even if they never sold as well as they might, and Geoffrey Russell commissioned Bill to translate Dürrenmat's play, *An Angel Comes to Babylon*, from the German. The first English production, at the Bristol Old Vic in 1963, was not a great success, but this appears to have been the fault of the play's dramatic construction rather than the translation. Bill celebrated his fiftieth birthday during the one Spanish Culture Tour, and in December 1955 they had a riotous party to mark their Silver Wedding. They felt this was truly something to celebrate. Divorce was beginning to become more common, and at Oswald and Grania Normanby's wedding reception in 1951, they had been delighted to hear some prewar acquaintance say in surprise, 'Look, there's Bill and Patience, still together.' Bill and Patience's party was given in the elegant Stowe Library, the drink served being nothing but champagne cocktails. They asked all their friends, which meant that the lady of the manor, Mrs Close-Smith, brought along her groom. The Historians had a whipround and presented them, in a Georgian silver mug, with one of the splendid flimsy fivers then current, for every year they had been married. Patience always alleged that she did not believe that the fivers were real, and that Hamish St Clair Erskine, who was staying at the time, had only just managed to stop her rolling one into a spill in order to light a cigarette. The money probably got used up in paying for the party. Throughout the latter part of the fifties, Bill was a popular lecturer to the Worker's Education Association, the series based round the Congress of Vienna being particularly successful. In the wider world it was pleasing that in 1959 he was made a fellow of the Royal

Society of Literature. This was an affirmation of his literary skills and a measure of the solidity of his achievements.

Historians did well and were affectionate and entertaining, while the plays continued to be enjoyable and successful. Horses and ponies added an extra dimension, though they were also a constant source of worry to Patience. She fretted over where they were to be kept, since grazing had to be arranged with local farmers, and whether the vet's bill could be paid when there was trouble with their notoriously fragile legs. The possibility that I would fall off one of the horses and break my neck, or be humiliated in some show was also a constant worry. However, the satisfaction when things went right and the varied people they met at equestrian events provided compensation. Bill suffered two serious bouts of pneumonia, one of which landed him in hospital in a state of delirium. It was characteristically self-inflicted. He chose to go out hunting on an appallingly cold, wet day, with a severe cold in the head. 'Today will be kill or cure' he remarked to the Huntsman, and it was damn nearly kill. Bill was saved by his responsiveness to penicillin, and within two days was expressing fury that the hospital could only provide the *Telegraph* rather than *The Times*. The crossword was a daily pleasure and, at that time, he regarded the *Telegraph*'s puzzle as too easy. Patience's health remained variable, with regular fearful episodes when she was convinced that she had some life-threatening illness.

Neither Bill nor Patience gave much thought to my future. By the age of 15 I was virtually working as a full-time girl-groom looking after Bill's Irish hunter, Wicklow, and her beautiful daughter, Caprice. There was then a national scheme to improve horse stock in the country, which was to be achieved by mating not quite top-drawer mares like Wicklow, with well-bred stallions. A much lower fee was asked than would have been required for a mare of equal standing. Not wanting to hunt for a season or so, Bill took advantage of this arrangement to mate Wicklow with a handsome stallion called Whim. I was allowed to watch the entire process from behind a hedge, so at least my sex education continued. The result of this union was a delightful foal that exactly fulfilled the ambition of the scheme. I broke her in and trained her with great care, managing to curb the worst excesses of Alec Tait, my riding master, so that his skill rather than his brutality prevailed. By the age of five, she was the perfect three-day-event horse. Her only drawback was a tendency to move with such speed when she was startled that staying on her was impossible. There were several occasions when, although I was prepared for such an eventuality, she whipped round while I went straight on. I did not have the temperament or the capital to exploit her ability, and with parental overdrafts pressing, she was sold. Sadly, the woman who bought her attempted to jump her over an iron gate which swung back as the horse went over, causing a horrendous fall from which, apparently, Caprice never recovered. At least the overdrafts were paid off. A second foal bred under the same scheme failed to grow properly and was a comparative failure.

In March 1957, when I was 14, we were interviewed as a family by a journalist from the *Northampton Mercury and Herald*. Under the headline 'Author and Authoress educate their only child at home', some of the criticisms they had received were described and our views expressed. '"She will never be able to earn her own living – she will never be able to mix with company." Such have been some of the criticisms aimed at author Mr William McElwee and his authoress wife Patience since they decided to educate their only child, Harriet, themselves. I spoke to all three at their home last week about this individualistic stand over the daughter's education.' She went on to outline Bill's literary achievements and his statement that as Chairman of the Governors of the Royal Latin School, he was 'right in touch with school overcrowding problems and the consequent disadvantages.' Patience was quoted as saying that she had 'found school an awful strain myself mentally and physically', and that 'the awful thing about school is the time that is wasted – one forgets most of what one has learnt afterwards.'

They made their teaching of me sound wonderfully planned: 'Like her mother, Harriet could read by the age of five and at about that time was given an old typewriter – to "get used to the shape of the 26 letters in the alphabet." Once you have got a young child to read, half your education problems are finished. With a young child, education is going on all the time because they are always asking questions. "And as she wanted to know about various subjects, we got her the suitable books," said Mrs McElwee.' Mendaciously, Patience said that I had been taught to write copperplate since script had ruined her writing, quite ignoring the fact that my handwriting was awful. 'Her mathematics lessons finished when I thought she had learnt as much as any woman decently ought to, said Mr McElwee.' According to Bill and Patience, I had learnt to play the piano, to dance, to speak French and was shortly to start German, none of which was strictly true. 'I think it is very important that a girl should know at least two languages,' stated Patience. She also extolled the culture with which I come in contact at home, saying that 'ordinary school life turned out thousands of girls from the same mould which had left them little time for studies of their own choice.' Patience's final sally was a statement about girls being allowed to wear 'discreet make-up' when they began to mind about their appearance and to be allowed some choice in their own clothes.

The only quote from me came at the end of the article, when I said that I thought being educated at home 'was terrific fun, but if you don't have some outside interest, life at home could soon become very boring.' 'Harriet has always had her horses,' said the final paragraph, 'she took up riding at the age of six, has a list of showjumping successes (another bit of mendacity) and has hunted with the Grafton.' What a little horror I must have been.

Bill and Patience were convinced that travel abroad, even if quite brief, would enable me to learn the two languages they thought so important. However, without money to send me to any kind of institution or as a paying guest with a family, they were reliant on contact with generous friends to promote this idea. Patience did once harbour a fearful plan to pack me off to work in a French racing stable, but to my enormous relief, failed to pursue that idea. My first foreign travel took place when I was 12 and arose from one of Bill's interesting extracurricular activities. In the mid-fifties, he became involved in a series of Anglo-German conferences for Historians, taking place in Oxford and Bamberg, which were aimed at reaching a broad agreement in describing 'Anglo-German relations, 1918–1933'. A pamphlet produced after the conferences outlined their task. It noted that at the time, many necessary documents of the period were still inaccessible and that there had not been time to study the material that was available. They decided that it would be impossible to reach final conclusions and outlined their task as being 'To reach agreement as far as possible upon the main events of these years and upon their effect on the home and foreign policies of the respective governments, and to prepare a summary of such agreements as could be reached by an exchange of views from each side for the further guidance of historical textbook writers.' There followed 27 paragraphs of varying length, outlining their agreed version of events.

It was during one of these conferences that Bill met Herr Kellermann, who ran a highly successful screw factory in the Harz mountains. It was arranged that two of his adolescent children should come to stay at Vancouver as paying guests for three weeks, taking me back with them for five weeks for nothing and all expenses paid. Edda and Manfred's stay at Vancouver appeared successful, though Patience alleged that the only English words Edda learnt were 'boyfriend', 'blue-eyed boy', 'poppers' and 'hooks and eyes' – being July, the production of *Coriolanus* was in hand and everyone was required to sew. For much of my stay in Germany, however, I was bored and unhappy. Apart from staying with the nearby and much-loved Connors when Vancouver was full of old Historians, I had never been properly away from home and the five weeks seemed endless. There were some compensations, such as being able to ride the high-powered horses bought when the children had expressed an interest in riding, using the indoor and outdoor schools equipped with a fine set of show-jumps, and the cross-country course built in the mountains. By then, the children hardly ever rode, and the member of the German equestrian team hired to teach them was delighted to have a willing pupil. However, because during August in the Harz mountains there are quantities of flies, the horses had to be exercised early in the morning, leaving little for me to do for the rest of the day. In sheer self-defence, I had learnt to read as fast as Bill and Patience and so my stock of books soon ran out. A Kellermann cousin gave me *Animal Farm* and *How to Be an Alien*, but these did not last me long.

Weekends were enlivened by long drives in the Harz Mountains, stopping at intervals to admire, with many expressions of enthusiasm, the totally uniform views of endless fir trees. The expensive and jerkily driven Mercedes caused me to return from all these trips an alarming shade of green, so I began trying to avoid them. However, being taken to see the 'Iron Curtain' winding its way endlessly across the countryside, slicing through back gardens and brooded over by the sinister watchtowers, was a powerful experience for which I was grateful. My journey home, in contrast to the flight out with Edda and Manfred, was an endless, frightening affair of broken-down trains and wrongly booked ferry tickets. I was triumphant at surviving it, however, and at reaching Liverpool Street where, characteristically, Patience had arranged for me to be met by Piers Plowright, who escorted me across London to Marylebone. Nothing could more clearly illustrate their delightfully erratic concern for their just 13-year-old's welfare.

In fact, I must have been a pain to have around when I was in

Germany, and the five weeks must have seemed just as long to the Kellermanns. I was much younger than any of the children, and my behaviour cannot have been attractive. I was resentful, insular and intolerant, clearly failing to enjoy any of their regular entertainments and making little attempt to overcome their gales of laughter at my halting German. My passport photograph shows a lumpish child with an oily skin and lank, untidy plaits. At Bill's insistence, my hair had not been cut for years, and Christabel Ampthill convinced Patience that pulling the right plait forward would eventually persuade my sticking-out ear to return to its proper position. The ear was supposed to have been caused by a nurse allowing it to be folded forward when putting me, newly born, in my cot. This theory failed to take account of the fact that my Uncle Alan had ears that stuck out so badly that he had been sent to Germany to have them corrected. It was only when my own first child appeared with a similar ear to mine, that I realised the futility of that unattractive plait. The summer following my return from Germany, Patience realised what a burden my long, thick and greasy hair had become, and took me to have it cut without telling Bill.

In spite of bouts of homesickness, the other travel arranged for me was more enjoyable once I got over my strong resistance to leaving home. Bill and Patience met Meyer and Helen Handler at a party given by Oscar Hahn about two years after my visit to the Kellermans. Meyer was a distinguished foreign correspondent with the *New York Times* and was then working in Bonn. They had a daughter about to go to Bedales. I stayed with them briefly in Bonn, which, after I tried everything I could to avoid going, was a success. Three years later, when I was 17, I spent four months with them in Vienna during which they generously included me in many of their activities. Vienna in 1960 was, in places, still battered by the war, but seemed generally prosperous and lively. The regular singers at the Staatsoper were outstanding, and in the monthly repertoire there would be Christa Ludwig, Hans Hotter or Graziella Sciutti performing. Herbert von Karajan was in charge of the opera and appeared to be regarded by the Viennese as a satisfactory replacement for the Emperor Franz Joseph. Von Karajan dropped in briefly to a concert conducted by Klemperer, who was back in Vienna for the first time since the war, and instantly distracted the audience from the powerful performance of a Beethoven symphony to which they were supposed to be listening, causing a buzz to run round the concert hall.

247

Meyer Handler was now a Central European correspondent, which meant that their flat, which also contained his office, was constantly buzzing with news. There were gatherings of the other distinguished and articulate newspaper men covering the area, endlessly discussing and arguing. When Gary Powers and his U2 spy plane were brought down in Russia, the excitement was huge, with the mostly democrat journalists heaping contempt on Eisenhower's handling of the crisis. When the fuss had died down, Meyer and Helen entertained a powerful Russian diplomat who cheerfully predicted that Powers would be given 30 years imprisonment and then quietly swopped for a Russian spy, which was precisely what happened. Then, with the Cold War going strong, contact with this man felt exciting and dangerous. He had enormous charm, a great sense of humour and exuded ruthlessness. Like a goat, his eyes had a sinister unchanging quality. The Iron Curtain was after all, just up the road from Vienna, and on this visit I was able to cross it.

The regime in Warsaw had, some months earlier, expelled the *New York Times* correspondent there for probing some issue too deeply. Now, relaxing a little, they were prepared to allow Meyer in for a month to catch up on affairs. Helen and I joined him for a week, driving up through the lush farmlands of Czechoslovakia to find ourselves in a much more primitive country once we crossed the Polish border. Gone were the Czech cars and tractors, with horses and carts being the only vehicles we passed. There were extensive-sounding menus in the Polish hotels, but little food was actually available. I remember chiefly living off delicious bread and radishes. Vodka flowed, however, and Bill would have been proud of my being able to toss it back in one gulp. Warsaw was poor, beautiful in parts and exciting. The plays in the hideous Palace of Science and Culture were wildly satirical, and one of Meyer's contacts was a Jew who had been given the name of Tommy Atkins when he escaped to England at the start of the war. He had never bothered changing it, and bravely continued to give information to journalists despite having been arrested in the past and being unable to leave the country. He and his wife lived in dread of heavy footsteps on the stairs of their shabby tower block, but entertained us royally. At the end of our week, Helen and I travelled back to Vienna in the Moscow express, of which the rolling stock had been made in Leeds. It was extremely comfortable and policed by incredibly glamorous customs officers.

My four months had not been entirely easy. Meyer, though funny and prepared to talk endlessly to me about Central European affairs, was an angst-ridden Russian Jew with whom it must have been very difficult to live. Helen clearly found him so and, also struggling with their demanding social life, had become stressed and unhappy. I got caught up in family dramas, taking the side of Helen, whom I loved dearly, without thinking that there might be other aspects to the story. No doubt my being asked to stay for so long was to give her company and interest, but in the end it all became a considerable strain, and I was relieved to get home.

I went back with some German but not enough to be fluent, an abiding passion for Mozart operas sung by the very best voices, and a short-lived taste for Baroque architecture. I had seen most of the sights, eaten at Sachers Hotel, Demels and the Café Mozart, heard *The Merry Widow* and *Die Fledermaus* done as they should be, with maximum glitter and, when missing my horses, had comforted myself by going and talking to the famous Lippizaner horses in the stables of the Spanish Riding School. All this was probably what Bill and Patience intended, though Patience would possibly have been happier if I had come back engaged to an Austrian aristocrat. Bill tried to build on the German I had learnt by giving lessons to me and one of his senior Historians. He made us read poetry from the *Oxford Book of German Verse* and Bismark's *Memoirs*. These were printed in German script and were extremely difficult. My sole legacy of those lessons is being able to recite chunks of *Die Lorelei*.

Patience would quite possibly have liked me to have a London season, which was of course, out of the question. Instead, some weeks after my return from Vienna, she arranged a 'Northern Tour' for me. The first stop was with Iain Moncreiffe and his then wife, Diana, Countess of Errol, known to her friends as Puffin. They had young children and no time for entertaining young people to meet me. Puffin spent all her time managing the children, curbing the excesses of the exuberant Spanish couple who were supposed to help in the house, and keeping Iain supplied with the only brand of vodka he would drink, which had probably been originally brewed for the Tzars. My ability to drink this came in useful, and I avoided being seduced by Iain simply by being too naive to realise that he was making the attempt. Iain was exciting company, though. He put on a great double act with Don Pottinger, who was also staying while he and Iain worked on one of their successful books on heraldry, and told gleeful stories about his ancestors and those of their neighbours. Iain was entranced at being descended from Gilles de Rais and that alarming Hungarian Countess who liked to refresh herself by bathing in virgins' blood. 'That's a descendant of the Wolf of Badenoch,' he would say with relish, pointing out a mild-looking man at some drinks party. Iain was far too serious a genealogist to make any of this up.

Staying with Bill's ex-mistress and Patience's great friend, Ismay Ross, and her husband Donald in Edinburgh was also fun, but not fruitful from Patience's point of view. However, eating at the Ross's restaurant, the wonderful l'Aperitif, was exciting, and Ismay improved my cultural education by taking me to the local big houses, including Falkland Palace, of which her brother was keeper, and the Roslin Chapel. She had a theory that ordinary people in Scotland had lived in holes in the ground until the nineteenth century, which might account for the almost complete absence of attractive village houses. A room at l'Aperitif was later to become the meeting place for a club founded by Iain Moncreiffe and called Puffins. Members came entirely from the Scottish aristocracy, but foreign grandees could be associates and Bill was enormously flattered to be included in this category.

I moved on to stay with John Hunt and his parents near Dunfermline, a visit that did include a Reel Party and some rather more youthful company as well as more sightseeing, but the final visit of my tour, to my godfather, Oswald Normanby, was back to being with older adults and young children. The Normanbys clearly did not know what to do with me, and I suspect I got off on the wrong foot by telling a faintly risqué story on my first evening. Fed on Bill and Patience's stories of the prewar Oswald, I thought it would reveal me as a woman of his world. He had changed, however, and his wife Grania did not approve. I was further disconcerted when I got to my room, to find that most of my tatty underwear had vanished. It reappeared, beautifully clean and ironed, first thing the next morning. Patience did not think that underclothes and nightwear mattered. One of her favourite sayings was that she would never be able to commit adultery since she would not have a clean, mended nightdress at the strategic moment.

Having grown up in such an adult world, I was more comfortable with people of my parents' generation than my own and therefore did not repine over the lack of younger company during my tour. Patience was probably disappointed that no wider social world had opened up for me after her hard work in arranging these visits, but her desire to see me marry 'well' was implicit rather than stated. Being fundamentally realistic, she probably realised that there was little chance of my forming the relationship of her dreams. Though my looks had improved, I did not possess the sort of beauty that could override my social background. Stoics would seem an obvious source of relationships for me, but the only serious one I formed, was too 'boy and girl' to have lasted. Otherwise, the boys either, as Jeremy Jessel said, did not know what to make of me, or as Colin James said in his address at Bill's memorial service, regarded me as a 'favourite younger sister'. I did not at all wish to be so regarded, but in spite of the open discussion of sex to which I had been privy, I remained ignorant and naive in many ways, with a strong awareness of the dangers of pregnancy current in those pre-pill days.

Bill and Patience disapproved deeply of young women who appeared sexually aware, rather unpleasantly spreading stories about some girl whose parents wished to remove her from the co-educational Royal Latin School because she was distracted by having boys around her. Bill had a theory that girls who had full sexual experience in their teens would become wholly promiscuous. This could have arisen from a misreading of what can happen to women who have been sexually abused, seeing them as being desperate for sex rather than suffering from a sense of worthlessness. Adrian Evans remembers being impressed by Bill's having noticed that someone's visiting sister revealed a lack of knickers when climbing over a style. To Adrian this showed a worldliness unexpected in a middle-aged schoolmaster. Fundamentally, though, both Bill and Patience regarded themselves as failures in the performance of sex and were at pains to ensure that I was taught how very difficult it was to achieve it successfully. They gave me a fearful book to read when I was about 16, entitled the *Psychology of Sex*. It was written by an Austrian, probably a follower of Freud, who detailed a lot of difficult relationships and no successes that I can remember.

It was Patience who realised that I was in danger of becoming wedded to home and began a push to get me out. I was clear that working with horses was not something I wished to pursue, but I had no qualifications whatever in any other field. She therefore pulled strings and persuaded David Part, who was by now running a large part of The General Trading Company, to take me on as a salesgirl. I was 18 and wholly without experience. However, my erratic upbringing had apparently equipped me better than I feared, and I turned out to be a reasonably efficient saleswoman. Through an agency I found a flat to share with the Lady Katherine Courtenay, which pleased Bill. John Hunt

251

remembers him in the Master's Common Room stirring his gin and orange with a pencil while announcing that I had 'got in with the upper classes'. I mostly enjoyed my work, though I missed Vancouver passionately and rushed home every weekend.

I was close to both my parents, but to each in very different ways. With Patience I talked endlessly. We discussed relationships, animals, books, her past, and, obliquely, her marriage. Once, when very angry, she said she was going to divorce Bill. I was furious with her and she backed down instantly, leaving me surprised by my own power. I now realise that she never had any intention of leaving him. With Bill I did things like going hunting and to pubs. It was probably because he had driven me home from one of these outings having had a considerable amount to drink that caused Patience's rage, and she was quite right to be angry. His being late for meals, which was frequently because he had been boozing and gossiping, and his failing to pay bills so that we were threatened with the telephone or electricity being cut off were, understandably, strong sources of grievance. Their mutual care for the Historians, however, always overrode such clashes.

In spite of my devotion to them, a year working in London loosened their hold on me and I began to hanker after wider worlds. The ending of the relationship that, however youthful, had been a powerful element in my life since I was 15, was a catalyst, and I decided to follow what was a conventional path for young women of my generation, and go to America. I said at the time that I needed to get far enough away from Bill and Patience to test out my ability to be independent, which was probably an accurate assessment of my motives. Through a colleague at the GTC, I got an introduction to someone who recommended me to Scribners Bookshop as a suitable saleswoman, a pleasing achievement since it was on my own merits. I organised my admission to America as an immigrant and, failing to realise that the lavish-sounding $18 a week was less than I was earning in London, set off full of optimism in October 1962 at the height of the Cuban missile crisis. My departure horrified Patience. She wanted me to stay at General Trading, where she thought I would have a good chance of finding a suitable husband and was anxious about what might happen to me. She would have been even more frightened had she realised how serious the Cuban crisis was or how dangerous a place New York was thought to be. Heroically, she concealed all her misgivings from me and paid my fare. When we parted, she characteristically offered me her cheek to kiss with her mouth screwed sideways. Demonstrations of affection were never her strong point and I had few presents from her. An exception was a copy of *A Shropshire Lad* by A. E. Housman, poems that she adored, so it was a deeply significant gesture, but there was no inscription or note to go with the book. Bill was much more comfortable with showing his feelings.

Bill and Patience had arranged for me to be met by their delightfully named American literary agent, John Tiffany Elliot. I nonetheless arrived in New York quaking with terror and was not much helped by John, who was clearly fed up at the lateness of my plane. However, having started work in the children's book department of Charles Scribner's Sons, taken up some of the numerous introductions I had been given and moved out of the very expensive hotel recommended as 'safe and suitable' by my godmother Lee Kennard, I began to find my feet, make some friends and survive, albeit close to the breadline much of the time. I obeyed the exhortations not to walk home from work via the darker streets, not to travel by public transport at night and on no account to go near Harlem, and remained unmolested. John Tiffany Elliot took me out once. He was sadly mean, and a trip on the Staten Island Ferry was about the cheapest activity possible in New York.

I was puzzled by Pop Art, then just getting into its stride, regarding it with insular prejudice. One of my introductions arranged for me to attend a party given for Andy Warhol, whom I duly met. I was unable to dredge up anything complimentary to say about his pictures of Campbell's soup tins, which I found baffling, while he left no impression on me at all. It was years before I realised how privileged I had been and how regrettable it was that I had been unable to take advantage of my luck. Instead, the Frick Museum, full of familiar artists, became a comforting bolthole.

My other celebrity introduction was much more manageable. At a party given by Fabers to which Bill and Patience had taken me just before I left, they had met Wystan Auden, whom they probably had not seen since before the war. It was a happy encounter and when I rang him as instructed, he and his partner, Chester Kallmann, asked me to supper. Armed with my experience of the Viennese opera, I was able to hold my own and was deeply touched when Wystan gave me my taxi fare home. He subsequently asked me to a party on Christmas Eve, at which I was the only woman. On this occasion keeping my end up was harder, but it was unnecessary to make much effort since, after a time, Wystan became rather maudlin and insisted that we all listen to records of trains running through cuttings in Devon. Later, he enormously increased my kudos in the shop by coming in to ask for a copy of *The Hobbit*. His next invitation was to go with him and Chester to a new production of *The Rake's Progress* for which he had written the libretto. He promised to introduce me to Stravinsky after the performance, but at that point I had to return to England. During all this time Bill and Patience's lives had been going through a series of massive upheavals.

23

Changes

For a time in the fifties, Stowe went along cheerfully enough, but the discipline was reputed to be dire and there was a sense of drift. Eric Reynolds had continued to feel the ill-effects of his fall from the Cuillins and was without the drive needed to pull the school together. In 1958 he retired, and there was much excitement about who should succeed him. At Vancouver, a list of runners and prices was drawn up, which included genuinely possible names together with some lurid figures currently hitting the headlines. Donald Crichton-Miller was quoted at short odds, but Bill, who had known him when he had taught briefly at Stowe in the thirties, was deeply perturbed at the thought that he might be the successful candidate. He travelled to Cambridge to see Noel Annan, then Chairman of the Governors, to express his doubts. When Crichton-Miller was finally appointed, Noel wrote reassuringly to Bill, stressing his strength and experience. The fact that the man had an excellent track record, having turned round first Taunton and then Fettes, inspired the Governors to think that he could do the same for Stowe.

In his *Times* obituary, Crichton-Miller's achievements at Taunton and Fettes were noted and it went on: 'Moving to Stowe at the height of his powers, aged fifty-two, he should have looked forward to winning still more golden opinions, particularly as he had taught there as a young man. But then things went badly wrong. His robust authoritarian style which according to Rae, had "inspired great loyalty" at Taunton and later at Fettes, was resented by a number of Stowe's senior housemasters. Moreover, some of these, as is often the way in such closed communities, maintained their own private lines to the governors – especially to those of them who were old boys of the school.'

Probably Bill was one of those complaining, but for once, he was

in the majority, since dislike of Crichton-Miller and his 'robust authoritarian style' actually succeeded in uniting all eight Housemasters, a
unique event. My personal view of what happened is that, with the
advent of a new Headmaster, the school's morale had lifted, discipline
had improved and there was a greater sense of purpose in the place
before Crichton-Miller arrived. Instead of taking time to find out what
was actually happening, he set out at once to be the new broom with
a style that was the antithesis of Roxburgh and, indeed, Reynolds.
Boys and staff resented the fact that their efforts had gone unnoticed,
becoming rebellious and uncooperative.

Another of Crichton-Miller's achievements at Fettes had been to
make it one of the best sports schools in the country, and his passion
for all sports, but particularly rugby, was another cause of major
clashes at Stowe. From the start, Stowe had, I think, always been
ambivalent about sporting prowess, J.F. being particularly anxious that
there should be a balance with sport being varied and not an obsession. (There was a legend to which, naturally, Patience gave credence,
that a Stoic had once been overheard in a rugger scrum saying
piteously, 'Humphrey, for pity's sake, you are standing on my hair.')
Donald Crichton-Miller, who had played rugger for Scotland, placed
great emphasis on the First Fifteen doing well, and it became known
that good rugger players could get away with murder. No action was
taken over one member of the First Fifteen who, before a match, had
too good a lunch with quite a lot of brandy, causing him to throw up
on the field. However, Paul Whitfield, who was not a rugger player,
was caught returning to his study by a teetotal master after a modest
consumption of vodka, which he had thought would not be detectable
on his breath, and was partially expelled. This was a curious punishment. He was suspended from living in the school, but was allowed
to stay at Vancouver for a term while he worked for an exam. He was
later to become a Governor of the school. Francis O'Neill, who was,
with Paul, one of the wits of the History Side, suggested in the
Debating Society to loud cheers, that 'members of the First Fifteen
should take care to wear their scarves at all times in case they got
expelled by accident.' Obviously, such inconsistent discipline failed to
inspire respect and exacerbated the clashes between Crichton-Miller
and his staff.

Bill thought that there was a conflict in Crichton-Miller between the
authoritarian sportsman and the tenets handed down by his father, who
was a distinguished psychiatrist. Bill intolerantly branded Crichton-

256

Miller *père* a 'charlatan' which, given that he founded the highly thought of Tavistock Clinic, is unlikely, but his assessment, that no one knew which side of the son would appear in which situation, was probably accurate. Although Bill felt that all he stood for was being undermined, he did not retaliate in all the ways he might. Adrian Evans, who was Head of School in Crichton-Miller's second year, said that he never felt a clash of loyalties or any suggestion that he should not carry out policies agreed with the Headmaster. It is, perhaps, symptomatic of the erratic discipline however, that Adrian's varied reasons for trips to London were never questioned.

The Times obituary charts 'Arguments over discipline and admissions, fuelled by this damaging clash of personalities'. This led to a struggle for power, and, in the end, to an inquiry led by Queens Counsel, during which Crichton-Miller was suspended. The inquiry cleared him, but he was then accused of leaking the findings and offered the choice of instant resignation or being sacked. He chose to resign, and thus ignominiously ended what had been a successful career up to the point of his moving to Stowe. It is possible, however, that his time at Fettes was not the sweetness and light portrayed, but then Patience's story, that the staff there danced a jig on the table in the master's mess when they heard he was leaving, may have been apocryphal. Stephen Whitwell knew Crichton-Miller after he had left Stowe and liked him.

Bill, however, was not part of the final cabal against Crichton-Miller. Increasingly unhappy with the job and finding it difficult to continue running the History Side as he wanted, Bill was, for the first time, seriously considering his future. He had continued to feel that his 1959 Culture Tour was a comparative failure, and it was probably symptomatic of his feelings that the 1961 production of *Macbeth* was not marked with the usual pasting of the reviews and programme into his press-cutting album. The problems at Stowe had naturally affected the intake of boys, and while many of his later Historians were as cherished and appreciated as ever, he was not enthusiastic about the prospects for the future.

Not that Crichton-Miller was, apparently, anxious to be rid of him. An additional Senior Tutor post seems to have been planned, and the Headmaster offered it to Bill. In reply Bill wrote:

'After very careful consideration I have come to the conclusion that I shall have to ask you to find someone else to do the new

Senior Tutor job for you. Though I fully understand, and in many respects wholeheartedly appreciate, the objects which you have in view, and have no doubt that I could manage the job to your satisfaction, it is clear that the sort of supervision you require will involve a great deal of administrative work of the kind which I most dislike and would cut me off altogether from the sort of teaching which I enjoy and do best.'

Bill goes on:

'Whether there will remain a niche for me within your recon-structed syllabus is a separate question which needs more care-ful and lengthy thought than I have yet had time to devote to it. I feel, however, that you should know my decision on the Senior Tutorship at once so that you may start looking for someone else right away. I *am* grateful to you for offering me the post and much regret that I feel obliged to decline it.'

The final tantalising sentence reads:

'The points raised in your private covering note I have answered also privately and under separate cover.'

The mind can only boggle at what issues might have been raised.

Now aged 55, finding another job could have been difficult for Bill, but for once he had a stroke of solid luck and the consideration of what place he might have had in an academically reorganised Stowe did not arise. A civilian was needed at the Royal Military Academy Sandhurst to head the Modern Subjects Department, and Bill was pro-posed as a candidate by General Jim Wilson, known as 'Swinging Jim', who had heard Bill holding forth on the Battlefield Tours, and was deeply impressed. In March 1962, Bill wrote again to Crichton-Miller, this time addressing him as 'Donald' rather than 'Headmaster'.

'Sometime ago I was asked to stand for the Directorship of Modern Studies at Sandhurst and agreed to do so. It is a £2,400 a year job [considerably more than Bill was earning at Stowe] and from what I have been told at the Sandhurst end sounds very much my cup of tea. They want the whole of their Arts curricu-lum livened up and liberalised, and the problem of educating the

258

soldier has always been one that interested me anyway. So I hope you will not feel that I am doing the wrong thing. The matter has now come rather abruptly out of the clouds of Civil Service Commission muddle and delay, and I am invited to an interview on the 30th. There are, of course, many slips twixt cup and lip and invited to stand by no means implies appointment. But I thought I should let you know as soon as the matter became definite, lest you should feel I was manoeuvring behind your back. I imagine, anyway, that at some stage you will be asked to answer some enquiries. I need not tell you that my feelings about it all are excessively mixed. But once in for a job one can't help wanting to get it. So I hope you will be able to give me a reasonable character.'

Bill did get the job and Sandhurst announced that they wanted him to start within a month. This meant an incredibly abrupt departure from Stowe, with the History Side abandoned to its fate. A letter to Crichton-Miller written at the beginning of May reveals some of the haste and complications involved:

'Dear Donald, I rushed off in terrible confusion and without formal goodbyes and am only just beginning to surface this end. But formal goodbyes are always trying, and I daresay you were as busy as I was on Thursday morning. I must however just put on record my very great sense of the patience and tolerance extended to me by three consecutive Headmasters and my gratitude for them; and for the kind things you said on Wednesday evening.'

He goes on to propose a master to take over the fencing, suggests that Joe Bain might prefer to put on the Shakespeare play rather than one with the Congreve Club, and says that he has briefed the master designated to take over the History Side. Bill implies that he is feeling somewhat adrift at Sandhurst, but adds that he has been warmly welcomed. He ends:

'I hope to get over for an occasional weekend in the intervals of house-hunting to see you all. Meanwhile, very many thanks for much kindness.'

Bill had taught at Stowe for 24 years, though Patience would call it

259

28 as if the war had never happened. The speed of his leaving now seems almost brutal, but does seem, in some respects, to have been eased by Crichton-Miller who had initially made the reasonable assumption that he would give a term's notice, but agreed to let Bill go immediately without his having undergone the medical required by Sandhurst.

However, his swift departure does seem to have left Crichton-Miller floundering a little, and apparently deeply concerned about the issue of whether or not Bill's name should be removed from the *Blue Book*. The *Blue Book* was produced every term and listed the staff, all the boys, their forms or sides and gave details of who taught them. A soothing letter to Crichton-Miller from Patrick Hunter, the Senior Tutor, which begins by detailing the disposition of Bill's work, goes on to address this matter: 'What I was trying to say about the *Blue Book* was this. The other day you expressed a considerable doubt about whether Bill would pass his medical. If that is in fact the case, my feeling was this. The circumstances compel our making and, unless the case is by then confirmed, implementing plans for the taking of Bill's work for next term. If he were failed on the Medical and came back, it would be embarrassing but not very embarrassing for him.' Hunter goes on to say that he felt the embarrassment would be worse if alterations had already been made to the *Blue Book*, and wondering if these could not be left until regular revisions were made, or, finally, whether the whole issue was really so crucial.

Crichton-Miller replied that the arrangements for the disposal of Bill's work were most satisfactory, but that the matter of the *Blue Book* was 'most unsatisfactory'. He admits that he had changed his mind about it, adding that his hand had been forced by alterations having been made without his authority. He suggests that he had been indiscreet in mentioning the possibility of Bill failing his medical, saying that he had been influenced by the Stowe tradition that Bill had only one lung along with 'various other deficiencies'. He goes on to detail his decision to compromise by removing Bill's name from the list of tutors, but not his initials from besides the names of his tutees. However, he had then found office staff busily removing all traces of Bill from the *Blue Book* and had felt that it would be impossible to tell secretaries why the process should be delayed.

There is an element of farce in this exchange. Had Bill been aware of it, he would have been fascinated by the way in which his departure could only be coped with by a partial denial that it was going to happen at all and by focusing on what must have been the most trivial aspect of the upheaval he caused. Since he was not required to take Sandhurst cadets across the Brecon Beacons, Bill's lack of a lung did not tell against him. David Farmer, Bill's successor, can have had only the briefest of handovers, but I suspect that Bill had become sufficiently detached from the History Side to be able to leave them to their fate in a way that would have been unthinkable only a few years earlier. He would have been pleased, however, that, some years later, his post was taken by Andrew Rudolph, one of the mid-fifties Historians of whom he was both fond and proud.

Though the actual leaving of the school cannot have been marked at all, the Historians did him proud. A group of them, inspired by my then boss, David Part, arranged a dinner for Bill and Patience at the Cutler's Hall, at which there were nearly 70 of them across the generations. Noel Annan presided, and Bill was presented with a bound volume of all the Historians' photographs.

Patience's departure was less dramatic. It had never occurred to either of them, that they might one day need to own a house. They could have continued to postpone this decision had not Patience said that she would rather be dead than live in the Army 'Quarter' offered to them by way of accommodation. This made the acquisition of a house essential, and by June a pleasant enough turn-of-the-century house had been found in Yateley. The fact that one of her favourite Victorian tear-jerkers had been set in that village overcame her memories of stressful occasions staying with her formidable aunt who had lived there in her girlhood, and she was prepared to settle for the house which, though smaller than Vancouver, she thought would do. There then arose the problem of paying for it. Their hand-to-mouth finances had never included saving money for the future, and the only capital available was tied up in a marriage settlement in my favour that could not be touched before I was 21. At this point I was almost 20 and attempts were made to persuade Coutts, as trustees of the settlement, to break the trust. My assurances that I would honour the arrangement were countered by the assertion, put with maximum charm and diplomacy, that I might meanwhile marry a 'bounder'. They were rescued by Old Historians. Geoffrey Russell and George Corbett who, being more trusting of me than Coutts, lent them the money until I could repay them. It was blithely assumed that the house would be of greater value to me than £5000, but the arrangement gave little thought to the future.

261

For Patience the move was a huge upheaval. Bill was to some extent familiar with the army world he was moving into, but to her it was unknown and would require her to perform in a more adult social milieu, where her duffle coat and sneakers would not suffice. To start with, responding to the drama of it all, she threw herself into preparations for the change with gusto. She travelled to London, actually bringing herself to use the Underground, of which she had always been terrified, and acquired a splendid wardrobe from an upmarket second-hand clothes shop. This included a particularly smart Hardy Amies dress and jacket in which she looked splendid.

She set about packing up Vancouver with a vengeance, labelling the whole exercise *The Fall of the House of Usher* and becoming carried away by the enthusiasm of the various Historians helping her and the sight of bonfires consuming the accumulation of years. Much of value disappeared, though some clearance was necessary given that The Hollies was considerably smaller than Vancouver. All was eventually ready, and the leaving of Vancouver Lodge was appropriately toasted in gin drunk out of jam jars. Christopher Gauvain and Patience between them commemorated the house as a second home for Historians in the back of the visitors' book: 'Total number of guests at Vancouver Lodge Jan 20th 1934 – 10th August 1962 Approx 1,270. Since the war, 1,008 approx. Stephen Whitwell stayed 50 times, Christopher Cash 45. Paul Whitfield stayed the longest.'

24

A New Life and a Tragedy

In the aftermath of the war, it had been decided that the British Army needed to extend the education of the Officer Corps. The two-year course at the Royal Military Academy, Sandhurst, therefore added to the military training provided, with departments teaching military history, languages, a range of scientific subjects, and the department Bill had been appointed to head, Modern Subjects, which was concerned with modern history, economics and political sciences. The then Commandant of the Academy, Major General Geordie Gordon-Lennox, felt that the syllabus in Modern Subjects needed to be revised to take account of the rapid changes taking place in British and International affairs. Bill's task was therefore to ensure the relevance of the teaching with this in mind and to enhance the department's credibility with the soldiers and the outside academic world. Philip Warner, the distinguished author, who was already a member of the department when Bill arrived, thinks that Bill was well fitted to build bridges. He cited his successful career as a teacher and historian together with his war record, as making him acceptable on both counts. It was a good start that Bill enjoyed the company of soldiers. He also became close friends with Brigadier Peter Young, legendary soldier, author and creator of the Sealed Knot, who had no trouble in maintaining the prestige of the Military History Department, which he ran. The two of them were able to do much to promote academic studies to the military. Both enthusiastic drinkers with a fund of amusing war stories, they made a highly entertaining duo.

Bill therefore began his new career on a good wicket. Patience, after her initial optimism, struggled to find her feet. It was particularly difficult for her that, immediately after the drama of the move, the Academy was shut for the holidays and nothing was happening.

Thrown in on herself, she became depressed and only began to revive when term began. Projecting her feelings about other Stowe masters' wives, she was suspicious of the wives of Bill's fellow academics and, before she really knew them, was concerned to think that her social life might revolve round coffee mornings and drinks parties given by members of his department. However, her morale was boosted by the arrival of old friends to stay at The Hollies and, like Bill, she enjoyed the company of soldiers enormously. When I left for America in October, she was beginning to get interested in Bill's work and to make friends, a process that escalated and was vividly described in her letters.

She was an assiduous correspondent, writing at least once a week, almost invariably typing on air letter forms and beginning with the day of the week and no other preamble. To save space, she used a telegraphic style and mostly did without paragraphs, ending as abruptly as she had started as in: 'Feet now dropping off, so must stop. Both bathroom basin and my cigarette holder stopped up. Bad butter.' They described enjoyable parties with the military, mostly what she felt were boring events with the civilians, and mixed entertainment in the village. She was also concerned to keep me posted about the affairs of David Hall, a young officer I had met a week before leaving.

One of Patience's earliest involvements was in helping to run a stall at some pre-Christmas fair in the Academy. The woman in charge of the stall was a comparatively senior officer's wife, but this in no way protected her from Patience, who described her as being 'exactly like a superior housekeeper, dressed in frock though middle of the morning, perched on the edge of her chair nibbling biscuits like a rabbit. Cannot imagine her at siege of Lucknow or any other where mem [*sic* – short for memsahib] heroism called for, nor indeed coping with Judy O'Grady.' The sale itself provided another vivid description:

'R.M.A. sale totally exhausting, owing to rebellious behaviour of Judy Swinton, who said how could we have been such fools as to let ourselves be roped in for this and then spent most of the time the wrong side of the counter with children and splendid nanny, who refused to let children buy solid bar of bright yellow icing sugar how right she was. The General appeared in full regimentals and bought a tin of sardines. Cannot think how and when he will eat them in Government House.'

Patience was also distracted by 'long wails' from two other helpers, one about her writing, which she thinks is out of touch – 'and so I should think after reading pretty nauseous poem in the *Lady*, and the other from the befrocked housekeeper.

> 'She hates Sandhurst, can't fit in, always doing the wrong thing, and she has four daughters 21–16, and she can't get hold of cadets for them and they tell her she is a dreary old hag. Oh dear. Could not in all honesty say that all daughters like that.'

Judy Swinton was the wife of the Adjutant and mother of the actress Tilda Swinton. The Adjutant is an important figure in Sandhurst life. At the Sovereign's Parade, at which those of the cadets who have completed their training 'pass out', he is expected to ride his horse up the steps and into the main building behind their retreating forms. The big double doors then close symbolically behind cadets and horse. The Swinton's nanny was a formidable figure, and Judy would tell with relish the story of Nanny's planned holiday in what was then Yugoslavia. This was a coach trip with other nannies, and, before departing, Nanny was given to talking intolerantly of foreigners. 'But Nanny', said Judy, 'when you are there, you will be the foreigner.' 'Oh no I shan't' said Nanny, 'and what's more they'll know it.' I was later startled when I was a Captain's wife, struggling to make ends meet, when Judy remarked cheerfully that 'John's pay just about covers the housekeeping.'

I had written to Patience, telling her that I had been asked out several times by a man called Biddle, using the quote 'how can I marry a man called meatsafe' from one of the beloved Nelson classics to demonstrate my feelings about his name. Patience's next letter began: 'Wed. You say how can you marry a man called meatsafe, but I would remind you of Social Register saying that the Cabots only speak to the Biddles and the Biddles speak only to God. You say 0 [sic] about your job, want to know about fellow workers, customers and what Kropotkin [the manager of the shop] looks like.' Having then described a number of looming parties, 'wine and cheese with the Rs weighing on me like ton of bricks and I shall be asked fifteen times if I write under my own name', but 'cheered' by the thought of dining with the Deputy Commandant, she writes of the first time she had cadets to dinner.

> 'Pa worried about it as he feared I would find the first ones he

had asked dull and charley [a current McElwee euphemism for common], as two from grammar schools and the other only from Worksop, but it was most successful, all talking subjects like mad and only one from Gloucester Cathedral School really common. All three pathetically grateful. When you really get them talking and when object of party intellectual and not sexual intercourse they really are much more mature than the average schoolboy, and one can see dedication to their profession burgeoning in them, maybe because they have had to make a real effort to get to Sandhurst and are not just doing it because they can't get to a university and don't like the idea of business. Boy from Worksop very well read.'

A subsequent cadet party was: 'so successful that they said, when I began my Company Commander panic at 10.45, that they would risk white belts if they could stay a bit longer'. The wine and cheese party lived up to all Patience's worst expectations:

'accents one and all shattering and I found myself saying pleased to meet you and phone for the fish knives Norman before I had been there half an hour. Pa took your flask, very wisely, but felt we couldn't both of us say we could only drink spirits so swallowed three glasses of tepid cough mixture and woke up next day with hang-over of a lifetime.'

Now successfully back on some familiar territory, Patience also began enjoying village activities as well. She even went to the Women's Institute, something she never did in Dadford, leaving me to be the family representative from the age of 15. (Bizarrely, I was secretary by the time I was 17.) Of her first visit to the WI she wrote,

'Hilarious afternoon tasting British wines, utter filth, purveyed by determinedly jolly man called either Hoberman or Hamburger. Achieved no doubt lasting fame by saying "yes I have" when he asked if any of us had been in Vienna and answering ensuing spate of German with one polished sentence. About fifty people there so reedy pipe was drowned in Jerusalem, played with startling inaccuracy by elderly Miss Stilwell. Feel no time at all will elapse before I am asked to give a Talk.

266

She also described Yateley society in general:

'You wouldn't think, there could be so many women in twinsets and pearls in the world, all with miniature poodles and tottering old Colonels in the background.'

Of the academic wives she was intolerant:

'Am truly appalled by attitude of wives to R.M.A., nervous break-downs right and left, chips on their shoulders about the military, husbands in consequence either neglecting their work or break-ing up their homes. Cannot get used to people oiling up to me as though I were headmaster's wife. So strange to me, after having been kicked around by generations of Stoics, thankful to be allowed to sit in the Pavilion, elated to be treated to nasty cup of Maxwell House in Temple Prefectory. Whole place too vast a con-cern for me to be able to turn it upside down, but do see how very wrong these women are, saying how glad they are they Keep Out or have Dropped Out.'

A party with old friends, someone to stay for the weekend, an outing to hear *HMS Pinafore* at Wellington with a friend ('familiar Tiber coloured coffee and fancies afterwards'), and entertaining some cadets to dinner was described by Patience as an 'otherwise blank week'. No wonder that in another letter she remarked that 'As you can imagine, my Hardy Amies is doing overtime.'

Patience also wrote that she had revamped an unpublished novel and had an idea for another, and that she was keeping The Hollies, which she always referred to as 'The Doll's House', immac-ulate. Not without help, though. 'Peter Leslie's weekend made by discovering that stains hitherto defying OMO, Ajax, Brillo etc, on gas stove could be removed by Duraglit, madly expensive and thought whole thing would blow up.' Bill's specific activities were mentioned occasionally, along with those of the young man I had met before I left:

'Pa had a batch with the military on Friday night, crawling home at two thirty. He said there was a night exercise going on and that David managed to retain his early nineteenth charm and elegance even with his face blacked.'

267

She described the fearful weather of the 1962 winter:

'Getting a bit sick of blasted winter wonderland, everything out-lined in white for days, no let up and people dying like flies in London. Am put in frenzy by command to meet Queen Mum at party in Indian Army Room on Sunday week, not because I wouldn't like to make my curtsey to the old girl, but because do not see that I can go in my boots, David's hockey shirt and old green sweater, topped by that red cap of yours.'

This 'David' was the last of her specially beloved Stoics.

Before she could meet the Queen Mum however, Patience had dis-turbing news.

'Dec. 14th. Know you will not fall into strong hysterics when I tell you I am going into Cottage Hospital to have a cyst or gland or something out of my breast on the 27th. You remember I had a swelling and a rash and a very sore nipple in August, and it has not got better. The Dr did give it a name, something like Packet's Disease, and as it hasn't yielded to drugs they think it better to hack it open. Specialist madly glam in world-weary sort of way, and all at hospital very nice. I shall be in there some time as they will do a skin graft over the scar, cannot think why, as I don't earn my living as a fan dancer. Asked doctor if any need to fuss and he said none in the world, so no need for you to, nor to waste substance on telephoning. Shall use it as an excuse for months to come not to have to entertain bores, just have nice little parties of cadets lying about like Madame Recamier.'

Later in the same letter she wrote:

'Am not keeping ausflug to hospital dark, as wish for as many letters, flowers and visitors as possible, but as mere mention of hospital and the knife gives rise to fantastic rumours warn you not to take anything anyone writes to you seriously. Only person I am not telling – repeat not – is Mary [my Godmother], or she would be here at once, feeding Pa on macaroni and chocolate shape and hopefully planning her nuptials with him.'

She then went off on another tack before returning to the subject, saying that she only wanted glamorous and useless presents in hospital so that she could impress the nurses and the surgeon. 'Odd fact of life that all surgeons have surnames instead of Christian names, Dill Russell, just like Sir Watson Cheyne, Sir Lenthil Cheetle, Sir Crisp English and Sir Omicron Pi.'

In her next letter Patience described the moving response of Sandhurst staff to her news. Everyone, from General Gordon-Lennox to members of Bill's department whom she had not even met, enquired and offered help. 'I am quite amazed to find how terribly kind people are and what a mark we have made here.' One Colonel said she should ask him for anything in the world she would like, 'so he is sending me some port. Only hope it doesn't arrive before I go in, or it will all be drunk and I shall have gout into the bargain.' Characteristically, she then describes the party given to meet the Queen Mum, which 'all agreed was pretty dull, drinks not on the house which was a shock, no food and Queen Mum obviously only wanted to talk to cadets, for which I don't blame her.' The final paragraph returns to her health: 'as I said in my last, do not attach any importance to anything you hear about my health. You know my instinct for drama and if people want to think it's serious and that I'm being a heroine, so much the better.' I cannot remember if I believed the fiction she sold me.

I obeyed her injunction against telephoning. Spending on long-distance telephone calls, even when she was not paying, was something Patience hated, and conversations were therefore deeply unsatisfactory. Her grandmother had died of breast cancer, and though an aunt had survived it, living to a ripe old age, it had always been one of her greatest fears and we had lived through a good many apparent false alarms. Four years earlier, she had been to the doctor with a lump in her breast, but because it was painful he told her that it could not be malignant and was probably a manifestation of the menopause.

That this diagnosis had been quite wrong was confirmed by a letter from Bill, written on Christmas Day. He wrote 'in the teeth of P's prohibition, because I think you would hate to be kept in the dark.' He was reassuring, acknowledging that because the cancer had been ignored, a lot would have to be taken away, but quoting the surgeon as saying that she would have an 80 per cent chance of survival. He wrote that: 'There will be a good deal of immediate discomfort, I'm afraid, especially for a person as unamenable to hospital discipline as your Mum, God bless her.' He hopes that she will be well by March and fuller of energy than she has been, which suggests that the positive picture she had painted of her life in Yateley had not been a full one. Above all, he stresses, she would hate me to come home, and assures me that it would be quite unnecessary. 'P herself entirely brave and cheerful – quite wonderful though apt to wake in the night to tell me what she wants done with the cats or about your stored clothes in the cupboard in case she dies "under the knife".'

Three days later he wrote again:

'The news to date is good. The operation was done this morning and according to all accounts, took much less time than was expected. The sister tells me, also, that they aren't proposing to do a skin graft, which argues that they've had to take way less than they feared. Still more reassuring, your Mum, when I crept in on her this evening, though still very dopey, splendidly trucu- lent – always a good sign – stoutly protesting that they had removed her entire chest, but also assuring me at slightly tearful intervals that all the staff of the hospital were angels. Anyway, no immediate need to worry. I think myself that we're probably out of the wood, and in the nick of time, though I expect we shall have some scares over the next year or two.'

He is concerned by a letter from me that clearly suggests that I should come home and reiterates the lack of immediate concern, adjuring me to continue to write 'cheerful loving letters. Thanks to her enormous courage – always much in evidence in a real crisis – Mum's cancer and Mum's prospective falsies are already on the way to becoming great jokes among the cognoscenti, and all I feel we can do is to help along these lines.' In his next sentence, Bill allows his distress to show: 'I wish I had time and opportunity for a good long talk about it all. Letters are such an inadequate medium, and I feel that I sound cal- lous, when in fact I am consumed with love and anxiety, not only for darling Patience, but for you.' He goes on, more positively, to detail the support and concern he was receiving from the Church services that included prayers for Patience and gave him great comfort, to the kindness of Peter and Joan Young, who made him spend the day of the operation with them. However, 'The cats, I need hardly say, are entirely uncooperative and much resent the whole situation.' Bill then returns to Patience's way of dealing with it all: 'I feel that what is really building is another splendid chapter in the saga, and my one preoccupation is to prevent your mother drawing up a black list of

270

those who haven't enquired, sent flowers or entertained me in her absence.'

Shortly after this I got a pencilled letter from Patience herself. She repeated much of the information Bill had already given me, and said that 'No words can describe kindness of nurses, also divine sort of male orderly who has just backed Brown Diamond for me.' She went on: 'Have been prayed for twice in Church, though mercifully I didn't need it health-wise, and it worked courage-wise, which was all I minded about. So hard on Pa and angelic friends if I had allowed myself to be stampeded into terror by the mere words. Must have presented strange appearance for operation, wearing long white stockings, snazzy little dark green pants and sort of white middy blouse. Far the worst aspect of it all is that I have promised Dr not to smoke for a week in case I cough to detriment of stitches.'

Throughout the early part of January the news continued to be positive. Bill wrote that Patience's recovery was remarkable, largely thanks to her high morale. He also said that her social standing in the hospital was enormous thanks to the masses of flowers, including a huge bunch of carnations from Oswald Normanby. The weather, this being the awful winter of 1963, clearly added to Bill's difficulties, and though he wrote that he had been able to get his ancient Rover out every day, Patience described him having to be pushed out of a drift by 'prettiest nurse and Matron herself.' Bill described 'siege conditions at The Hollies', for which the five cats apparently held him personally responsible. 'They sit gloomily round me all day with their arms folded remarking at intervals that the Mistress managed better.' His strain shows particularly in one brief sentence: 'The only snag is that Sandhurst starts up again on Wednesday. Hardly feel I have had a holiday at all.'

Patience began to find the hospital wearing, though she remained funny about it. 'Most sinister Bad Leg in today. Glad her leg is bad as she is clearly a murderess. Also another dotty old Gran. Foresee most disturbed night of bedpans, chokes and slipping down in bed.' She was cheered by her literary agents being pleased with her revised novel and fascinated to discover that what she had lost would be replaced by birdseed: 'so entranced by this discovery that it nearly makes whole thing worthwhile – Pa told Kitty Cunliffe this when she rang for news and she wrote and said it must be Swoop. The only perfectly *balanced* birdseed.' The hospital filled up with difficult patients, and though the flow of flowers and visitors continued, she longed to be at home.

'Major op, (not as major as mine) playing up like mad, screaming to go home. Hope they will knock her out tonight or we shall get even less sleep than last when sinister old gran walked in her sleep – oh my goodness, minor op now crying her head off – Nurse Taylor promised me an improper story three hours ago, but has not yet got round to telling it. Pa, needless to say, life and soul of the ward – nurses and patients alike mad about him.'

Patience's next letter was written from The Hollies and reveals how difficult it had been for her in hospital:

'Heavenly cold, dark silent bedroom. I slept 13 hours straight through last night. Could not have stood central heating, telly or fellow patients one night longer, though parted from nurses with great regret. Drove Dill Russell against the ropes yesterday and said as he had not minced words at first interview could I have the same plain speaking now to which he said that he had found it very widespread and had done an enormous operation, but that I had made a first class recovery and that I had every chance of it being a complete success. The odd thing is that all that depression and nerviness has completely gone. I feel limp of course and have to sit about, but I feel quite a different person in myself. I must have had it for years sapping me. Am v glad that I emerged from hospital with unblemished reputation for being perfect patient. Cannot think how I managed it as hospital life not my cup of tea in any way except for having more flowers than anyone else and roughly fifteen letters a day. Even the butcher sent me a get well card. Pussies all entranced to see me and never had less than three on my lap from the moment I got home.'

After describing some of her visitors, she went on:

'I suppose people might think I've asked for this, always being pretty pleased with myself and really having an astonishing run of luck, But I must in all honesty admit that not at any moment in this last month, from when Dill Russell told me to the moment when I looked at the devastation for the first time, have I felt that

272

it outweighed all the fun and love and luck I've had. And I really think as regards actual minding, there have been lots of things I have minded more, like getting books returned, and your being made unhappy and Christopher (another beloved Historian) failing to get into Cambridge.'

This euphoria was short-lived. A letter from Bill is dated January 16 and written in his elegant, but illegible Germanic style, because 'it is slightly warmer by the sitting-room fire than in the study and conditions just now resemble siege of Haarlem though not yet reduced to eating boots or even Fergusson' (his favourite cat). He went on:

'Life not very easy just at the moment, tho' nothing you or anyone else can do anything about. I think they let your Mum out of hospital too soon. She has been bitterly disappointed to find herself very weak and pulled-down, having been badly misled over this by hearty physiotherapists. But the dry heat of the hospital gave her a ticklish cough, which of course pulls damaged muscles and nerves about quite cruelly. And as a result she has an attack of paralysing muscular rheumatism. V depressing for her, poor sweet as she can neither read, write nor knit, since the drugs which kill the rheumatic pains do her eyes in.'

My aunt, who was due to come and help out, had not arrived, and life must have been hell for him. Old friends visiting clearly helped, though – company was always the greatest tonic Patience could have.

A week later she wrote herself, apologising for lack of communication from either of them and describing 'muscular spasms, adhesions, shortness of breath and sweats etc, and have really been very sorry for myself.' The David she loved so much had come to see her and been deeply distressed by her plight, but my aunt Tonti had arrived and had cheered her greatly. The weather continued dire, and power cuts added to the misery. She described a visit from a doctor: 'my own off duty and had sinister woman from Eversley who started by saying was I sure they had taken off the right breast and that I had pleurisy. All a hum, of course, and perhaps excusable by light of guttering candle in sherry bottle.'

The sinister doctor, not being party to the hopeful fabrications of the truth by which Bill and Patience were surrounded, was right to question Patience's state. The next letter from either of them was a

273

shakily written note from Patience dated 4 February and written from St Luke's Hospital in Guildford. She wrote: 'I was removed here in a hurry last Thursday, to have a lot of fluid removed from my lungs. Am still a bit breathless and the deep x-rays are playing me up a lot, but I hope that Pa's charm may be able to arrange for me to have the whole treatment as an inpatient.' She went on to say that the food was filth, but that kind friends had supplied her with quantities of smoked salmon 'which pops out of the fridge whenever I want it, also they don't mind if you don't eat provided you will drink stuff like boiled down operation stockings in sufficient quantities. They also have the most potent pain killer referred to as jungle juice.' The next bit is hard to read and rambles rather though it includes speculation as to whether the 'jungle juice' is really curare.

The final paragraph says: 'Your David is being so angelic driving Pa over and loading me with flowers. He really is so decorative and sweet, though adamant on the subject of never having called a pavement a sidewalk.' – a reference to a running joke about my language becoming Americanised. Uncharacteristically, she ended 'Much love and don't worry'. I knew, though, from that letter that she was seriously ill, and was unsurprised when later that same evening, Bill rang me and said that she was dying. The doctors had continued to waffle on about recovery and another five years of life at least, but the Ward Sister took him aside and said that there was no hope of her surviving. The operation had of course revealed that the cancer had spread into her lung, exacerbated no doubt by her smoking, and they had known full well that she had no chance of recovery – hence, no doubt, the decision not to do a skin graft.

I told Bill that I would come home at once, at which he sounded hugely relieved, but a weekend and a public holiday for Lincoln's birthday intervened, delaying my obtaining the necessary tax clearance without which I would not be allowed to leave the country. I was clear that I was leaving America for good in order to look after Bill. He had told me that he felt I should not see Patience when I got back, since she would then know she was dying, but while still organising my departure, I got a telegram announcing her death. Perhaps Bill could not bring himself to tell me over the phone. I arrived the day before her funeral, which took place on Valentine's Day, and only properly realised she was dead when I saw her coffin carried into the church. She was cremated, and I remember feeling miserably that I was nowhere near ready for my 52-year-old mother to disappear like

274

that. The hymns we sang, the *Trumpet Voluntary* and Bach's *Jesu, Joy of Man's Desiring*, are still hard to hear. However, the lunch following her funeral was a riot. Alan Taylor, who had wept copiously earlier, became the life and soul of the party.

25

Picking up the Pieces

There was no question of Bill and me being left to ourselves to get over Patience's death. We were endlessly asked out to dinner, lunch and drinks. In addition, I was being traditionally courted, which added another layer of entertainment and companionship to a life in which I was also struggling with learning to manage a house. Patience had, by example, taught me to make cakes, but had neglected general instruction in cookery. With hindsight, all this activity prevented me mourning Patience properly, but Bill talked endlessly about her during those evenings when we were alone. He went over and over the events leading up to her death, how he would not have let me see her, not only because she would then have known she was dying, but also because of her changed appearance. He would then tell me that she had wished to see me again, which hurt. He was not with her when she died, but the Sister had told him that she had been reading and was found with the book drooping and her glasses slightly awry, which sounded peaceful and appropriate for Patience.

Bill detailed the difficulties of the period before she was taken into St Lukes, how she had been convinced that a little girl was trying to steal her breath, and, when she was lucid, how she had acknowledged the enormous mutual support and value of their relationship. It moved him deeply that I had found a copy of the poem he had written to her as the dedication of his novel, *The House*, tucked into a handkerchief case I had made for her one Christmas. The whole of their marriage was raked over, many of his memories being negative, such as Patience at the Normanby's wedding reception, saying: 'Well Oswald, so you have decided to remember your old friends after all?' and of the struggle he had to get her to return to Vancouver after the war. Yet underlying all the anger, which probably stemmed from his feeling

276

that she had abandoned him, was the sense of how enormously she had mattered to him. The difficulties involved in living with her challenged and stimulated Bill and this, together with the passionate interest she had always shown in his work, pupils and colleagues, gave him the grounding and structure from which he functioned. Without this particular companionship and the strong support she gave him in real crises, he was adrift and was never to recover entirely.

In the immediate aftermath, he ran his department, went to parties, embarked on a book and was both sustained and overwhelmed by the letters he received about Patience. The abundance of affection and sympathy was heartwarming, but writing answers, which Bill felt he had to do, was an added stress for one of the most reluctant letter-writers in Britain. The most eloquent tributes came from those who had found life at Stowe difficult. Not that this was true of Nicholas Lyell, later to be Attorney-General, who felt that 'in many ways Patience epitomised the highest form of human life on Earth.' He went on: 'This seems a silly and meaningless statement perhaps, but I have met few people who were so truly kind, so deeply interested in others, and such delightful company all in one. I don't believe I can ever remember a dull moment in her company.' The letter written by Donald Crichton-Miller did not survive, which is sad because Bill's answer suggests sensitive and appreciative comments:

'Dear Donald, Thank you for writing and for saying so much that was comforting and sustaining. Patience loved Stowe with all her heart and talked of it to the last. The knowledge of the affection and loving kindness of that great world helped very much to sustain us all in the last awful weeks and both Harriet and I will always be grateful for it. Illogically and, I suppose, sentimentally, I feel so sad that Patience can't read all the nice things people have said of her in the mountain of letters which lies in front of me. Of all of them I think she would have chosen yours as an obituary.'

After a message of thanks to Crichton-Miller's wife for her separate note, Bill ends:

'You said not to acknowledge, but I have found to my own surprise, so much comfort in all these letters that I feel bound to write and say thank you.'

A month later Bill was able to write to Christopher Kenyon: 'Now that the shock is over, to grieve overmuch for so complete and valuable a life as Patience's would be sentimental folly. I have no need to remind myself how lucky I have been, and am, with Harriet to take charge and provide me with a future to get excited about.'

Bill was very conscious that he and I could become mutually dependent, and was anxious that I should not drift into being 'the daughter at home'. At the end of March, he declared that David's courtship resembled a siege by Vauban, a seventeenth-century general given to a particularly lengthy investment of a town, and bore us off to France on a mini-Culture Tour. An added purpose to this was to inspect those Normandy beaches at which he had not been present in 1944, since one of the books he had undertaken to write in order to pay for the move from Stowe was a short history of D-Day. The tour duly included the beaches together with chunks of Normandy, a selection of the great cathedrals and of the Loire Châteaux. He had thought that the nightingales who sang so beautifully in the environs of the Abbey of Solemnes would be inspirational for us, but in fact it was the bullfrogs inhabiting the village pond in Cour Cheverny that did the trick, and Bill was duly delighted with our engagement.

With my future settled, but the wedding not planned until December, the summer should have enabled Bill to recuperate, but in May his brother Patrick died suddenly of a heart attack, leaving him even further bereft. Contact between the brothers had only ever been intermittent, but they had always been there for each other and Patrick was the repository of the family history. A number of cousins remained, but Bill had never had regular contact with them, and it was now too late to form any real links. He had chosen to let Patrick be the family one, and a further anchor had now gone. At the time, I failed entirely to comprehend the depth of his loss. However, he continued to attend parties and to entertain, helped David study for his Staff College Exams and gained satisfaction from, in effect, cherishing a son who shot and fished.

Patience would have adored organising my wedding, alternating between wanting a slap-up musical comedy affair, with herself dressed as a parody of the traditional mother of the bride, and an absolute minimum of fuss, with a couple of witnesses and her in her sneakers and duffle coat. Without her, Bill decided on an enormous party in the Indian Army Room at Sandhurst, to which he asked 300 people and served champagne cocktails. The choice of venue was appropriate

278

since my intended, unlike the general run of young officers at Sandhurst, with their round, pink faces, had a lean, tanned look that resembled the figures round the room, modelling the various Indian Army uniforms. Once, Bill found Brigadier Peter Young contemplating one of the cases and speculating as to whether I would fit beside the swarthy, mustachioed dummy. The absence of Patience's caustic comments on the celebration, the guests and our wedding presents was palpable. We were married quietly with just family present, in Yateley Church.

It seemed highly practical for us to move into The Hollies while Bill took over David's bachelor flat in Sandhurst, and it was only with hindsight that I realised that the early part of our marriage would have been much easier had we started afresh. The weakness of the arrangement was obvious to David from the moment when we returned from our honeymoon to find Bill waiting for us at The Hollies. Still enormously close to him and concerned for his loneliness, I was tolerant of his frequent visits, but we both chafed at his objections to our changing anything in the house and his consumption of the gin we struggled to afford. However, he was a sterling babysitter when our first daughter was born, a little more than a year after our marriage. Bill was entranced by her and remained an enormously proud grandfather, never hinting that he might have liked one of the three to be a grandson. The eldest, however, remained his particular pride and joy.

The proximity of the Officer's Mess to Bill's Sandhurst flat was a mixed blessing. Philip Warner says Bill could 'start a frantic discussion out of nothing and enliven pre-lunch or pre-dinner drinks in a way which many remembered years after they had left'. Richard Snailham, who was a member of Bill's department, recalls Bill gathering young officers around him before dinner to discuss and argue, but above all, to tell stories. There was an element of the Ancient Mariner in the way he would detain his company until even his most devoted fans would insist that they must eat before the dining room closed. Some found his repeated stories highly irksome and would escape to the television room, knowing that his dislike of the medium would prevent his pursuing them. They could not escape his deep disapproval, however, at their preferring to watch a screen rather than talk. There were those who could argue with him and would greatly enjoy the dialogue, but as his alcohol consumption increased, so discussion was apt to turn into monologue. Bill, invariably late for his meals, failed to eat enough and was then late in going to bed, so his already poor health suffered further. A bout of shingles was particularly debilitating and left him with intermittent pain for the rest of his life.

More positively, he got much pleasure from a Jack Russell terrier bought from a friend in Yateley. Evans, named after the Siamese cat they had had in Vienna, was a delightful companion to him with a number of engaging party tricks, the most famous of which was his ability to catch and collect large quantities of old pennies in his mouth. He would be thrown ever more of these, and then would sit quite still for a while, before opening his mouth to expel a dozen or more coins. He and Bill developed a nightly ritual when the bar closed. They would make their way across the parade ground to the Luneberg Stone, a monument particularly dear to Field-Marshal Montgomery, since it commemorated the German surrender on Luneberg Heath. Bill and Evans would both solemnly pee on this stone before finally going to bed. Monty, making a surprise visit to Sandhurst, went to inspect his stone and found it in a dire state. Instantly, minions were set to work with scrubbing brushes and bleach, but Bill and Evans were undeterred and happily continued with their nocturnal routine. I never asked Bill why he targeted this monument. Probably it stemmed partly from mixed feelings about Montgomery, and partly from his having acquired the army habit of peeing against something.

Bill's effectiveness as a head of department appears to have been mixed. Bill Jenkins, who taught geography, says that he 'didn't push us around in the slightest' and points out that the academic work took second place to military studies, so that Bill was able to 'coast' rather more than he would had he still been in a school. Richard Snailham, who joined Modern Studies halfway through Bill's tenure, found the department 'very laid-back', and Bill 'intelligent and easy going'. As a subsequent author, he was impressed by the way in which Bill had managed to get his most recent book, *Britain's Locust Years*, taken on as a set book. This was a move that undoubtedly did begin to bring some of the material presented to the cadets up to date, apparently a necessary process. However, as Richard pointed out, it did not go nearly far enough, since it was the legacy of various postwar settlements which soldiers were having to confront in the sixties. Having decided, though, that he would concentrate on the earlier part of this century, Bill brought aspects of it to life for the cadets by hiring relevant films. I remember *The Battleship Potemkin* and Charlie Chaplin's *The Great Dictator* being used to illustrate the events of the first half of the century and the power of compelling oratory.

Richard Snailham remembers no departmental meetings, and both he and Bill Jenkins give the impression of 15 lecturers being able to get on with teaching their particular subjects in peace. Philip Warner points out that the academic staff as a whole were, in the main, highly qualified, and chose to be at Sandhurst because it offered greater freedom than would a school or university. They saw themselves as separate from the military staff rather than, as Patience thought, at loggerheads with them. There had been some initial resentment when an outsider was brought in to run the Modern Subjects department, but Philip feels that Bill's understanding and sense of humour overcame the resistance. He has a different slant to the 'laid-back' quality of Bill's department, seeing the lecturers as being encouraged to develop ideas rather than just being left to get on with it. Philip also feels that Bill was good at identifying and solving problems. He cites as an example, Bill's arranging for the Captains and younger Majors working for the Staff College exams to be linked to a member of the academic departments. This not only provided professional tutoring for what was a demanding task, but also helped enormously in breaking down barriers between the military and academics. A number of long-lasting friendships were created by this system.

The picture of a number of individualists working, each in their own office, is reinforced by Kathleen Rumbold, who was secretary to the department for many years. She was seems to have been a unifying force and a huge support to the all-male staff, dealing with practical issues for them and ensuring that she kept a supply of appropriately coloured cotton in order to mend torn trousers. She remembers having to wake Bill up during the afternoons, taking work and messages to his flat when he was ill, and generally protecting him. At intervals she would be called upon to clean his typewriter, which would become gummed up with cigarette ash and spilt gin and orange.

Throughout his life Bill had alternated periods of energy and lassitude, and while there were still bursts of achievement and inspiration, the lassitude was gaining the upper hand. One of the successes, however, and a case where he worked closely with others, was in the creation of the Communication Course. This was something he undertook with Philip Warner, someone to whom he was close both personally and professionally. Philip was an English specialist, and they were both passionate about teaching soldiers to communicate clearly, both also having extensive wartime experience to inform their goals. While Philip was mainly concerned with setting up particular courses,

281

Bill used his contacts to get successful communicators to come and lecture. Paul Johnstone and Colin Welch were the old Historians he chose, and he also found, probably via Paul, a senior figure from the BBC concerned with the training of announcers. From this man Bill delightedly acquired a clutch of new stories concerning such hazards as having to announce the *Flight of the Bumble Bee* or the discussion of any situation involving the Chief Constable of Kent. Philip Warner recalls the setting up of a Communication Centre in an old mortuary. Here, cadets were required to read maps and to pass on vital information while being bombarded by noise from tapes simulating battle conditions. This area of work must have appealed enormously to military staff and provided an excellent model of cooperative teaching.

Professor Kenneth Ingham, who was Director of Studies at Sandhurst and thus held responsibility for the whole range of academic teaching, paints a picture of Bill that confirms the impression of a mixed performance. He also acknowledges that he knew Bill less well than any of the other heads of departments. This, he says, was due to 'unnecessary reticence' on his part. 'As a fellow historian I should have had a close bond with Bill, but just because I was a historian I hesitated to intrude too obviously into the work of Bill's department.' Professor Ingham felt he could take more interest in the teaching of science and mathematics since 'no-one could believe for a moment that I was trying to interfere in how science or mathematics should be taught.' He also notes the 'devastating impact' of Patience's death, the result of which he feels, is that he never knew the 'real Bill'.

He goes on: 'Although I think Bill found a measure of contentment in the comradeship of the RMAS I do not believe that he ever recovered the state of mind which made him such a distinguished student and teacher of history in the past. It was almost as if he were, intellectually, floating rather than swimming. Yet he was able to convey to the cadets the pleasure of scholarship – something which the inevitably utilitarian character of academic work at Sandhurst must often have failed to do. This, I believe, rubbed off on some of the officers at the Academy too, though I think there may have been some more senior members who were a little wary of what they probably misconstrued as too casual an approach to work.' I suspect that the senior officers were right to be wary in the sense that Bill was not doing enough work, but that this sprang, not so much from a casual approach, but from a lack of energy.

Professor Ingham also recalls that he asked each head of department to inaugurate an after-dinner discussion of their particular discipline among the other academics and the senior officers. He writes: 'Bill was not in the mood for it, probably because of his own state of mind at the time. I was not even sure he would agree to do it. But after Arthur Lakin had given what I can only describe as a brilliant introduction to mathematics Bill was obviously put on his mettle. A few weeks later he produced a similar case for the study of history which had us all enthralled.' Remarkably, this paper has survived, albeit tatty and stained, and it reveals Bill at his most fluent.

Bill first deplores the need for having to justify the teaching of a subject, quoting Macaulay, who had written 'a butcher of the higher class disdained to ticket his meat', but then goes on to accept that his Director is right in asking that his particular meat should be ticketed. Bill goes on to quote Houseman's inaugural lecture at London University in 1892, contrasts Aristotle saying that 'all men possess by nature a craving for knowledge' with Plato's opposing statement that 'there is a large body of men who wallow in ignorance with the complacency of a brutal hog', and suggests that experience of teaching schoolboys or cadets inclines teachers to believe the latter. He feels that if the young are to be coaxed or compelled out of that complacency, 'we must convince both ourselves and them that we have something better to offer; and so we are forced back to external justifications after all. However pure and disinterested our own studies may be – whether they are concerned with breeding canaries or stamp-collecting or nuclear fission – some justification is needed for including them in a curriculum for general education.' He concludes that not only does the meat have to be ticketed, but that it should also have 'its calorific value extolled and documented.' Bill cites the parents who asked what history leads to and fears that 'the answers I shall give will not be of the kind to satisfy that particular sort of parent, who probably only wishes to see his son a prosperous stock-broker.'

The paper ranges through and condemns the 'philosophy of history' and 'scientific history', which, he says, is a misnomer. He cites, among many historians, Professors Pibram in Vienna and Mommsen in Berlin, uses Churchill as an example of a historian and a user of history, and concludes that the study of history instils the ability to think creatively and analytically. Bill acknowledges that while there are documented facts, the interpretation of these will vary individually, according to experience and temperament. History, he feels, is an ideal subject for

283

a soldier since successful strategies depend on informed, thoughtful guesswork.

Bill ends: 'For, though scientific knowledge becomes an ever larger ingredient in the essential equipment which a soldier must have at his disposal, war itself, from the level of the highest strategy to that of the most minor tactics, will always remain an art. The ability to assess correctly the effects of events often bewilderingly complex; the painstaking visualisation of what is going on on the other side of the hill; the faculty of seeing a situation in reverse and penetrating an opponent's mind and intention, these are the qualities which the so-called discipline of history is peculiarly fitted to cultivate; and I know of nothing besides the field sports which will do it half as well. When I became a soldier I taught myself to write military appreciations by applying to them the methods by which I had learnt to write history essays. Since the war I have always taught boys to write history essays by instructing them in the rules governing military appreciations. I would claim that a modest success in both processes justifies my claim. Enough, at any rate, to make me hope that, whatever becomes of the teaching of history elsewhere, it will remain as a severely practical part of the Curriculum at Sandhurst.' While the paper is a clear exposition on Bill's belief in the value of studying history, it is also a brilliant piece of showing off. The paper was in fact given comparatively early in his Sandhurst career and illustrates vividly how much was lost in his decline.

Bill's loss of energy and enthusiasm extended into his own written work though he did manage to complete the short history, *The Battle of D-Day* for the Men and Events series, published by Fabers. It was an effort to finish it and he was well behind his deadline, but it did fulfil the brief he had been given. It was aimed at adolescents, but was also reviewed as an adult book, notably by Alan Taylor in *The Observer*. He commends a 'clear, effective account of the essential points both on the Allied and on the German side', but questions the political background. He wrote: 'It is carrying patriotic devotion rather far to present Churchill as the long-term planner of D-Day, when in fact he opposed a landing in northern France from first almost to last.' Other reviews agreed with *The Stirling Journal*, who hailed the book as 'a masterly summary, which also brings out D-Day's importance in the perspective of the war as a whole.'

The other contract Bill had signed in the flush of successfully achieving a new job and the need to pay the debts incurred in moving house, was for an ambitious book on Corps d'Elite, commissioned by Secker and Warburg, for whom he had never written. This required extensive research going back to the early Greek armies and covering specialist forces throughout history. Some chapters were completed, but Bill found himself slipping ever further behind with the struggle to complete the work adding unmanageable pressures. He finally, and sensibly, called it a day and returned the advance royalties. This at least was less of a problem than it might have been in the past. For the first time in his life, Bill was adequately paid and, with only himself to support, was actually quite well-off. Quite a lot of money went on drink, though not only for himself, since he was a generous host and would be much revived by people gathering in his flat, but his bank balance nonetheless stayed in the black. The only drink he was mean about was tonic consumed without gin.

When he arrived at Sandhurst, Bill had been given a five-year contract. In 1967, when he was approaching 60, this came up for renewal, and when he was not given a further term, Bill felt, inevitably, hurt, rejected and a failure. Alongside this feeling, however, there was also relief at being able to give up what had become a real struggle to keep going and, with time, an acceptance that, fundamentally, it was his health and circumstances that had let him down. Given a summer to plan for his retirement, he decided not to remain within the environs of Sandhurst – he had a theory that if you stood in the middle of Camberley High Street and called out Brigadier, every other head would turn – and chose the village of Micheldever near Winchester as being somewhere that was central and would be within reach of military centres where we were likely to be stationed. He found a dilapidated thatched cottage, for which he paid so little that he could afford to have it satisfactorily done up, and was delighted to discover once installed, that what was officially called Winchester Road was known locally as Gin Hill.

26

Fin

Bill's existence at 99 Gin Hill was probably the most satisfactory that could have been arranged in the circumstances. His lack of other immediate family was intractable, and our regular moves, though all within the British Isles, made his living with us impossible. This was just as well, since he had quite enough power over our lives even at a distance. He was inevitably lonely, and seeing him standing in the road waving us off after a visit wrenched my stomach. However, he did not allow himself to wallow in self-pity and got on with rather haphazard cultivation of his extensive garden, cooked for himself and his visitors with varying results, and took an active part in the activities of the village. In the garden he grew runner beans, which he salted in huge glass jars, continuing to feed them to us all in spite of the fact that they turned a sinister shade of yellow. He also cultivated roses, generally choosing yellow which, with his red-green colour blindness, was a shade he could see. A rose called Grandpa Dickson was his pride and joy. On the cookery front, Bill invented a hay box in which he prepared casseroles with patchy results, being more successful with a conventionally cooked chicken dish. His *pièce de résistance*, though, was an incredibly sweet concoction that involved stewing pears in treacle *and* brown sugar. This would be served with lashings of cream, which had become one of his favourite forms of food. At The Ely, a restaurant local to Yateley and much favoured by Bill and ourselves, Bill had spotted under the list of puddings, 'Cream 1/-'. Initially resistant to his demand to be served with cream on its own, the staff subsequently agreed happily to what they came to see as an engaging eccentricity in a regular and generous customer.

The church was a solace and a source of friends. Bill became a parochial church councillor and sometimes attended the Synod as the

Council's representative. It was through the church that he met people who would entertain him, give him lifts into Winchester and allow him to go and watch the television programme *Softly Softly* every week. Bill remained implacably opposed to owning a television, but was furious if anything prevented him seeing something to which he had become attached. If, when he was staying with us, we had arranged some other entertainment on a *Softly Softly* evening he would be furious, but would also complain if we wanted to watch something of which he disapproved or when he wanted to talk.

From some items it became necessary to steer him away. Watching the *Last Night of the Proms* towards the end of his life was disastrous. He became angry and tearful at this celebration of something that we had long lost. In his paper on *The Use of History,* he might castigate Churchill for allowing 'his tremendous sense of the glorious achievement of the British in India to blind him to current realities', but emotionally he mourned the loss of the Empire deeply. Always an emotional man, his long years in public schools had schooled him to suppress tears, but with increasing age, this restraint broke down. However, his frequent visits to us provided him and us with much entertainment. We had to ensure that the house was supplied with gin, Special K cereal and a large thermos for the six cups of tea he liked to drink before getting out of bed in the morning, but he was mostly much appreciated by our friends and remained a companion with whom I could talk endlessly. His grandchildren were an abiding source of pleasure to him. He welcomed our visits enthusiastically, cooking his chicken and sweet pears, and being quite prepared for the cottage to be turned upside down or to be left with a small baby. He would recount with pride that he had regularly changed my nappies and was delighted to find that he was equally competent when undertaking this task for his granddaughters. When two daughters and I, pregnant, got mumps, he managed the household splendidly.

His retirement did not lead to an abandonment of intellectual activity, however. Among his press cuttings are reviews he wrote for the *Sunday* and *Daily Telegraph*s, including one of William L. Shirer's *The Collapse of the Third Republic* and of Alistair Horne's *The Fall of Paris*. While noting that this last book was 'extremely readable and historically profoundly interesting', he accuses Mr Horne of 'changing escalators halfway.' The Shirer he praises for 'holding the reader's interest for every one of its 921 pages.' Above all, however, Bill wrote one more book. *The Art of War: Waterloo to Mons* grew out of some of the research he had done for the abortive book on Corps d'Elite. Having written as much as he wanted about the seventeenth century, he had turned to his other great love, nineteenth-century Europe and to military history, his interest in which had been increased by his experiences at Sandhurst. Weidenfeld and Nicholson commissioned the book and must have waited patiently for it, since it was not published until 1975. It was probably the most successful of all his books, being published and enthusiastically reviewed on both sides of the Atlantic simultaneously. Field-Marshal Lord Carver, reviewing the book at length in *The Times Literary Supplement*, cavilled at the title, saying that it should actually have been called 'The Management of the Business of War in the Age of Moltke', which is hardly snappy, but which he uses as a starting point for the thesis, pursued in the review, that war is a business rather than an art. He goes on to say that the book is at once 'a fascinating and an irritating book: fascinating in the amount of detail and in the trenchant and lively criticism which Mr McElwee bestows on all and sundry; irritating just because of the detail, which tends to divert one's attention from and to obscure the main theme.' This clear theme is, he writes, 'that throughout the period all the principal armies, and to a certain extent the navies also, were imprisoned in the conservative outlook of their very elderly senior officers and their sovereigns.' It was a constant theme of Bill's that generals would persist in fighting previous battles instead of looking at their strategies afresh. In the case of the nineteenth and early twentieth centuries, the European leaders persisted in using tactics that they felt had been successful in the Napoleonic wars rather than learning lessons from the American Civil, Boer and Russo-Japanese wars. Lord Carver described Bill's arguments across several columns and concluded that 'Mr McElwee has made a most valuable contribution to the history both of the period and of warfare generally.'

Bill clearly asked Alan Taylor to review the book. Alan wrote from the Beaverbrook Library in characteristic terms:

'Dear Bill, Fancy your writing a letter! I do what I can about your book but I can't promise. Literary Editors even of *The Observer* are unpredictable. Friedjung has not paid up so far this year, probably run out of stock. But never despair. The dollars will roll again one day. Family all well. I have seven grandchildren. This library is to close at the end of March. Damn! Much love, Alan.'

His review in *The Observer* was warm and personal, stating that Bill was one of his oldest friends and recalling that they had started their academic careers together by translating Friedjung. He then sums up the main themes, remarking in passing that 'Moltke was the first general to master railway timetables and hence moved his armies even faster than Napoleon had done', and ends by saying 'All these lessons can be learnt from McElwee's book and a great deal of European history, to say nothing of American, can be learnt as well.' Following the review Alan wrote again, asking: 'Was Alamein a battle of flanks and movement? I thought it was the great slogging match of the Second World War. Have a look at the map of the Balkans 1878 in your book. The Serbian frontiers are 1913; the others are First World War.' Bill no doubt particularly cherished this review and the paragraph in the Parish Magazine that said: 'The research and hard work of five years has gone into this book, which will almost certainly become required reading for students of military history around the world.' Now out of print in this country, *The Art of War* is still selling in America. Roughly every other year, I receive a surprisingly generous royalty cheque, which suggests that the book has indeed become required reading in some circles.

This success cheered Bill, but it did not halt a continuing decline of his health and, to some extent, his morale. As Colin James remarked, he depressed himself by too close a reading of *The Daily Telegraph*, leading to an increasing gloom about the state of politics and the world. His isolation left him too much time to brood and meant that when he was in company, while there were still flashes of charm and wit, he could be exhausting and domineering, riding roughshod over the views of our guests. Attacks of bronchitis became more frequent and were not helped by the alcohol and the cigarettes that he continued to roll. A particularly virulent infection was exacerbated by a fall following an injudicious visit to his local pub, situated as it was, conveniently just across the road from 99 Gin Hill, and from this he never quite recovered. When he came to us for Christmas in 1976, he could clearly no longer live on his own. At this point, we still owned The Hollies, which had been let during our travels and could now be sold along with 99. We were then able to buy an ancient Essex farmhouse which provided Bill with his own sitting room as well as a bedroom containing some of the oldest timbers in an Essex house.

During this last period of his life Bill became a shadow of his former self. Now suffering from emphysema, his shortness of breath resulted in an uncharacteristic quietness, and for much of the time he was withdrawn into himself. He did manage to hang on to some activities, however. Pruning and tying up raspberry canes had always been a favourite task, and a satisfactorily lavish crop rewarded his efforts for two years running. For a long time he insisted on doing the washing-up, always a mixed blessing since it was a matter of pride with him to stack everything so that no drying up was required, the resulting pyramid being highly insecure.

He continued to enjoy his granddaughters' company, particularly that of the eldest, Susannah, with whom he played chess. Their behaviour was constrained, however, and balancing the needs of children ranging in age from early adolescence to the first stages of primary school with those of an aging man with high expectations of their behaviour and intellects, together with little tolerance of bad behaviour, was difficult. To my chagrin, Bill happily accepted their conventional schooling and was delighted when Susannah won her school history prize. In doing this, she showed herself a true chip off his block. Deciding to enter an essay the night before it was due, she wrote into the small hours. The most painful aspect of the changes in Bill was that, apart from the family, he lost his enjoyment of company, and while he liked the idea of seeing old friends, he quickly tired and retreated to his own room. His main sources of entertainment were the stacks of thrillers I culled from the mobile library.

With heart and lungs failing, a downstairs study became his bedroom and he had to have an oxygen cylinder from which he was supposed to inhale regularly, but he disliked it and had to be bullied into using it. His consumption of gin and tobacco continued, in spite of the admonitions of doctors. We refused to follow this line, feeling that he had little enough to enjoy and was perfectly entitled to shorten his life if he wished. A pulmonary embolism, which formed just when we were about to put him in a nursing home for a week while we went on holiday, meant that I stayed with him while David had a harassed week on a narrow boat with three argumentative daughters. This episode further weakened him, and throughout the autumn of 1978 he drifted towards death. During the last days of his life he was only intermittently conscious, but was quite clear that he did not wish to go to bed. This was probably because breathing sitting up was easier, but I have always wondered whether he was subliminally influenced by the death of Elizabeth I, whom he much admired, telling the story of her refusal to go to bed when she was dying, with relish. Clear that he wanted to die, he remained sitting at his desk with a glass of gin and orange and a freshly rolled cigarette to hand, until the morning of 22 November 1978, when we came down to find him gone. He was 71, which is no age now, but considering that he had been told in 1930 that he would be lucky to live for five years, he had done well.

Bill decided that he did not want a funeral and had long since bequeathed his body for research. Since the advent of antibiotics the diseases that had attacked his lungs had vanished, and he was delighted to find that he could leave his therefore interesting body to the 'Inspector of Anatomy'. He made us promise that we would not take it back for burial. Stephen Whitwell wrote an obituary for *The Times* which appeared in the last edition before it was closed by a lengthy strike.

Later we held a memorial service in London, during which Colin James' address recalled the vital Bill that for us, his close family, had become dimmed by the final years of his life. Colin cited his 'alert, incisive mind', his ability to have the last word, remembering 'his account of being sent for by J.F., and incurring some rebuke which he felt he had not merited; but Bill was able to leave the presence with unaccustomed meekness; he had completed J.F.'s obituary only a day or two before, and the last word he knew would be his.' Bill's teaching, writing, war service, and hunting were all noted, as was Vancouver and his religious position. This, Colin said, 'might not unjustly be described as that of a God-fearing Low Churchman, with a penchant for High Church company, which could perhaps ease his conscience in his enjoyment of non-puritanical tastes.' Colin also recalled that Bill had 'effectively rallied the forces of his Deanery Synod against the innovators in Church order and worship.' He ended with a quotation from Sir Thomas More's final letter to his daughter: 'Pray for me, and I shall pray for you, and all your friends, that we may merrily meet in Heaven.' Bill would have undoubtedly have been delighted to be associated with this statement.

Colin subsequently told Peter Leslie that all the time when preparing and delivering his address, he was conscious of 'a sardonic voice over his shoulder correcting a phrase here and there.' No doubt both Bill and Patience would have commented pungently on the gathering that was inevitably about Patience too, since they could not be separated. That there was a good party afterwards would have delighted them, and both would have appreciated Iain Moncrieffe's wonderful coat, lined, as he gleefully told us all, with 'wolf's tummy'. Given

Bill's determination to have no traditional headstone, I remembered that for a time after the war, he made every Scholar plant a beech tree in the extensive Vancouver grounds. His memorial is therefore a group of trees planted by the Woodland Trust.

Had Patience not died when she did, it is possible that Bill's career at Sandhurst would have ended on a happier note and that the whole of the latter part of his life could have had at least some of the serenity that should come at the end of a busy successful life. As it was, he coped courageously with his loneliness and found the discipline to produce a final successful book in spite of his ill-health. Overall, it was not a career that has lasted publicly as has those of his contemporaries, Wystan Auden and Alan Taylor. Highly though it was thought of at the time, his style of history has not lasted and the novels were never quite the success that reviewers felt they deserved to be. I think he felt himself that he never quite lived up to his undergraduate promise. However, 20 years after his death, three of his books are still listed in the Battersea District library, and *The Art of War* continues to sell in America. His most lasting legacy, though, exists in his pupils, most of whom have pursued useful, and many highly successful, lives in worldly terms. A large proportion of them feel that his teaching and the joint influence of Bill and Patience at Vancouver were strong factors not only in their achievements, but in their enjoyment of their lives.

Together, in spite of their areas of intolerance, their uneasy childhoods and their battles with ill-health, Bill and Patience were a powerful entity. The differences between them were considerable, exemplified perhaps by on one level their attitudes to travel, and on another by their eating habits. Patience, had she lived, might easily have become as reclusive as her mother, while after her death, Bill relished the new experience of visiting Aden, where Stephen Whitwell had been posted. With regard to their eating habits, Bill ate very slowly, talking all the time, while Patience would eat at the speed of light and then talk. Conversation, accompanied by cigarettes, over the remnants of a meal was very much a part of Vancouver life. Sometimes they argued, but always they talked – about the boys, their books, the horses, about me and about ideas. They would take a thermos of tea up to bed with them every night, and I would hear the drone of their voices through the bedroom wall as they drank it. It was this communication, I think, that forged the bond between them. They were united in their aims for the Historians, but I suspect they sometimes disagreed about me, with Bill trying to soothe Patience's worries that I would turn out to be either delinquent or unhappy. Patience appeared to be the most vulnerable, and yet she provided a framework from which Bill could function successfully. No one thought she would predecease him. 'When I am left a widow,' she would say, 'I shall become a house-keeper for a gentleman farmer.' I cannot imagine why this seemed such a desirable position to her. She would have been bored to tears.

A tangible memorial to them both is an annual travel scholarship open to Stoics during their first year in the Sixth form. A small group of old Historians devised and organised a system whereby members of the school submit a plan of travel, the best being awarded a sum of money with which to carry out the plan. On their return they have to give a talk describing their achievements. The generosity of Old Stoics in subscribing to the scholarship would have delighted and touched Bill and Patience. Sometimes I picture them sitting on a cloud, wreathed in cigarette smoke, Patience with a glass of whisky and ginger ale and Bill with his gin and orange, discussing with relish, the looks, accents, plans and presentations of the participants, disapproving deeply of a boy and a girl travelling together and of everybody's clothes. With the entertainment finished, Patience, reluctantly aware of things to be done, would say 'The bell invites me' (in spite of her superstitions, *Macbeth* was her favourite play) and take herself off to some nether region. Bill would pour himself another drink, settle back and reach for his book.

BIBLIOGRAPHY

Annan Noel, *Roxburgh of Stowe* – Longmans 1965.
Annan Noel, *Our Age* – Weidenfeld & Nicholson 1990.
Botting Douglas, *Gavin Maxwell, A Life* – Harper Collins 1993.
Carpenter Humphrey, *W. H. Auden, A Biography* – George Allen & Unwin 1981.
Hailsham of St Marylebone, Lord, *A Sparrow's Flight* – Collins 1992.
Hunter Eileen, Christabel, *The Russell Case and After* – Andre Deutsch 1973.
Robinson John Martin, *Temples of Delight, Stowe Landscape Gardens* – George Philips Ltd in association with the National Trust 1990.
Taylor, A. J. P., *A Personal History* – Hamish Hamilton 1983.
Townsend-Warner, Sylvia, *T. H. White: A Biography* – Cope with Chatto & Windus, 1976.
Worsthorne Sir Peregrine, *Tricks of Memory* – Weidenfeld & Nicholson 1993.

Books by Patience McElwee

Roman Holiday – Geoffrey Bles 1939.
Love or Money – Andrew Melrose 1946.
Pride of Place – Faber & Faber 1950.
Wintersweet – 1954.
Gainfully Employed – 1955.
Beggar my Neighbour – 1956.
Time's Fool – 1957.
Malice Domestic – 1958.
A House for Olivia – 1961.

All published by Hodder & Stoughton.

For Children:

Match Pair – 1956.
Dark Horse – 1958. } All published by Hodder & Stoughton
The Merrythoughts – 1960.

Books by W. L. McElwee

History

The Struggle for Supremacy in Germany, 1859–1866 by Heinrich
   Friedjung – Translation from the Gerrnan with A. J. P. Taylor –
   Macmillan 1935.
The Reign of Charles V, 1516–1558 – Macmillan 1936.
*History of the 2nd Argylls (Reconstituted) – European Campaign
   1944–45* – Thomas Nelson 1949.
The Murder of Sir Thomas Overbury – Faber & Faber 1952.
The Story of England – Faber & Faber 1954.
England's Precedence – Hodder & Stoughton 1956.
The Wisest Fool in Christendom, The Reign of King James I & VI –
   Faber & Faber 1958.
History of England – In the *Teach Yourself* series – English University
   Press, 1960.
Britain's Locust Years, 1918–1940 – Faber & Faber 1962.
Argyll and Sutherland Highlanders – For the *Men-at-Arms* series –
   Osprey 1972.
The Art of War: Waterloo to Mons – Weidenfeld & Nicholson 1974.
An Angel Comes to Babylon – Translation from the German. Published
   as *Four Plays* by Friedrich Dürrenmatt – Grove Press 1964.

Novels

The House – Geoffrey Bles 1938.
The Cure – Andrew Melrose 1946.
Final Objective – Andrew Melrose 1950.

INDEX

The references to Bill and Patience McElwee, to Vancouver Lodge, the house they lived in for most of their married lives, and to Stowe School are so numerous that I have not listed the individual entries. An initial description of Vancouver Lodge appears between pages 55 and 58 and there is a brief description of Stowe's history and of the School's beginings between pages 50 to 52.

297

299

302